Human Relations in the Hospitality Industry

Authors

Walker, DBA, FMP, CHA • Cooper, PhD • Bagdan, Ph.D., C.H.E. • Barrows

ISBN 9781119919193

Printed in the United States of America 10 9 8 7 6 5 4 3 2

List of Titles

Table of Contents

The Supervisor as Leader

Overview

If you were to ask any hospitality leader what his or her greatest challenge is, the likely answer would be finding and keeping great employees motivated. Given the high turnover in the hospitality industry and the resultant cost, we begin to understand some of the leadership challenges that supervisors face.

The idea that a supervisor must be a leader comes as a surprise to people who have never thought about it before. The term *leader* is likely to be associated with politics or religious movements or guerrilla-warfare situations in which people voluntarily become followers of the person who achieves command. Although it is not necessarily true, it is generally assumed that the one who is followed is a "born leader" whose influence is based at least partly on charisma or personal magnetism. A definition of leadership is: "The ability to articulate a vision, to embrace the values of that vision, and nurture an environment where everyone can reach the organization's goals and their own personal needs."[1]

Leadership begins with a vision, a mission, and goals. *Vision* is the articulation of the mission of the organization in such an appealing way that it vividly conveys what it can be like in the future. Vision instills a common purpose, self-esteem, and a sense of membership in the organization. The *mission statement* describes the purpose of the organization and outlines the kinds of activities performed for guests. Mission statements normally have three parts:

1. A statement of overall purpose.
2. A statement explaining the values that employees are expected to maintain in the daily decision-making process.

vision
The articulation of the mission of the organization in such an appealing way that it vividly conveys what it can be like in the future.

mission statement
Describes the purpose of the organization and outlines the kinds of activities performed for guests.

39

3. A declaration of the major goals that management believes is essential to attain. Goals should be relevant to the mission, specific and clear, challenging yet achievable, made in collaboration with employees, and written down with the strategies and tactics of how to meet the goals.

The importance of vision, mission, goals, strategy, and tactics is critical to the success of the company, and much of the crucial work is done by supervisors.

In a work situation, the supervisor is in command by virtue of being placed there by the company and its superiors. In the hospitality industry, the term *supervisor* refers to a manager at a lower organizational level who supervises entry-level or other employees who themselves do not have supervisory responsibilities. The employees are expected to do what the boss tells them to do—that's just part of the job, right?

But if employees simply do what they are told, why is labor turnover so high, productivity so low, and absenteeism so prevalent? Why is there conflict between labor and management? The truth of the matter is that the boss is in charge of the employees, but that does not guarantee that the employees will put all of their efforts into the job. This is where leadership comes in.

In this chapter, we explore the kinds of interactions between a supervisor and the employees that relate to the building of leadership in work situations. After completion of this chapter, you should be able to:

- **Identify typical hourly jobs in foodservice and lodging establishments.**
- **Outline the demographics of the labor pool typically hired for hourly jobs in the hospitality industry.**
- **Explain the concept of leadership.**
- **Describe the characteristics of leadership.**
- **Compare and contrast the concepts of formal authority and real authority.**
- **Compare and contrast Theory X and Theory Y management styles.**
- **Describe and give examples of leadership styles—autocratic, bureaucratic, democratic, laissez-faire, situational, transactional, and transformational.**
- **Outline leadership practices.**
- **Develop your own leadership style.**

You and Your Employees

More than one out of every eight Americans now working have worked in a McDonald's since the first one opened over 50 years ago in California.[2] It seems an incredible statistic, but keep in mind that 8 percent of American employees work in foodservice, and many young people find their first job in foodservice or a hotel. You may already have worked in a hospitality operation yourself.

The hospitality industry is composed of 70 percent part-time, short-term people. They are "only working here *until*"—until they get out of high school, until they get out of college, until they have enough money to buy a car, or until an opening comes up someplace else. It is not uncommon to hear a young hourly employee say, "I'll keep this job until I can get a real job," for what they often mean is that they plan to switch from an hourly to a salaried position.

Characteristics of Leaders

If we were to examine great leaders of the past, we would likely come up with a list similar to the 14 leadership traits from the *Guidebook for Marines*: justice, judgment, dependability, initiative, decisiveness, tact, integrity, enthusiasm, bearing, unselfishness, courage, knowledge, loyalty, and endurance (known by the acronym JJ DIDTIEBUCKLE). Of these, a Marine would likely say that integrity is the most important. Integrity to a Marine means to do something right even if nobody is aware of it.[3]

Several studies have shown that effective leaders have six traits that distinguish them from nonleaders: drive, the desire to influence others, honesty and moral character, self-confidence, intelligence, and relevant knowledge (see Figure 2.1).

A person's *drive* shows that he or she is willing and able to exert exceptional effort to achieve a goal. This high-energy person is likely to take the initiative and be persistent.

Leaders have a *desire to influence others*. This desire is frequently seen as a willingness to accept authority. A leader also builds trusting relationships with those supervised, by being truthful. By showing consistency between their words and actions, leaders display *honesty and moral character*.

Leaders have *self-confidence* to influence others to pursue the goals of the organization. Employees tend to prefer a leader who has strong beliefs and is decisive over one who seems unsure of which decision to make.

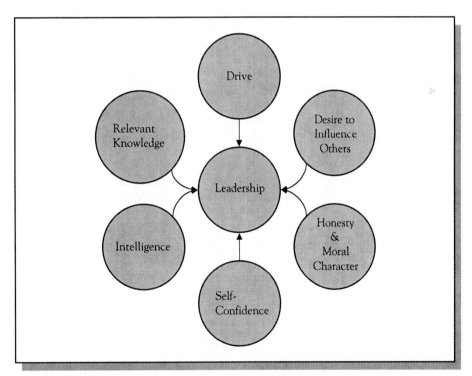

FIGURE 2.1: Characteristics and traits of effective leaders.

Influencing others takes a *level of intelligence*. A leader needs to gather, synthesize, and interpret a lot of information. Leaders create a vision, develop goals, communicate and motivate, problem-solve, and make decisions. A leader needs a high level of *relevant knowledge*—technical, theoretical, and conceptual. Knowledge of the company, its policies and procedures, the department, and the employees are all necessary to make informed decisions.[4]

John C. Maxwell in his *21 Indispensible Qualities of a Leader* rightly suggests that leadership truly develops from the inside out. If you can become the leader you *ought* to be on the *inside*, you will be able to become the leader you *want* to be on the *outside*. People will want to follow you.[5] Followers love leaders with charisma, and John C. Maxwell has the following suggestions for improving your charisma:[6]

- *Change your focus.* Observe your interaction with people during the next few days. As you talk to others, determine how much of the conversation is focused on yourself. Determine to tip the balance in favor of others.
- *Play the first-impression game.* Try an experiment. The next time you meet someone for the first time, try your best to make a good impression. Learn the person's name. Focus on his or her interests. Be positive. And most important, treat them as a "10." If you can do this for a day, you can do it every day. And that will increase your charisma overnight.
- *Share yourself.* Make it your long-term goal to share your resources with others. Think about how you can add value to five people in your life this year. Provide resources to help them grow personally and professionally, and share your personal journey with them.

Reflecting on John C. Maxwell's *21 Indispensible Qualities of Leadership*, there are several that stand out, and there are hospitality leaders to match them. You can explore more about each hospitality leader if you like—just Google them.

- Commitment = Caesar Ritz of hotel fame
- Communication = Herman Cain formerly of Godfather's Pizza and the NRA
- Competence = Escoffier, chef of kings and king of chefs
- Focus = Ray Kroc of McDonald's
- Initiative = Max Shoenbaum of Shoney's
- Listening = Dave Thomas of Wendy's
- Passion = John Schnatter of Papa John's pizza
- Positive attitude = Steve Wynn of Wynn Resorts
- Relationships = Chris Sullivan of Outback Steakhouse
- Responsibility = Chef Charley Trotter
- Self-discipline = Bill Marriott
- Vision = Walt Disney

power
The capacity to influence the behavior of others.

Effective leaders are able to influence others to behave in a particular way. This is called *power*. There are four primary sources of power:

1. *Legitimate power* is derived from an individual's position in an organization.
2. *Reward power* is derived from an individual's control over rewards.

Approximately half of the foodservice workforce, as well as a big presence in hotels, are employees from 17 to 34 years old, referred to as Generation Y.
Courtesy of PhotoDisc, Inc.

3. *Coercive power* is derived from an individual's ability to threaten negative outcomes.
4. *Expert power* is derived from an individual's personal charisma and the respect and/or admiration the individual inspires.

Many leaders use a combination of these sources of power to influence others to goal achievement.[7]

leader
A person in command whom people follow voluntarily.

The Nature of Leadership

You are going to be a ***leader***. Now, you may wonder, "What is a leader, and how is it any different from being a manager?" These are good questions. As a part of the management staff, one is expected to produce goods and services by working with people and using resources such as equipment and employees. That is what being a manager or supervisor is all about. As discussed in Chapter 1, an important managerial function is to be a leader.

A *leader* can be defined as someone who guides or influences the actions of his or her employees to reach certain goals. A leader is a person whom people follow

leadership
Direction and control of the work of others through the ability to elicit voluntary compliance.

formal authority
The authority granted by virtue of a person's position within an organization.

real authority
The authority that employees grant a supervisor to make the necessary decisions and carry them out.

formal leader
The person in charge based on the organization chart.

informal leader
The person who, by virtue of having the support of the employees, is in charge.

voluntarily. What you, as a supervisor, must do is to direct the work of your people in a way that causes them to do it voluntarily. You don't have to be a born leader, you don't have to be magnetic or charismatic; you have to get people to work for you willingly and to the best of their ability. That is what *leadership* is all about.

Although it is true that many leadership skills are innate and that not all managers make great leaders, it is also true that most managers will benefit from leadership training. Moreover, natural leaders will flourish in an environment that supports their growth and development.

There are seven steps to establishing a foundation for leadership development:

1. Commit to investing the time, resources, and money needed to create a culture that supports leadership development.
2. Identify and communicate the differences between management skills and leadership abilities within the organization.
3. Develop quantifiable measurables that support leadership skills. These include percentage of retention, percentage of promotables, and percentage of cross-trained team members.
4. Make leadership skills a focus of management training. These include communication skills (written, verbal, nonverbal, and listening), team-building skills (teamwork, coaching, and feedback), proactive planning skills (transitioning from managing shifts to managing businesses), and interpersonal skills (motivation, delegation, decision making, and problem solving).
5. Implement ongoing programs that focus on leadership skills, such as managing multiple priorities, creating change, and improving presentation skills.
6. Know that in the right culture, leaders can be found at entry level.
7. Recognize, reward, and celebrate leaders for their passion, dedication, and results.

In theory, you have authority over your people because you have *formal authority*, or the right to command, given to you by the organization. You are the boss and you have the *power*, the ability to command. You control the hiring, firing, raises, rewards, discipline, and punishment. In all reality, your authority is anything but absolute. *Real authority* is conferred on your subordinates, and you have to earn the right to lead them. It is possible for you to be the *formal leader* of your work group as well as have someone else who is the *informal leader* actually calling the shots.

The relationship between you and your people is a fluid one, subject to many subtle currents and cross-currents between them and you. If they do not willingly accept your authority, they have many ways of withholding success. They can stay home from work, come in late, drag out the work into overtime, produce inferior products, drive your guests away with rudeness and poor service, break the rules, refuse to do what you tell them to, create crises, and punish you by walking off the job and leaving you in the lurch. Laying down the law, the typical method of control in hospitality operations, does not necessarily maintain authority; on the contrary, it usually creates a negative, nonproductive environment.

do the right things right
To be a leader and manager; to be both effective and efficient.

MBWA, management by walking around
Spending a significant part of the day talking to employees, guests, and peers while listening, coaching, and troubleshooting.

Check Your Knowledge

1. What is a leader?
2. What is the difference between formal and informal authority?
3. What is real authority?

What it all adds up to is that your job as a supervisor is to direct and oversee a group of transients who are often untrained, all of whom are different from each other, and many of whom would rather be working somewhere else. You are dependent on them to do the work for which you are responsible. You will succeed only to the degree that they permit you to succeed. It is your job to get the workers to do their best for the enterprise, for the guests, and for you. How can one do this?

As a distinguished leadership expert noted, "Managers are people who do things right, and leaders are people who do the right things." Think about that for a moment. In other words, managers are involved in being efficient and in mastering routines, whereas leaders are involved in being effective and turning goals into reality. As a supervisor and leader, your job is to *do the right things right*, to be both efficient and effective. An effective supervisor in the hospitality industry is one who, first, knows and understands basic principles of management, and second, applies them to managing all the resource operations.

In the hospitality industry we use a technique referred to as *MBWA, management by walking around*—spending a significant part of your day talking to your employees, your guests, and your peers. As you are walking around and talking to these various people, you should be performing three vital roles discussed in this book: listening, coaching, and troubleshooting.

leadership style
A pattern of interaction that a supervisor or manager uses in directing subordinates.

Choosing a Leadership Style

The term *leadership style* refers to your pattern of interacting with your subordinates: how you direct and control the work of others, and how you get them to produce the goods and services for which you are responsible. It includes not only your manner of giving instructions but also the methods and techniques you use to motivate your workers and to assure that your instructions are carried out.

There are several different forms of leadership style—autocratic, bureaucratic, democratic, and laissez-faire being the most popular styles today (Figure 2.2). Before choosing a style of leadership, one must identify the pros and cons of each and then decide if it will be the most effective style in the hospitality industry.

Autocratic leadership style can be identified with the early, classical approach to management. A supervisor practicing an autocratic style is likely to make decisions without input from staff, to give orders without explanation or defense, and to expect the orders to be obeyed. When this style of leadership is used, employees become dependent on supervisors for instructions. The wants and needs of the employees come second to those of the organization and the supervisor.

In bureaucratic leadership style, a supervisor manages "by the book." The leader relies on the property's rules, regulations, and procedures for decisions that he makes. To the employees, their leader appears to be a "police officer." This style is appropriate when the employees can be permitted no discretion in the decisions to be made.

Forms of Leadership Style			
Autocratic	Bureaucratic	Democratic	Laissez-Faire
Sees him/herself as sole decision maker	Strictly by the book	Almost a reversal of autocratic	Hands-off approach
Shows little concern about others' opinions	Relies on rules and regulations	Wants to share responsibilities	Turns over control; delegates authority
Focuses on completing goals	Acts like he/she is a police officer	Collaborates on opinions when decision making	Style works well when employees are self-motivated
Dictates tasks to be accomplished	Appropriate when employees are permitted no discretion	Is a concerned *coach* of the team	Little application in the hospitality industry

FIGURE 2.2: The pros and cons of each leadership style.

Democratic (also called *participative*) leadership style is almost the reverse of the autocratic style discussed previously. Democratic supervisors want to share decision-making responsibility. They want to consult with the group members and to solicit their participation in making decisions and resolving problems that affect the employees. Employers strongly consider the opinions of employees and seek their thoughts and suggestions. All employees are informed about all matters that concern them. One could compare a democratic supervisor to a coach who is leading his or her team.

Laissez-faire (also called *free-reign*) leadership style refers to a hands-off approach in which the supervisor actually does as little leading as possible. In effect, the laissez-faire supervisor delegates all authority and power to the employees. The supervisor relies on the employees to establish goals, make decisions, and solve problems. At best, the laissez-faire style has limited application to the hospitality industry.

✳ THE OLD-STYLE BOSS

reward and punishment
A method of motivating performance by giving rewards for good performance and by punishing poor performance.

In the hospitality industry, the traditional method of dealing with hourly workers has generally been some variation of the command-obey method combined with *carrot-and-stick motivation* of *reward and punishment*. The motivators relied on to produce the work are money (the carrot) and fear (the stick)—fear of punishment, fear of losing the money by being fired. All too often, the manner of direction is to lay down the

Choosing your leadership style will be one of your most important career decisions.
Courtesy of Digital Vision.

law in definite terms, such as cursing, shouting, and threatening as necessary to arouse the proper degree of fear to motivate the worker.

autocratic method
Behaving in an authoritarian or domineering manner.

People who practice this ***autocratic method*** of managing employees believe that it's the only method that employees will understand. Perhaps that is the way the supervisor was raised, or perhaps it is the only method the supervisor has ever seen in action. In any case, it expresses the view of the people involved that "employees these days are no good."

Some employees are simply bad workers. However, cursing, shouting, and threatening seldom helps them improve. Many employees do respond to a command-obey style of direction, but those employees often come from authoritarian backgrounds and have never known anything else. This style is traditional and military—perhaps the style of dictatorship in countries from which some immigrants come. However, for your average American employee, it does not work. It might be enough to keep people on the job but not working to their full capacity.

When coupled with a negative view of the employee, this style of direction and control is far more likely to increase problems than to lessen them, and to backfire by breeding resentment, low morale, and adversary relationships. In extreme cases, the boss and the company become the bad guys, the enemy, and workers give as little as possible and take as much as they can. In response, close supervision and tight control are required to see that nobody gets away with anything. In this type of atmosphere, guest service suffers and patrons go somewhere else.

We are also learning more about what causes employees to work productively, including many of the things we have been talking about, such as positive work climate, person-to-person relations, and other people-oriented methods and techniques. At this point, let us look at some current theories of leadership and see how—or whether—they can be applied in hotel and foodservice settings. These theories emerged in the 1950s and 1960s, following the discovery that making employees happy does not necessarily make them productive. The theories are based on what behavioral scientists, psychologists, and sociologists tell us about human behavior. They explore what causes people to work productively and how this knowledge can be used in managing employees.

✳︎ THEORY X AND THEORY Y

Theory X
The managerial assumption that people dislike and avoid work, prefer to be led, avoid responsibility, lack ambition, want security, and must be coerced, controlled, directed, and threatened with punishment to get them to do their work.

In the late 1950s, Douglas McGregor of the MIT School of Industrial Management advanced the thesis that business organizations based their management of employees on assumptions about people that were wrong and were actually counterproductive. He described three faulty assumptions about the average human being as *Theory X*:

1. They have an inborn dislike of work and will avoid it as much as possible.
2. They must be "coerced, controlled, directed, threatened with punishment" to get the work done.
3. They prefer to be led, avoid responsibility, lack ambition, and want security above all else.

McGregor argues: "These characteristics are not inborn." He believed people behaved this way on the job because they were treated as though these things were true. In fact, he stated, "This is a narrow and unproductive view of human beings," and he proposed *Theory Y*:

Theory Y
The hypothesis that work is as natural as play or rest; people will work of their own accord toward objectives to which they feel committed.

1. Work is as natural as play or rest; people do not dislike it inherently.
2. Control and the threat of punishment are not the only means of getting people to do their jobs. They will work of their own accord toward objectives to which they feel committed.
3. People become committed to objectives that will fulfill inner personal needs, such as self-respect, independence, achievement, recognition, status, and growth.
4. Under the right conditions, people learn not only to accept responsibility but also to seek it. Lack of ambition, avoidance of responsibility, and the desire for security are not innate human characteristics.
5. Capacity for applying imagination, ingenuity, and creativity to solving on-the-job problems is "widely, not narrowly, distributed in the population."
6. The modern industrial organization uses only a portion of the intellectual potential of the average human being.

Thus, if work could fulfill both the goals of the enterprise and the needs of the workers, they would be self-motivated to produce, and consequently, coercion, and the threat of punishment would be unnecessary.

Theory X fits the old-style hospitality manager to a T, and it is safe to say that this pattern of thinking is still common in many other industries as well. However, behavioral science theory and management practice have both moved in the direction of Theory Y. Theory Y is a revised view of human nature with emphasis on using the full range of workers' talents, needs, and aspirations to meet the goals of the enterprise.

A popular way of moving toward a Theory Y style of people management is to involve one's workers in certain aspects of management, such as problem solving and decision making. Usually, such involvement is carried out in a group setting: meetings of the employees for the specific purpose of securing their input. The degree of involvement the boss allows or seeks can vary from merely keeping the employees informed of things that affect their work to delegating decision making entirely to the group.

The participative management style, mentioned in Chapter 1, results when employees have a high degree of involvement in such management concerns as planning and decision making. Enthusiasts of a participatory style of leadership believe that the greater the degree of worker participation, the better the decisions and the more likely they are to be carried out.

However, others point out that the degree of participation that is appropriate for a given work group will depend on the type of work, the people involved, the nature of the problem, the skill and sensitivity of the leader, and the pressures of time—the situational leadership approach, to be discussed shortly. The degree to which the boss involves the workers may also vary from time to time, depending on circumstances. You are not going to make a group decision when a drunk is making a scene in the dining room or when a fire alarm is going off on the seventh floor.

✳ SITUATIONAL LEADERSHIP

situational leadership
Adaptation of leadership style to fit the situation.

In the *situational leadership* model developed by Kenneth Blanchard and Paul Hersey, leadership behaviors are sorted into two categories: directive behavior and supportive behavior.[8] *Directive behavior* means telling an employee exactly what you want done, as well as when, where, and how to do it. The focus is to get a job done, and it is best used when employees are learning a new aspect of their jobs. *Supportive behavior* is meant to show caring and support for your employees by praising, encouraging, listening to their ideas, involving them in decision making, and helping them reach their own solutions. This method is best used when an employee lacks commitment to do a job.

directing style
Leadership style that is high on directive and low on supportive behaviors.

By combining directive and supportive behaviors, Hersey and Blanchard came up with four possible leadership styles for different conditions. When an employee has much commitment or enthusiasm but little competence to do a job, a *directing style* is needed; this is high on directive and low on supportive behaviors. Suppose that you have a new employee full of enthusiasm who knows little about how to do the job. A directing style is appropriate: You train the new employee by giving multiple instructions, you make the decisions, you solve the problems, and you closely supervise. Enthusiastic beginners need this direction. A directing style is also appropriate when a decision has to be made quickly and there is some risk involved, such as when there is a fire and you need to get your employees out of danger.

coaching style
Leadership style that includes lots of directive behaviors to build skills and supportive behaviors to build commitment.

As new employees get into their jobs, they often lose some of their initial excitement when they realize that the job is more difficult or not as interesting as they originally envisioned. This is the time to use a *coaching style*, with lots of directive

supporting style
Leadership style that is high on supportive behaviors and low on directive behaviors.

delegating style
Leadership style that is low on directive and supportive behaviors because you are turning over responsibility for day-to-day decision making to the employee.

transactional leaders
Leaders that motivate employees by appealing to their self-interest.

behaviors to continue to build skills and supportive behaviors to build commitment. In addition to providing much direct supervision, you provide support. You listen, you encourage, you praise, you ask for input and ideas, and you consult with the employee. As employees become technically competent on the job, their commitment frequently wavers between enthusiasm and uncertainty. In a situation like this, the use of a *supporting style* that is high on supportive behaviors and low on directive behaviors is required. If an employee shows both commitment and competence, a *delegating style* is suitable. A delegating style of leadership is low on directive and supportive behaviors because you are turning over responsibility for day-to-day decision making to the employee doing the job. These employees don't need much direction, and they provide much of their own support.

Using this view of situational leadership, you need to assess the competence and commitment level of your employee in relation to the task at hand before choosing an appropriate leadership style (Figure 2.2). As a supervisor, your goal should be to build your employees' competence and commitment levels to the point where you are using less time-consuming styles, such as supporting and delegating, and getting quality results.

✳ TRANSACTIONAL LEADERSHIP

Transactional leaders motivate workers by appealing to their self-interest. In other words, workers do their jobs and give their compliance in return for rewards such as pay and status. Transactional leaders stress communication of job assignments, work standards, goals, and so on, in order to maintain the status quo.

Transactional leaders motivate employees by appealing to their self-interest.
Courtesy of Sodexo.

James MacGregor Burns, a prominent leadership researcher, wrote a significant book titled *Leadership*.[9] In the book, Burns describes leadership as falling within two broad categories: transactional and transformational. Transactional leadership seeks to motivate followers by appealing to their own self-interest. Transactional leaders stress

PROFILE Laura Horetski

Courtesy of Laura Horetski.

I was asked what leadership means to me as the front office manager of a major hotel chain. When you look at the definition of a leader, it states, "one who leads or guides." And we've all heard the phrase "lead by example." I don't think that is enough. There are at least seven qualities of leadership that I can think of that make a good leader.

A good leader is someone who is not afraid to get his or her hands dirty. Someone who will do the same job, duty, or task alongside subordinates, peers, and supervisors, while keeping a positive attitude. This helps build and gain respect. Besides, how else can you expect someone to do the job you ask him or her to do if you do not know how or are not willing to do it yourself?

A person who listens, not just hears. Pay complete attention to what people are saying. Look them in the eyes, acknowledge them and don't interrupt. Ask questions of clarification, reiterate what they are saying, and ask the person if you understand correctly. But listening doesn't stop there. You need to follow through on the conversation and do what you said you would do. Build integrity and trust.

Make good business decisions but show compassion when needed. The bottom line is the bottom line. You don't have to be cruel to accomplish tough results. Be honest, state the facts, ask for suggestions, and make the best decision. A lot of times things look good on paper but don't really work in reality. Sometimes those who are on the front lines and performing the job everyday give the best answers. Not only do you get the answer you may be looking for, you also build confidence and develop future managers and supervisors.

Treat others fairly, including yourself. Favoritism has no place at work. Is it hard not to solely rely on those who are the strongest? Absolutely. But as a leader, it's your job to encourage and improve your super performers. Favoritism also provides an impartial playing field for everyone. Learn to delegate to improve teamwork and lighten the load for everybody.

Learning never stops. I try to learn something new every day, sometimes without even seeking it out. You also need to be open to learning from subordinates, peers, and supervisors. There is no one person who has all the answers. The workforce is always changing in every aspect, and you need to be able to adapt. It's important to stay fresh and current. Think outside the box; there's usually more than one way to accomplish a goal. If the way you tried doesn't work, you've learned, and it's what you take from the experience that's important.

Develop those under you. The fastest way to move up is to train someone to take your job. This is one of the best ways to show leadership. Too often, people are afraid of "losing their jobs" because someone else knows how to do their job. This is not the case. This frees up time for you to develop your skills in another position you are interested in, while developing your successor.

Finally, you need to be able to admit that you've made mistakes. As I said earlier, no one person has all the answers. You're going to stumble, trip, and even fall. But those who are honest and admit their failures will gain the respect of others and will learn the most. There's a saying, "No question is a dumb question." I say, "No mistake is a mistake."

I have had many teachers throughout my career, and I have taken pieces of their leadership styles along with me. You are never done learning how to lead. Each circumstance has its own manner in how to approach it. Above all else, a good leader is fair and ever changing. Have fun!

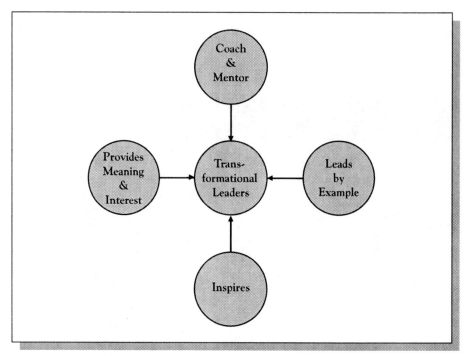

FIGURE 2.3: Transformational leaders.

communication of job assignments, work standards, goals, and so on in order to maintain the status quo. Its principles are to motivate by the exchange process. In other words, employees do their jobs and give their compliance in return for desired rewards such as pay and status.

Transactional leadership behavior is used to one degree or another by most leaders. However, as the old saying goes, "If the only tool in your toolbox is a hammer, every problem will look like a nail." Transactional leadership seeks to influence others by exchanging work for wages, but does not build on the employee's need for meaningful work or tap into their creativity. The most effective and beneficial leadership behavior to achieve long-term success and improved performance is transformational leadership.[10]

✳ TRANSFORMATIONAL LEADERSHIP

Transformational leadership is about finding ways of long-term higher order changes in follower behavior. It is the process of gaining performance above expectations by inspiring employees to reach beyond themselves and do more than they originally thought possible. This is accomplished by raising their commitment to a shared vision of the future. As illustrated in Figure 2.3, instead of using rewards and incentives to motivate employees, *transformational leaders* do the following:

1. Communicate with and inspire employees about the mission and objectives of the company.

transformational leaders
Leadership that motivates employees by appealing to their higher-order needs, such as providing employees with meaningful, interesting, and challenging jobs, and acting as a coach and mentor.

2. Provide employees with meaningful, interesting, and challenging jobs.
3. Act as a coach and mentor to support, develop, and empower employees.
4. Lead by example.

By appealing to employees' higher-order needs, transformational leaders gain much loyalty that is especially useful in times of change. Transformational leaders generally have lots of charisma. One of the most transformational leaders was Dr. Martin Luther King Jr. Dr. King dedicated his life to achieving rights for all citizens by nonviolent methods. In 1964, Dr. King won the Nobel Peace Prize and is perhaps best remembered for his "I Have a Dream" speech. Delivered in front of the Lincoln Memorial in the summer of 1963, Dr. King inspired his listeners to feel that history was being made in their very presence.

One hospitality example of a transformational leader was Horst Schultze, who developed Ritz-Carlton hotels and led the Ritz-Carlton Hotel Company (now part of Marriott International) to win the Malcolm Baldrige National Quality Award for service in 1992. A more recent example is the 2010 winner of the Malcolm Baldrige National Quality Award for health care, Advocate Good Samaritan Hospital. Its vision statement is to provide an exceptional patient experience marked by superior health outcomes and service.[11] Another example is Herb Kelleher of Southwest Airlines. Kelleher set a vision and was able to communicate it so well to all employees that they went the extra mile to ensure the company's and their own success.

✳ PRACTICES OF LEADERS

Leaders vary in their values, managerial styles, and priorities. Peter Drucker, the renowned management scholar, author, and consultant of many years, discussed with hundreds of leaders their roles, their goals, and their performance. Drucker observes that regardless of their enormous diversity with respect to personality, style, abilities, and interest, effective leaders all behave in much the same way:[12]

1. They did not start out with the question, "What do I want?" They started out asking, "What needs to be done?"
2. Then they asked, "What can and should I do to make a difference?" This has to be something that both needs to be done and fits the leader's strengths and the way she or he is most effective.
3. They constantly asked, "What are the organization's *mission* and *goals*? What constitutes *performance* and *results* in this organization?"
4. They were extremely tolerant of diversity in people and did not look for carbon copies of themselves. But they were totally—fiendishly—intolerant when it came to a person's performance, standards, and values.
5. They were not afraid of strength in their associates. They gloried in it.
6. One way or another, they submitted themselves to the *mirror test*—that is, they made sure the kind of person they saw in the mirror in the morning was the kind of person they wanted to be, to respect, and to believe in. This way they fortified themselves against the leader's greatest temptations—to do things that are popular rather than right and to do petty, mean, sleazy things. Finally these leaders were not preachers, they were doers.[13]

✳ EMPOWERMENT

empowerment
To give employees additional responsibility and authority over their decisions, resources, and work.

Empowerment, which is also discussed in Chapter 7, is a technique used by participative leaders to share decision-making authority with team members. Empowerment means giving employees more control over their decisions, resources, and work. When decision-making power is shared at all levels of the organization, employees feel a greater sense of ownership in, and responsibility for, organizational outcomes.[14] The relationship between employees and the company is more of a partnership, where the employees feel responsible for their jobs and have a share of ownership in the enterprise. Empowered employees take responsibility and seek to solve problems; they see themselves as a network of professionals all working toward the same goals.

An example of empowered employees making a difference happened at Hampton Inns after it began a program of refunds to guests who were dissatisfied with their stays. The refund policy created far more additional business than it cost, but a surprise bonus was the increased morale when employees—everyone from front-desk associates to housekeepers—were empowered to give refunds. With greater participation and job satisfaction, employee turnover fell by more than half.[15] Empowerment has strong links to total quality management, which is discussed at length in Chapter 7.

Developing Your Own Style

Applying theory to reality is going to be something you work out for yourself. No one can teach you. Since even the theorists disagree among themselves, the choice is wide open. But don't throw it all out; a lot of what the behavioral scientists are saying can be very useful to you. There does seem to be general agreement, supported by research and experience, that the assumptions Theory X makes about people are, at best, unproductive and, at worst, counterproductive, if not downright destructive.

However, an authoritarian style of leadership can be effective and even necessary in many situations, and there is actually no reason why it cannot be combined with a high concern for the workers and achieve good results.

As for Theory Y, probably two-thirds of the workforce has the potential for a Theory Y type of motivation—that is, working to satisfy such inner needs as self-respect, achievement, independence, responsibility, status, and growth. The problem with applying this theory in the hospitality industry is really not the workers. It is the nature of the work, the number of variables you have to deal with (including high worker turnover), the unpredictability of the situation, the tradition of authoritarian carrot-stick management, and the pressures of time.

The pace and pattern of the typical day do not leave much room for group activity or for planning and implementing changes in work patterns to provide such motivation. Furthermore, your own supervisor or your company's policies may not give you the freedom to make changes. In conclusion, Theory Y does not always work for everyone.

However, it is remarkable what is possible when an imaginative and determined manager sets out to utilize this type of motivation and develop this type of commitment. We will have more to say about motivation in Chapter 7.

> Success in life is measured by what we have overcome to become what we are and by what we have accomplished. Who we are is more important than what position we have.

The best style of leadership, for you, is whatever works best in terms of these three basics: your own personality, the employees you supervise, and the situations you face. It should be a situational type of leadership, just as your management style must be a flex style that reacts to situations as they arise.

You might give an order to Todd, but say "please" to Louis. You might stop a fight in the kitchen with a quick command when server Jenni and server Chris keep picking up each other's orders, and then later, you might spend a good hour with the two of them helping them reach an agreement to stop their running battle. You might see responsibilities you could delegate to Evelyn or John. You might see opportunities to bring workers in on solving work problems, or you might solve them yourself because of time pressures or because the problems are not appropriate for group discussion.

You can borrow elements and techniques of Theory Y without erecting a whole system of participative management. If something does not work for all three of you—yourself, the workers, the situation—don't do it.

Much attention has been focused on corporate leadership and the associated scandals including misuse of power, embezzlement, lack of moral and ethical behavior, lying, and other forms of improper behavior that have shaken the public's confidence in corporate leadership. Add to this the huge salaries many of these leaders are (and were) paid—even if their company did poorly, they still received a large salary increase. Events such as these have caused public opinion to turn against corporate leadership, with demands that corporate leaders become more ethical and moral in their behavior and make better decisions.

✳ VISION AND AWARENESS

As a leader, you will need to have a vision that is realistic and credible—a vision that everyone in the organization (or department) can rally around. Your vision—to be the best, or to be the most popular—needs to be complemented by the company purpose and mission statement. It needs to be ambitious and inspire enthusiasm. Leaders make things happen because they have developed the knowledge, skills, and attitude to positively motivate others to reach common goals.

What you need most in sculpting a vision and finding what works best is *awareness*: awareness of yourself and the feelings, desires, biases, abilities, power, and influence you bring to a situation; awareness of the special needs and traits of your various workers; and awareness of the situation, the big picture, so you can recognize what is needed as far as conceptual skills and human skills.

Leadership is also about change. As you develop awareness and vision, you will see an obvious need for change. Remember, there is a six-step method of making changes:

First, state the purpose;
second, involve others;
third, test the plan before you implement it companywide;

fourth, introduce the change;
fifth, maintain and reinforce the change; and
sixth, follow up.[16]

The best style of leadership is to be *yourself.* Trying to copy someone else's style usually does not work—the situation is different, you are different, the shoe does not fit.

Today, hospitality leaders are expected to have the communication skills to mobilize the energy and resources of a management team. Leaders are expected to be visionaries who see the future clearly and articulate the vision so that others can follow.

✳ EMPLOYEE ENGAGEMENT

As a people leader, your job is to inspire your employees to bring their personal greatness to work every day and to invest their best in your business—and that's a hard job. Getting the best is about building a culture of trust, connection, growth, and service. That culture is sustained and enlivened by supervisors and managers, one person at a time. That's employee engagement.[17]

Companies with a highly engaged culture have shown consistent growth and profitability. One study has shown that companies with 60- to 100-percent engaged employees report an average shareholder return of 20.2 percent. But companies with less than 40 percent engagement show a 9.6 percent return.[18] So, the message is to show personal interest and concern to all employees, even when you are so busy you think you don't have the time to spare.

Engaged employees are more productive.
Courtesy of PhotoDisc, Getty Images.

Ethics

ethics
The study of standards of conduct and moral judgment; also, the standards of correct conduct.

Although there are many definitions of *ethics*, ethics can generally be thought of as a set of moral principles or rules of conduct that provide guidelines for morally right behavior. To give you an idea of how ethics are involved in your job as a hospitality supervisor, let's look at three scenarios:

1. You've completed interviewing a number of candidates for a security position. One of the top three candidates is a relative of a supervisor in another department with whom you are close friends. You've been getting pressure from your friend to hire this candidate and you don't want to alienate him, so you hire his relative, even though one of the other candidates is more suited for the job.
2. Business at the hotel could be better on weekends, so you advertise 25 percent discounts on rooms. To keep profitability high, you inflate the room rate before taking the discount.
3. As purchasing manager, you know that the policy is not to accept free gifts from vendors. But one day when you are out to lunch with a vendor, he offers you free tickets to a Major League Baseball game and you accept them. You can't wait to take your son to the game.

As you can see from these examples, moral principles and standards of conduct are just as necessary in the workplace as they are in your personal life. There are ethical considerations in many of the decisions that you will make, from personnel management issues to money issues to purchasing and receiving practices. Unfortunately, the hospitality industry as a whole has not written its own code of ethics, but you will find that some operations have written their own.

Why is a code of ethics needed for hospitality operations? Just look at the temptations: stockrooms full of supplies that can be used at home and are often loosely inventoried, any kind of alcoholic beverage you want, empty hotel rooms, gambling, high-stress jobs, irregular hours, pressures to meet guests' needs. It can be easy to lose a sense of right and wrong in this field.

Stephen Hall suggests five questions that you can use to help decide how ethical a certain decision is:[19]

1. Is the decision legal?
2. Is the decision fair?
3. Does the decision hurt anyone?
4. Have I been honest with those affected?
5. Can I live with my decision?

These questions can provide much guidance.

The Supervisor as Mentor

This topic is a wonderful way to finish this chapter on supervision. As you become more experienced and proficient at being a hospitality supervisor, it is more likely that you will be a mentor to those who are less experienced and less skilled.

mentor
An experienced and proficient person who acts as a leader, role model, and teacher to those less experienced and less skilled.

A *mentor* is a leader, an excellent role model, and a teacher. A supervisor often functions as a mentor to a worker by providing guidance and knowledge on learning the operation and moving up the career ladder. The relationship often resembles that between a teacher and a student. At other times, the mentor simply provides an example of professional behavior with minimal or no interaction with the worker. Being a mentor can provide feelings of pride and satisfaction because you have contributed to someone else's career development.

Being a Winner! The Winner—is always part of the answer. The Loser—is always part of the problem. The Winner—always has a program. The Loser—always has an excuse. The Winner—says, "Let me do that for you." The Loser—says, "That's not my job." The Winner—sees an answer for every problem. The Loser—sees a problem for every answer. The Winner—sees a green near every sand trap. The Loser—sees two or three sand traps near every green. The Winner—says, "It may be difficult but it's possible." The Loser—says, "It may be possible, but it's too difficult." BE A WINNER

 # KEY POINTS

1. Being a leader means guiding or influencing the actions of your employees to reach certain goals. A leader is a person whom people follow voluntarily.
2. As a supervisor, you have been given the formal authority to oversee your employees. Your subordinates confer real authority, and you have to earn the right to lead them.
3. As a supervisor and leader, your job is to do the right things right.
4. Leadership style refers to your pattern of interacting with your subordinates, how you direct and control the work of others, and how you get them to produce the goods and services for which you are responsible.
5. The old-style boss uses an autocratic method of managing employees that relies on the motivators of money or fear.
6. According to McGregor, the autocratic style is typical of Theory X bosses. Theory Y bosses believe that workers will work of their own accord toward objectives to which they feel committed.
7. In situational leadership, the leadership style is adapted to the uniqueness of each situation. The four primary styles of leading are directing, coaching, supporting, and delegating.
8. Transactional leaders appeal to employees' self-interest. Transformational leaders appeal to employees' higher-order needs.
9. Employers and employees must develop mutual respect for success.

10. Ethics can be thought of as a set of moral principles or rules of conduct that provide guidelines for morally correct behavior. The five questions presented in the chapter provide guidance for making ethical decisions.

11. A supervisor often functions as a mentor to a worker by providing guidance and knowledge on learning the operation and moving up the career ladder. The relationship resembles that between a teacher and a student.

KEY TERMS

autocratic method

carrot-and-stick motivation

coaching style

delegating style

directing style

do the right things right

empowerment

ethics

formal authority

formal leader

informal leader

leader

leadership

leadership style

MBWA, management by walking around

mentor

mission statement

power

real authority

reward and punishment

situational leadership

supporting style

Theory X

Theory Y

transactional leader

transformational leader

vision

REVIEW QUESTIONS

Answer each question in complete sentences. Read each question carefully and make sure that you answer all parts of the question. Organize your answers using more than one paragraph when appropriate.

1. Identify typical hourly jobs in foodservice and lodging establishments. Include both skilled and unskilled jobs.

2. If a restaurant's turnover rate is 100 percent, what does that mean?

3. Define *leader* and *leadership*.

4. What is meant by "do the right things right"?

5. Compare and contrast the concepts of formal and real authority.

6. Why does a fear-and-punishment approach to supervision usually create a negative, nonproductive environment?

7. In two sentences, describe the essence of each of the following leadership styles: autocratic, Theory X, Theory Y, situational, transactional, and transformational leadership.

8. Identify the six practices of successful managers.

ACTIVITIES AND APPLICATIONS

1. Discussion Questions

- Why do you think turnover is high in hotels and restaurants? If you resigned from a hospitality job, what were your reasons? What could be done by management to reduce turnover?
- Why might it be difficult to supervise employees in minimum-wage or low-wage hospitality jobs that require no special skills? What kinds of problems might arise? What can be done to solve these problems or avoid them?
- Which view of people is more accurate: Theory X or Y? Give examples from your own work experience to support your view.
- Under what circumstances might you need to be an autocratic leader?
- Describe situations in which each of the four styles of situational leadership would be appropriate.

2. Group Activity

Using the three situations described in the Ethics section, use the five questions from Hall that are listed in that section to examine how ethical each decision was. Discuss each question as a group and have one person record your ideas.

3. Leadership Assessment

Using Figure 2.4, assess your leadership abilities.

4. L-E-A-D-E-R Activity

Using the letters in the word *leader*, think of a leader's qualities and actions that make him or her a good leader and fit as many as possible into L-E-A-D-E-R. For example, L—lends a hand; E—ethical; A—aware; D—. . ., and so on.

5. Case Study: Firm, Fair, and Open?

Latisha has just been hired as the dining-room supervisor on the noon shift in the coffee shop of a large hotel. She came from a similar job in a much smaller hotel, but she feels confident that she can handle the larger setting and the larger staff. Because she is eager to start things off right, she asks all the servers to stay for 10 minutes at the end of the shift so that she can say a few words to everyone. She begins by describing her background and experience and then proceeds to her philosophy of management. "I expect a lot of my people," she says. "I want your best work, and I hope you want it, too, for your own sake. You will not find me easy, but you will find me fair and open with you, and I hope you will feel free to come to me with suggestions or problems. I can't solve them all, but I will do my best for you." She smiles and looks at each one in turn.

"Now, the first thing I want to do," she continues, "is to introduce a system of rotating your stations so that everyone gets a turn at the busiest tables and the best tips and the shortest distance to the kitchen. I've posted the assignments on the bulletin board, and you will start off that way tomorrow and keep these stations for a week."

She says, "I will be making some other changes, too, but let's take things one at a time. Are there any questions or comments?" Latisha pauses for three seconds and then says, "I am very particular about being on time, about uniforms and grooming, and about prompt and courteous customer service. I advise you all to start off tomorrow on the right foot and we'll all be much happier during these hours we work together. See you tomorrow at 10:25."

Directions: Answer each question realistically using the following scale.
  1—I do this seldom or never.
  2—I do this occasionally.
  3—I do this always or most of the time.

If your total points are:

175–210   You are an excellent leader.

120–175   You are probably new to leadership and trying hard. Work on the areas where you rated yourself a "1."

Below 120   You need to improve in many areas.

Personal Qualities

SELF-CONFIDENT

_____   1. I believe in myself.

CONSISTENT/COMMITTED

_____   2. I stay focused on the vision.

_____   3. I keep my word.

UPBEAT/POSITIVE

_____   4. I am a positive thinker.

_____   5. I am an optimist—my glass is half full.

HONEST/OPEN

_____   6. I am up-front and honest with others.

_____   7. I do not get defensive in conversation.

INTEGRITY

_____   8. I honor my commitments and promises.

FUNNY

_____   9. I use my sense of humor.

_____   10. I love to laugh at myself.

RISK-TAKING

_____   11. I take calculated risks when appropriate.

_____   12. I let myself and others make mistakes.

CREATIVE/DIVERGENT & ABSTRACT THINKER

_____   13. I encourage and try to look at things in new and different ways.

INTELLIGENT/COMPETENT

_____   14. I am knowledgeable and competent in my field.

_____   15. I can make the complex simple.

_____   16. I am a lifelong learner.

WIN/WIN ORIENTATION

_____   17. In interactions with others, I want everyone to be a winner.

ETHICAL

_____   18. I maintain ethical standards.

ORGANIZED

_____   19. My work and paperwork are well-organized.

FIGURE 2.4:   Leadership assessment tool.

       LOOKS TO FUTURE

_____ 20. I keep an eye and ear directed to trends in my industry.

_____ 21. I try to innovate.

       CONGRUENT

_____ 22. I walk the talk.

       FLEXIBLE

_____ 23. I keep an open mind.

_____ 24. I can change my mind and change my plans when appropriate.

Vision

       VISION

_____ 25. I let my company's vision be my guide.

       PERSONAL VISION

_____ 26. I write and revise my personal mission statement yearly.

Managing Relationships

       SUPPORTING

_____ 27. I seek first to understand, then to be understood.

_____ 28. I genuinely show acceptance and positive regard toward staff.

_____ 29. I refrain from rudeness and treat others diplomatically and politely.

_____ 30. I maintain the self-respect of all individuals.

_____ 31. I have an open-door policy.

       DEVELOPING/MENTORING

_____ 32. I believe developing and mentoring others is part and parcel of being a professional, and that this will enhance, not detract, from my career.

_____ 33. I actively develop and act as a mentor.

       EMPOWERING

_____ 34. I actively empower staff to do their jobs in the manner they want as long as it supports our mission.

       RECOGNIZING & REWARDING

_____ 35. I use a variety of techniques to recognize and reward staff for their achievements and contributions.

_____ 36. I provide fair, specific, and timely recognition and rewards.

_____ 37. I recognize and reward more people than just the top performers.

_____ 38. I use recognition and rewards that are desirable to the recipients.

       MANAGING CONFLICT & CHANGE

_____ 39. I see conflict as an opportunity to grow.

_____ 40. I mediate conflicts and encourage constructive resolution of conflicts.

_____ 41. I work on building and maintaining cooperative staff relationships.

_____ 42. I realize that people generally don't resist change, but they do resist being changed.

       TEAMBUILDING

_____ 43. I understand the teambuilding process.

_____ 44. I model teambuilding skills.

_____ 45. I help form and monitor teams.

FIGURE 2.4:   *(continued)*

NETWORKING

_____ 46. I actively network with people both within and outside of the industry.

_____ 47. I keep in touch with members of my network.

_____ 48. I am good at remembering names.

Managing the Work

PLANNING

_____ 49. After considering input, I help establish clear priorities and goals for our unit/department.

_____ 50. Unit/department policies and procedures are spelled out.

_____ 51. Budgets are devised yearly and compared to monthly reports.

ORGANIZING

_____ 52. The work of my unit/department runs efficiently.

DECISION MAKING

_____ 53. I do much information gathering and get much input before making decisions.

_____ 54. I build commitment for my decisions.

_____ 55. I develop creative solutions.

PROBLEM SOLVING

_____ 56. I identify problems and take responsibility for them.

_____ 57. I use the problem-solving process including trying creative solutions.

_____ 58. I don't ignore problem behaviors and I deal effectively and quickly with them.

CLARIFYING ROLES & OBJECTIVES

_____ 59. My employees know what is expected of them.

INFORMING

_____ 60. I interact with and inform my colleagues.

_____ 61. I keep my supervisor informed about what I am doing.

_____ 62. I prepare meeting agendas for all meetings I conduct.

_____ 63. I keep staff informed about policies, procedures, and all changes.

MONITORING

_____ 64. I monitor the performance of staff.

_____ 65. I meet regularly with staff.

_____ 66. I periodically walk around to talk with employees and guests.

_____ 67. I attend monthly meetings of the local hospitality owners/operators.

MANAGING TIME

_____ 68. I set daily priorities and do first things first.

_____ 69. I set time aside every day for physical exercise.

DELEGATING

_____ 70. I delegate appropriate tasks.

FIGURE 2.4: _(continued)_

Case Study Questions

1. What kind of impression do you think that Latisha is making on the employees?
2. What are the good points in her presentation?
3. What mistakes do you think she is making?
4. Why did nobody ask questions or make comments?
5. From this first impression, what would you say is her management style?
6. Do you think that people will feel free to come to her with suggestions and problems?
7. Do you think that she will set a good example?
8. Is she fair in her demands?
9. Do you think that her people will "start off on the right foot," as she suggests?
10. Do you think that she sees herself clearly? Is she aware of her impact on others?

WEB ACTIVITY

- Go to the following website: www.valuebasedmanagement.net/methods_mcgregor_theory_X_Y.html. Here you will find McGregor's Theory X and Theory Y Model. Read the comparison chart and then scroll down to the links with comparison models. Pick two models that you feel are preferable over McGregor's Theory.
- Write a brief summary of these models and why you feel they are preferable. Bring the summaries in for the next class discussion.

RELATED WEBSITES

Society for Human Resources	www.shrm.org
Hospitality Magazines	www.restaurantresults.com
Hospitality Online	www.hospitalityonline.com
Hospitality Net	www.hospitalitynet.org
National Restaurant Association	www.restaurant.org

ENDNOTES

1. www.leadingtoday.org/onmag/jan01/leadership12001.htm. Retrieved May 14, 2010.
2. Eric Schlosser, *Fast Food Nation: The Dark Side of the All-American Meal* (New York: HarperPerenniel, 2005), p. 4.
3. U.S. Marine Corps Association, *Guidebook for Marines*, 19th ed. (Quantico, VA: U.S. Marine Corps Association, 2009), chapter 5, pp. 43–49.
4. Larry J. Gitman and Carl McDaniel, *The Future of Business*, 5th ed. (Cincinnati, OH: South-Western Publishing, 2005), p. 209.
5. John C. Maxwell, *The 21 Indispensible Qualities of a Leader* (Nashville, TN: Thomas Nelson, 1999), p. x1.
6. Ibid.
7. Stephen P. Robins and David A. DeCenzo, *Supervision Today*, 4th ed. (Upper Saddle River, NJ: Prentice Hall, 2010), pp. 235–236.

8. Paul H. Hersey and Kenneth H. Blanchard, *Management of Organizational Behavior*, 3rd Ed.– *Utilizing Human Resources* Upper Saddle River, NJ: Prentice Hall, 1977).

9. Transactional and transformational leadership are discussed in depth by James MacGregor Burns, *Leadership* (New York: Harper & Row, 1978). Also see Bernard Bass, *Leadership and Performance Beyond Expectations* (New York: Free Press, 1985); and Joseph Selzer and Bernard Bass, "Transformational Leadership: Beyond Initiation and Consideration," *Journal of Management*, vol. 16, no. 4 (1990), pp. 693–703.

10. www.leadingtoday.org/onmag/jan03/transaction12003.html. Retrieved May 24, 2010.

11. Malcolm Baldrige National Quality Award recipients can be found at baldrige.nist.gov/Contacts_Profiles.htm.

12. Peter F. Drucker, "Foreword," in F. Hesselbein, M. Goldsmith, and R. Beckhard (eds.), *The Leader of the Future* (San Francisco: Jossey-Bass, 1966), pp. xii–xiv.

13. Ibid.

14. Larry J. Gitman and Carl McDaniel, *The Future of Business*, 5th ed. (Cincinnati, OH: South-Western Publishing, 2005), p. 211.

15. Ricky W. Griffen and Ronald J. Ebert, *Business*, 7th ed. (Upper Saddle River, NJ: Prentice Hall, 2004), p. 445.

16. National Restaurant Association Educational Foundation, *Becoming an Effective Leader. Foodservice Leadership—Skills for the Professional*, v. 160 (Chicago: National Restaurant Association, 1994). Video.

17. Martha I. Finney, "The Truth about Getting the Best from People," *Financial Times Press* (Upper Saddle River, NJ: Prentice Hall, 2008), p. 6.

18. Ibid.

19. Stephen S. J. Hall, Ed., *Ethics in Hospitality Management: A Book of Readings* (East Lancing, MI: Educational Institute, American Hotel & Lodging Association, 1992), p. 75.

Chapter 3

Getting to Know People: Personality and Intelligence Differences

*P*art II of this book looks at employees; we can think of no better way to start Part II than by exploring how individuals differ, and how these differences impact the workplace. People have different hopes, fears, talents, experiences, beliefs, attitudes, and ways of thinking. You explore some of these differences in later chapters. But a lot of the differences between people can be said to boil down to personality, so in this chapter, you take a look at different theories of personality, at how personality is used in the workplace and how personality is linked to behaviour. We also discuss intelligence as another key difference between people and consider how intelligence is measured and used in the workplace.

So why look at individual differences like personality and intelligence? Well, understanding and measuring the ways in which people differ from one other enables you to see whether they act and perform in different ways at work because of those differences. Researchers have conducted many studies in these areas, which means that a lot is known about personality and intelligence. So, for example, knowing what type of personality is likely to be best suited to certain jobs and how levels of intelligence can affect job performance. This information is useful if a manager wants to hire somebody to work in his business.

Defining Personality: Type Versus Trait

Personality is people's tendency to act and think in certain ways. If you were asked what type of personality you have, you may reply with something like outgoing or adventurous, or perhaps reserved or quiet. In fact, how you decide to describe yourself reveals a bit about the person you are and the things you're likely to enjoy doing (assuming that you're telling the truth, of course; we discuss lying in the later 'Matching personality to the job' section). Of course, even a person who has an outgoing personality sometimes acts in a reserved and quiet way – for example, when he's attending a funeral. The situation a person is in affects his behaviour just as much as the type of personality he has.

Psychologists have proposed a lot of different ways of looking at personality over the years, which isn't surprising given people's interest in understanding why they and others act the way they do. This section gives you a whistle-stop tour of the main personality theories and then looks at the two most popular personality theories that psychologists use in the workplace to predict and explain behaviour, that is the type theory of personality and the trait theory of personality.

Reviewing personality theories

Psychologists have proposed several theories to try to explain and understand personality and how it affects behaviour. Different people agree with different theories and no *definite* agreement of personality exists – just suggestions for what it may be. The following list gives you an overview of the main theories.

- **Biological theory:** *Biological theories* of personality are based on the premise that personality and behaviour are related to purely biological factors (nature). Any difference between people is therefore based on biological differences and not differences in upbringing or experiences. Most people now accept that biology alone can't explain all personality differences.

- **Environmental theory:** *Environmental theories* go to the other extreme and propose that personality differences are all due to environment (nurture) rather than biology. In other words, your family and friends influence your personality. Of course, this theory is too simple a picture, too! Most theorists now agree that *both* biology and environment – both nature and nurture – are important to personality and behaviour.

- **Social learning theory:** *Social learning theory* is environmentally based but has been so influential, it deserves a bullet point of its own. This theory proposes that personality develops through socialisation with other people and that you find out how to behave by watching what other people do. In the most famous experiment of social learning theory, researchers found that if children watch adults being violent when they play with a doll and then see this behaviour approved of by another adult, then the children are more likely to be violent to the doll when they're given the chance to play with it. If, however, the children see an adult disapproving of the violent behaviour, then they were less likely to show aggression.

✔ **Psychoanalytic theory:** Psychoanalysts place a lot of emphasis on the unconscious mind and on how thoughts and motivations we are not aware of influence behaviour. The most famous psychoanalyst was Sigmund Freud, who, as well as talking about the unconscious mind a lot, also said that personality comprises three facets:

- **Id:** Controls instincts and looks to bring you pleasure.

- **Superego:** Provides you with a conscience and morals.

- **Ego:** Strives to meet the desire of the Id without compromising the superego's moral stance.

For example, say that you see a fantastic-looking slice of lovely, gooey, chocolate cake. Your id says, 'Eat it now'. Your superego says, 'But you're on a diet. You'll feel bad if you eat it, so leave it on the plate.' Your ego then mediates between these two and decides on your actual course of action. (To be honest, we'd probably have eaten the cake by now . . . .)

✔ **Humanistic theory:** *Humanistic theory* suggests that your personality is driven by the desire for self-development. You want to grow as a person and acquire new knowledge, and this desire influences the way you behave. Organisational behaviourists use humanistic theory in workplaces to try to understand and predict work behaviours, but mainly as a way of explaining motivation rather than as a true personality theory. Abraham Maslow and his hierarchy of needs is the most famous humanistic theory, and we discuss this more in Chapter 9.

✔ **Type theory:** *Type theory* sees personality as belonging to distinct groups (so you must be 'this' or 'that' type of personality).

✔ **Trait theory:** *Trait theory* sees traits as being on a continuum, so you can be anxious, a little anxious, or not at all anxious, for example, rather than being just one way or the other (as type theory would suggest).

Work psychologists measure personality and use the information they obtain to try to predict behaviour (check out the later section 'Assessing Personality to Predict Behaviour' to find out more) and their studies have revealed that personality is linked to performance at work. The two theories from the preceding list that they use most in the workplace when doing so are type theory and trait theory. The following sections provide more detail on type and trait theories.

Seeing personality as black and white with type theory

Type personality theory splits people into two main types when describing personalities. For example, in type theory, you describe yourself as introverted or extroverted, pessimistic or optimistic, disorganised or organised.

Take a look at Figure 3-1, which shows the personality types pessimistic and optimistic for four people: Alan, Becky, Colin, and David. If we accept that people can have different degrees of optimism and pessimism, then the curve shows how some people are low on optimism or pessimism, some people high and most people are around the middle. Type theory, though, forces people to be described as one thing or the other (here, pessimistic or optimistic). Under type theory, Alan and Becky are both described as pessimistic people, whereas Colin and David are seen as optimistic people. So far, so good. But an obvious problem exists. Look at the positioning of Becky and Colin. Despite being seen as having different personality types, they're actually the closest of all the people to each other, and so are the most similar of the four people. How does that similarity happen?

Type theory can be useful when making clear distinctions between people and is commonly used in the workplace in personality type questionnaires based on the Myers-Briggs Type Inventory (MBTI). The MBTI splits personality into four key areas, with two main personality types in each area, as shown in Table 3-1. Sixteen potential combinations derive from these personality types. How easy would you find it to place yourself in one of these types? Are you a thinker or a feeler? An extrovert or introvert? Looking at personality in this way can help to explain similarities and differences between people, but using distinct types means that you lose some detail.

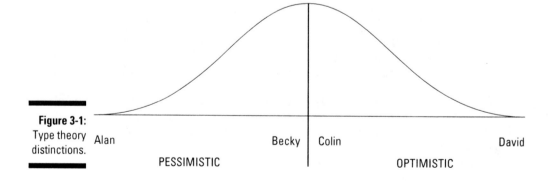

Figure 3-1:
Type theory
distinctions.

Alan   Becky   Colin   David

PESSIMISTIC   OPTIMISTIC

Table 3-1	MBTI Personality Types
MBTI Personality Type	*Description*
Extroversion/introversion	Extroverts enjoy interaction with other people, whereas introverts prefer to be alone. Extroverts like to work in teams, whereas introverts are more reflective and reserved.
Sensing/intuiting	Sensors have a preference of gathering information using their senses, so they enjoy working with facts and information. Intuitors, on the other hand, are good at working with possibilities and the abstract and theoretical.
Thinking/feeling	Thinkers like to make decisions in a logical, objective way, whereas a feeling person makes decisions in a more personal way.
Judging/perceiving	Judging people like structure and are decisive and time oriented. They like to be organised. In comparison, perceivers like flexibility and spontaneity. They prefer things to be open ended rather than rigid and organised.

One of the advantages of type theory is its simplicity. The theory is easy to understand and easy to communicate and use in the workplace. However, the simplicity of type theory is also the source of its major criticism: Can you really distinguish between people in such a simplistic way? Is everyone optimistic or pessimistic? Surely you could describe two people as optimistic, and yet they could be optimistic to different degrees? Another criticism is that by forcing people into distinct categories, type theory ignores some of the similarities between people. So, type theory can be limiting.

Taking the broader view with trait theory

The trait approach to personality has been influential in work psychology and has allowed work psychologists to make a lot of links between personality and work behaviours. (See the section 'Predicting Behaviour Using Personality,' later in this chapter.)

Trait theory is different from type theory (see the previous section) in that it sees personality characteristics as on a *normally distributed continuum*. This term sounds highly technical but it simply means that some people are low on a trait and some people are high, but most people are around the middle. Figure 3-2 illustrates this point, focusing once more on extroversion. (You may recognise this curve from Figure 3-1.)

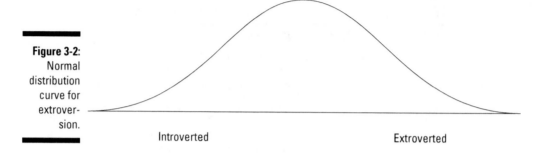

Figure 3-2:
Normal
distribution
curve for
extrover-
sion.

Introverted   Extroverted

Trait theory proposes that people can be at the extremes of a personality trait, but they can also be anywhere between the two. So unlike type theory, which allows you to compare people only in categories, trait theory gives you more detail. This additional detail makes comparisons easier and allows a better understanding of which personality traits are linked to which behaviours.

Trait theory proposes that personality traits influence the way people act and behave and that although behaviour differs depending on the situation, the underlying personality trait is still important in explaining why people behave the way they do. Trait theorists believe that traits are stable in adulthood, so although your personality may change a bit as you get older you're pretty much the same person in your 60s as you were in your 20s, 30s, 40s, and 50s.

If you've taken a personality test during a job interview, you may well have come across a personality questionnaire based on the work of Raymond Bernard Cattell, a famous personality trait researcher. The 16PT is a personality question-naire that provides information on Cattell's 16 personality traits. (Can you guess where they got the name from?) You can see these 16 traits in Table 3-2.

Compare Table 3-2 to Table 3-1 on the MBTI from the previous section and consider the amount of information provided by the two. Clearly, you discover a lot more about a person using trait theory rather than type theory. Remember also that type theory only tells you that a person is in one category or another, whereas trait theory tells you where a person sits on a continuum for each trait.

Trait theory is more useful than type theory in the workplace because it gives more detail about personality. However, some people disagree and argue that type theory is the one they feel more comfortable using.

Both type and trait theories are used at work but remember the limitations of type theory if you decide to use it.

Table 3-2	Cattell's 16 Personality Traits
Personality Trait	*Brief Description*
Cool/warm	From cool and reserved to warm and outgoing
Concrete thinking / abstract thinking	From *lower intelligence* (thinking based on facts and descriptions) to *higher intelligence* (thinking involving abstract mental processes)
Affected by feelings/ emotionally stable	From less stable and easily upset to emotionally stable and calm
Submissive/dominant	From co-operative and conflict-avoiding to forceful and assertive
Sober/enthusiastic	From serious and restrained to lively and enthusiastic
Expedient/conscientious	From a disregard to rules and self-indulgent to dutiful and conscientious
Shy/bold	From shy and easily intimidated to bold and thick-skinned
Tough-minded/ tender-minded	From unsentimental and tough to sentimental and sensitive
Trusting/suspicious	From trusting and not suspicious to sceptical and distrustful
Practical/imaginative	From practical and solution-focused to impractical and absent-minded
Forthright/shrewd	From open and forthright to discreet and diplomatic
Self-assured/apprehensive	From confident and secure to worried and insecure
Conservative/experimenting	From traditional and conservative to liberal and open to change
Group-oriented/ self-sufficient	From affiliative to individualistic
Undisciplined/controlled	From impulsive and careless to self-disciplined and a perfectionist
Relaxed/tense	From relaxed and patient to tense and impatient

Using Personality in the Workplace

In the previous section, we outline some popular theories for exploring personality. The next questions, of course, are, 'So what? Why examine personality? What does personality tell you?' Well, different personality theories explain quite a bit about behaviour. This section introduces three influential personality theories – Type A and Type B, locus of control, and the Big 5 – and describes what they reveal about behaviour and how they're used in the workplace.

Type A and Type B, locus of control, and the Big 5 are all based on trait theory, so they see personality as being on a continuum.

Considering Type A and Type B personalities

Are you a Type A or Type B person? If you've already come across these terms, you may already know. If you haven't yet heard these terms, you can do a personality test that tells you. Having said that, we reckon you'll have a good idea which type you are if you read this section.

Type A or Type B personality descriptors come under trait theory. (For more on trait theory, see the earlier section 'Taking the broader view with trait theory.') Traits are on a continuum, so, for example, you can be highly Type A or slightly Type B. Here's a basic overview of Type A and Type B personalities:

- **Type A:** High Type A means that you're competitive, high achieving, aggressive, hasty, impatient, time conscious, and hard driving. Type A people tend to be workaholics.

- **Type B:** High Type B is the opposite to Type A. Type B people are less competitive and tend to be more relaxed and fun loving.

The work attitudes and behaviours of Type A and Type B people differ, and both have their strengths and weaknesses, as outlined in Table 3-3.

What type of jobs suit Type A and Type B people? Well, Type B people may be more team or person-based and well-suited to jobs in which they can use their skills of empathy and patience. Type A people are well-suited to jobs in which they've a lot of control and are constantly faced with challenges they can throw themselves into. Type As can thrive in these kind of conditions and are commonly high achievers.

But health risks are associated with being Type A, especially if you've a high need for control in your job and you don't have it or it's taken away from you. In fact, in the 1950s cardiologists identified the Type A and Type B patterns of behaviour and discovered that in a study of more than 3,000 employees, Type A men had more than twice the rate of coronary heart disease than Type B men. (For more on stress, see Chapter 6.)

Table 3-3 Comparing Type A and B Personalities in the Workplace

Type A Personality	Type B Personality
Tend to work long hours	Tend to be productive under stress
Are constantly under deadlines and overload conditions	Are relaxed and patient and have a lot of self-control
Take their work home with them	Do not get irritated, angry, or frustrated easily
Find it hard to relax	Aren't particularly competitive
Have a habit of not taking vacations or cutting them short	May be tolerant and flexible and can change in order to adapt to situations
Like to compete with themselves and others	Tend not to overreact and do not mind waiting to get work done
Often drive themselves to meet high (and sometimes unrealistic) standards	Like to plan things in advance and keep aware of time available and deadlines
Can feel frustrated at work	Rarely complain or worry
May be irritated by the work efforts of subordinates	Do not constantly wish to lead or be in control
May feel misunderstood by superiors	Are emotional and not indifferent toward other people

Think about whether you'd rather be managed by a Type A or a Type B person? You may choose Type B because that person's likely to be the easiest to work with. But will a Type B manager keep the business going? Perhaps a Type A person who's hard driving and ambitious would be best for this role? Probably the best manager is someone who isn't too far in either extreme!

Looking at locus of control

How much control do you have over your life and the things that happen to you? If you believe that you're in control and can influence what's going on around you, you've what's called an *internal locus of control*. If, however, you think that events are out of control and things just happen to you, you've an *external locus of control*. Your belief about the amount of control you have over your life is an aspect of your personality and influence how you see your life.

People with an internal locus of control put good performance at work down to their abilities and effort and believe that they did well because they tried hard.

An internal locus of control means that you feel you can influence events around you, so if you work hard, you perform well. Compare this attitude to people with an external locus of control. If they perform well, then they believe it's because of luck or chance and that nothing they did influenced the outcome in any way.

Here are a few locus of control facts:

- ✔ People with an internal locus of control enjoy better health and greater job satisfaction, even more so for women than for men.
- ✔ People tend to get more internal as they age.
- ✔ People in management and leadership positions tend to be more internal.
- ✔ Internals tend to be better off financially (possibly due to being higher achievers and having better jobs).
- ✔ Some people believe that locus of control is linked to the situation and is not just a personality trait.

Generally, you're probably better off having an internal locus of control rather than an external. For example, imagine that you're the manager of someone with an external locus of control. How would you motivate the employee to work hard if he believes he can't influence the outcome and that doing well just boils down to luck and not effort? However, in some instances, having an external locus of control is useful. For example, if major work changes occur that are out of your control, having an internal locus of control can be more stressful than having an external locus of control. Overall, though, internals tend to fare better than externals.

The Big 5 personality traits

Probably the most famous and most commonly used personality theory in the workplace (and elsewhere) is the Big 5. Unsurprisingly, this theory has five personality traits. An easy way to remember the traits is to use the acronym OCEAN:

Openness

Conscientiousness

Extroversion

Agreeableness

Neuroticism

As trait theory (see the earlier section 'Taking the broader view with trait theory') dictates, the traits are on a continuum. Table 3-4 outlines the five traits of the Big 5.

Table 3-4	The Big 5 Personality Traits
Personality Trait	*Brief Description*
Open to experience/closed to experience	From open to new experiences and imaginative to less open to new experiences, narrow-minded, and unimaginative
Conscientious/disorganised	From well-organised, focused on targets, goals, and deadlines, dependable and good at paying attention to detail to impulsive, disorganised, and less detail-focused
Extroverted/introverted	From outgoing and good at dealing with people (managers tend to be above average on extroversion) to less outgoing, comfortable in own company or that of their close friends
Agreeable/tough-minded	From usually good natured, keen to co-operate with others, takes care to avoid conflict, easy to get on with, and not argumentative to unfriendly, strong-willed, and not averse to conflict
Neurotic/stable	From a tendency to experience negative states, such as anger, anxiety, and guilt, to stable, rarely upset, and typically calm

You can probably see how you may describe yourself in relation to these traits and recognise traits in friends and colleagues. You've no doubt got a tough-minded pal who tells the truth about something even if you don't like it and extroverted friends you'd invite out to the pub. You may also recognise the neurotic friend who panics over everything and blows the smallest problems into huge issues. Is this description ringing any bells?

Finding the Big 5: The lexical approach

Early personality researchers had the bright idea of looking at language to see the different ways in which people are described and created huge long lists of different terms that relate to personality. They argued that any important differences between people would have been recorded in language at some point, so where better to look when trying to find out about personality? As you can imagine, lot of words describe people – one of the surveys done discovered over 17,000 different words!

When investigated, though, these words all related to five basic personality factors, and the Big 5 was discovered. And the Big 5 exists across nationalities, such as American, British, Chinese, Czech, Dutch, German, Hebrew, Hungarian, Japanese, Korean, Polish, Portuguese, and Turkish. What is really impressive about this list is that researchers compiled it before computers were available, so all the analysis was done by hand.

What's really interesting about the Big 5 theory is that it can incorporate all other theories of personality. Research has shown that even where personality theories propose more than five factors (for example, Cattell's 16 factors; see the section 'Taking the broader view with trait theory'), they can all fit into the five-factor theory of personality.

The Big 5 is an excellent theory to use to predict behaviour in settings such as in the workplace. Take a look at the 'Assessing Personality to Predict Performance' section below where you'll find more on how the Big 5 is linked to work performance.

Assessing Personality to Predict Behaviour

The previous sections in this chapter demonstrate ways to measure and use personality theories, such as the Big 5 at work, to describe and compare people. So what? Is it at all useful to be able to say that one person is more extroverted than another? Well, yes, when knowing that someone's personality traits help you predict their behaviour.

Researchers have conducted lots of studies and have discovered that individual or combinations of personality traits predict:

- Job performance
- Academic success
- Mortality
- Divorce
- Alcoholism
- Health behaviours
- Drug use

Personality relates to academic success and job performance. As a result, you can use personality questionnaires in the workplace to look at what types of personalities are likely to perform best at different types of jobs. Employers commonly do this kind of thing when selecting employees.

This application of personalities makes sense when you think about it. Say that you want to employ a sales manager. Would you want an introverted person who isn't hugely outgoing or an extroverted person who's outgoing and good at dealing with people? Now, unless you've an odd idea of what a sales manager does all day, you've probably decided that an extrovert would suit the job best.

Some people are clearly better suited to certain jobs than others. Looking at personality and job characteristics allows you to match up people to jobs in a logical manner.

Performing and personality

A recent study of the Big 5 personality traits (see the earlier section 'The Big 5 personality traits') showed that four of the five factors were related to job performance:

- ✔ Conscientiousness predicts performance across most jobs and organisational settings.
- ✔ Openness to experience predicts training performance.
- ✔ Emotional stability predicts job performance.
- ✔ Extroversion predicts performance for some jobs (for example, sales).

As well as overall job performance, personality traits relate to detailed aspects of work, such as how dedicated people are to their jobs and how likely people are to be absent from work. Table 3-5 shows areas in which researchers have found links between personality and work behaviour.

Table 3-5	Work Behaviours Linked to Personality
Overall Job Performance	*Counterproductive Work Behaviour*
Getting ahead	Procrastination
Task performance	Absenteeism
Training performance	Team performance and teamwork
Learning and skill acquisition	Job and career satisfaction
Organisational citizenship	Subjective wellbeing
Altruism	Innovation
Job dedication	Creativity
Overall managerial effectiveness	Goal setting
Promotion	Managerial level
Turnover	

Matching personality to the job

When interviewing for a job, organisations commonly ask candidates to complete a personality questionnaire. But what does a personality test look for?

Take the following example ad:

> **DATA PROCESSOR REQUIRED.** *CLS Ltd. Hours of work 9–5. You will be required to manage incoming data, check for duplications and errors, mail merge data, and produce weekly reports. Good IT skills are essential.*

Just by reading the advertisement, you can identify some of the qualities a person who would do well in the job would possess. For example, he needs to be happy working on his own because he'll likely spend most of his time working with data rather than people. He also needs to have good attention to detail because he'll be required to check for errors and mistakes and produce reports. What personality traits would you look for in the applicants then? Probably a more introverted than extroverted person and somebody who's conscientious rather than disorganised.

Of course, personality assessment isn't as crude as this example, and you wouldn't just guess at the personality factors that would fit the job. Loads of research in this area can tell you what to look for and how to go about it – flick to Chapter 17 for more on using personality tests in selection.

You may be thinking at this point that personality testing is all very well, but what's to stop somebody lying when he fills out his questionnaire? For example, an applicant may pretend he's extroverted to get a well-paid bar manager job he wants rather than staying in work as a data processor. Well, for one thing, why would somebody want a job that he's obviously not going to be suited to and may hate? More seriously, though, most personality measures have lie scales built into them that assess whether or not people are providing the answers that they think people want to hear rather than telling the truth. An example of a lie scale is a simple question like, 'Have you ever told a lie?'. The assumption is that nobody can really say 'no' to this question, so if you do you must be lying!

Measuring Intelligence

The previous sections look at how people differ in terms of their personality, but that's not the only difference between people. Another important difference between people, often used in the workplace during selection as a way of identifying the best candidate, is that of intelligence.

Intelligence – also known as general intelligence (g), cognitive ability and general mental ability – is a person's general mental ability to understand things around him. You use your intelligence to try to figure out solutions to the problems you're faced with. Researchers believe that intelligence is inherited, to a point; some researchers say up to 80 per cent of intelligence is inherited whereas others suggest environmental factors can contribute up to 50 per cent.

Intelligence has a normal distribution curve (see the earlier section 'Taking the broader view with trait theory'), so some people have low intelligence, some people have high intelligence, but the majority of people are around the middle and have average intelligence.

Researchers also believe that in addition to general intelligence, you can measure different types of intelligence, such as

- **Visual/spatial:** Being able to make sense of visual images, such as reading a map (if you struggle with map reading, you're probably low on visual/spatial intelligence).
- **Perceptual speed:** Being able to identify and understand objects quickly.
- **Reasoning:** Being able to solve complex problems.
- **Numerical skills:** Having good mathematical ability.
- **Learning and memory:** Having the ability to recall knowledge.

Looking at intelligence in more detail allows you to assess how well people are likely to perform in different tasks. This assessment is especially useful in the workplace. Some jobs, such as being a pilot, require good visual perception, whereas others, such as acting, call for good memory skills. Measuring intelligence can therefore help you match people to job requirements.

Having higher-than-average levels of general intelligence is thought to increase the chances of being successful at work and in life in general. Intelligence has been linked to educational achievement, better finances, social status, and – most important for this discussion – work performance. People with higher general intelligence are more likely to be effective at work, especially in complex or difficult jobs. They're able to pick up jobs quicker and are more likely to acquire knowledge and succeed in training.

To best predict success at work, you can look at specific types of intelligence that are relevant to the job. For example, an accountant will probably perform better if he has high numerical skills and may have less need for visual/spatial skills.

Testing intelligence

You can assess somebody's intelligence by how well he performs at problem solving. You can probably think of somebody you believe to be low on intelligence because of his poor problem solving. (We won't ask you to name names, of course.)

Many intelligence tests exist that are designed to measure general intelligence or the subscales of intelligence. Most people have at some point completed an intelligence test for fun (you can find plenty of intelligence tests online if you fancy a go) or as part of a career interview (to see what your skills are) or job application (to see whether your skills match the ones needed to do the job).

Intelligence tests often standardise the scores and results, so the test reviewer can compare people easily. When standardised, the midpoint of the normal distribution curve (that is, the average intelligence level) is set at 100. About two-thirds of people have scores between 85 and 115. Any score below 100 is seen as below average intelligence, and any score over 100 is seen as above average intelligence.

One study looking at predicting job performance compared many different assessments of new recruits, such as interviews, references, personality tests, intelligence tests, and work sample tests. Intelligence was the best predictor of performance of all the different assessments except the work sample test. A work sample test, where the candidate spends time completing work similar to that he would do on the job, can be expensive and time consuming to set up. An intelligence test, in comparison, is quick, cheap, and reliable. No wonder they're used so much in the workplace to identify good candidates for a job! (To find out more about intelligence assessments and other tests, see Chapter 17.)

Intelligence tests have issues, so you need to use tests that don't discriminate and are fair. See Chapter 11 for more on fairness at work.

Valuing emotional intelligence

Emotional intelligence is often seen as a new concept, mainly due to the popular success of psychologist Daniel Goleman's book *Emotional Intelligence: Why It Can Matter More Than IQ* in 1995 (Bloomsbury Publishing Plc). The idea that people have emotional intelligence isn't really that new, though. Researchers have been discussing emotional intelligence since the 1930s.

Emotional intelligence is the ability to

- Perceive emotion
- Reason using emotion
- Understand emotion
- Manage emotion

Studies looking at performance and emotional intelligence have reported links between the two, suggesting that the higher your emotional intelligence levels, the better your performance (for some tasks at least). Emotional intelligence has been shown to predict

- ✔ Classroom performance of managers
- ✔ Sales performance
- ✔ Performance on group tasks
- ✔ Potential leadership ability
- ✔ Good customer interaction
- ✔ Leaders ability to manage employee job satisfaction
- ✔ Supervisory ratings of work performance

Emotional intelligence is important when you're working with other people. If a job involves working with colleagues, employees, or customers, then having good emotional intelligence is likely to make the job easier to do for many reasons:

- ✔ **Customers respond better to emotionally intelligent staff.** Think about being faced with an angry or upset customer. Understanding why the customer is angry and controlling your own emotions during the customer interaction are both really important to how well you perform your job and how happy the customer is. (We discuss these emotional demands of jobs in Chapter 7.)

- ✔ **Managers with higher levels of emotional intelligence are better able to understand the feelings of their employees and can use this information to better manage the workplace.** If a manager giving a performance review understands that an employee may be disappointed or upset by negative feedback, he may take care to handle feedback sensitively and ensure that the employee has the opportunity to ask any questions. If the manager doesn't realise the possible emotional reaction of the employee (because he has low emotional intelligence, for example), he may be too blunt with his comments and leave the employee feeling demoralised and upset.

Dispute exists as to whether emotional intelligence is an ability you're born with or something you can develop and improve. However, some organisations and business schools train people in emotional intelligence and they report success, so it seems that emotional intelligence can be taught to some extent. The development of emotional intelligence training proves that a demand exists for these types of skills in the workplace.

How emotional intelligence benefits organisations

The following examples illustrate the impact of emotional intelligence in the workplace.

✔ Salespeople selected partly on the basis of their emotional abilities outsold sales people selected using 'normal' methods. They were also less likely to leave the organisation.

✔ In an insurance company, salespeople high in emotional abilities sold more than double the policies of those salespeople who had lower emotional abilities.

✔ Executives who were low in emotional ability encountered problems with handling change and working in teams and also had poor interpersonal relationships.

✔ Following supervisor training in emotional skills at a manufacturing plant, accidents and complaints plummeted. Similar training in another plant led to increased profits.

✔ High-performing debt collectors were found to have better emotional skills than lower performing debt collectors.

Chapter 1

The Basics of Guest Service

Chapter Objectives:

After reading this chapter, you should be able to:

Identify and describe the history, ages of change, and current status of guest service in the United States.

Identify the various reasons why guests may not complain outwardly.

Identify and explain the reasoning behind why guests share their poor experiences with others.

Describe the expectations of guests as they relate to hospitality.

Explain and apply the concept of using quality service as a competitive advantage.

Describe details regarding the legends of guest service.

Terminology:

Age of Communication
Age of Service
Age of Technology
DRIFT
MBWA
Moment of Truth
PDCA
Quality Customer Service

Introduction

Guest service cannot be studied in a vacuum. The concepts of this book are a unique blend of the materials essential to deliver quality guest service in the hospitality industry. It involves history, terminology, tools and instruments, human resources, problem-solving, strategy, marketing, and technology. Furthermore it, must also be applied to each sector of the hospitality industry.

This book is aimed toward hospitality management students in the first, second, or third year of their college studies. It may also be easily used by practitioners, laypeople, and those in other secondary education areas.

❦ A SCIENCE AND AN ART

This book aims to explain the primary aspects in customer service management within the hospitality industry. We all know that you should be nice to people, so why are there so many negative guest experiences in the hospitality industry? This is because good service doesn't just happen by itself. It requires a special blend of procedure, technique, and skill combined with the human element. It is, essentially, both a science and an art.

❦ INTEGRATION OF CUSTOMER SERVICE

Providing service is a concerted effort. There is much more to providing good service than simply being nice to people. In order for customer service to be successful, it must be integrated into the overall business model. Customer service must be part of the company's identity, or brand. It must be tailored to the individual operation and customized, planned, and executed with systems that support it. Employees must be knowledgeable about the brand, the products, and the operations. Also, the customer must be properly gauged or assessed to ensure proper alignment with the brand image.

So, the brand image, operations, and employees of the business must all align with the target customer whom they are aiming to attract, serve, and retain. In other words, providing quality customer service is more than being friendly. **It is part of the core of the business. It is integrated into nearly every decision. It is calculated and planned. It is evident in all of the operations, the people, and the plan.**

❦ MEETING GUESTS' EXPECTATIONS

Quality Customer Service

Meeting and exceeding the individual expectations of the customer.

There are a variety of definitions for customer service. Essentially, anytime patrons, or even prospective patrons, interact with a facet of the organization, customer service is rendered. **Quality customer service** is meeting and exceeding the individual customer's expectations. If service meets or surpasses customer's expectations, in any situation, it is said to be quality customer service.

Meeting or exceeding the expectations of customers, or quality customer service, can occur anywhere and at any level of establishment. Good service can occur at a concession stand, at a fine-dining establishment, at a show, or on a tour.

The Significance of the Pineapple

The pineapple is the most appropriate symbol for this book on guest service. Welcoming guests is central to all of the industry.

The pineapple's origins date back several hundred years. As ships returned from the Caribbean with pineapples, this sweet fruit was embraced in Europe and Colonial America. Hosts used it both as a centerpiece and dessert when entertaining. Hence, the pineapple came to represent hospitality. It is rumored that sea captains, once home, would place a pineapple on the front porch to signify their return. Neighbors then were welcome to stop by.

Hospitality is what we do. We make guests feel welcome.

❦ OVERVIEW OF HOSPITALITY– HOW IT RELATES TO CUSTOMER SERVICE

The hospitality industry is a service industry. The guest is served through many different means. The industry has many segments. Food, lodging, and travel have traditionally been the primary three. Controversy has recently entered the industry. Arguments support that events, sports, gaming, health care, and assisted living are other major segments. Some argue that "almost all of the industry is travel and tourism," or "marketing" or "business management." Despite this controversy, most would agree that all of these disciplines fall within the service sector of the economy.

Being a service industry means that customers determine the success of the operation and business. The customer can make a business the most popular business in town. The customer can also shut down a giant operation by choosing not to patronize it.

This text dedicates specific chapters to the food, beverage, hotel, casino, travel, and events sectors of the industry, recognizing the individual nature of each.

❦ EXAMPLES OF BAD SERVICE

Why does bad service exist? There are many reasons for bad service. The reasons are endless and often appear to be out of direct control. Some appear acceptable to the staff, the manager, or even the guests. Following is a list of common excuses. While many may appear legitimate, none is truly acceptable.

Service Insight

I'm in Training

A name tag states, "I'M IN TRAINING." Employee turnover, cross-training, system changes, and employee development means that there will always be someone in training. How should this best be handled? Does it always have to be simulated behind the scenes? Or, can it be assisted training in front of the guest? Surveys suggest that customers are generally more patient and have lower expectations of service when they see that an employee is in training. Others, though, are immediately intolerant because they feel that the business has provided them with less-than-adequate attention and that errors are likely.

Suggestions: Do as much training as possible behind the scenes. Don't release employees to the public who aren't ready. Use role plays and simulations until trainees are competent. The customer service setting is not a training ground. Always give direct supervision when training in front of a guest. Make it obvious they are training and that support is immediately available. This will show the customer that the business cares about providing them with service.

❦ EXCUSES FOR BAD SERVICE

Staffing

They are understaffed.
They aren't paid enough.
They aren't properly trained.
They are just having a bad day.
No person or system is present to monitor.
They are in training.
They are overworked and tired.
It isn't their responsibility.
The boss isn't present or doesn't care.

Systems

The computer is slow.
The kitchen is slow.
The _____ is broken.
We just got a new _____.

Capacity/Customers

There are too many customers.
They didn't expect this many customers.
The customer is rude.
The customers are too demanding.
The customers don't know what they want.
The customers don't pay attention.
The customer doesn't seem to mind. No one has complained to corporate.
The party next to us or in the other room is too loud.

Setting

Everything in this neighborhood stinks.
This place is all about low cost.
We are renovating.

There are numerous reasons why poor service is delivered. Most of these reasons are common to all customer service settings. They are used regularly. **It is important to have a mindset that none of them is truly acceptable.**

Renovations

Renovations are inevitable. Some upgrades can be made with little or no disturbance to the customers. Sometimes, however, this is not possible. How should a business communicate to the customer that it is performing renovations?

Some businesses announce: "Please pardon our appearance." Others decide to say nothing and simply conduct business as usual. If it is mentioned before customers arrive, some customers will avoid coming altogether. If it is noticed at the time of service, some will forgive and others will be very disappointed. Their expectations will not have been met.

There are advantages and disadvantages to informing guests about construction, which must be carefully weighed. There is no one best way to approach a renovation. Keeping the inconveniences and loss of expectations to a minimum is key. Customers will be inconvenienced, and allowances must be made, so it is important to have a good service-recovery program in place. Also, a good contractor and project manager will greatly add to your success. Make sure they are aware of your expected level of service during the construction period.

✵ REASONS WHY CUSTOMERS DO NOT COMPLAIN

Most customers do not and will not complain. They will not give the business a chance to know what is wrong. Instead, they simply will not return. They may not tell you because they think you do not care or that you don't deserve to know. They may think that you should figure it out for yourself or that it would be too difficult for them to complain and actually be heard. Or they tried to complain and their concerns fell on deaf ears. Perhaps no system was in place to receive or correct the issue.

Lack of complaints doesn't always imply that service is great. Even the best-run companies struggle with issues. Also, it has often been said that *if you think that you have no problems, then you aren't listening hard enough.* Below is a list of reasons describing what might be going through the minds of guests.

- I don't think it's worth it.
- I tried before and no one listened.
- I am in a hurry.
- I don't want to make a scene.
- I feel bad for the staff.
- It isn't the staff's fault.
- I don't want to get anyone in trouble.
- There seems to be no solution in sight.
- I'm afraid that they'll mess with the food.
- I don't think that it will make a difference.
- I don't think anyone cares.
- I just hate this place and I want to leave.

You may not always know the reason why a customer doesn't complain. While they won't tell you, they will be sure to tell many of their friends.

✵ GOOD SERVICE CAN MAKE UP FOR BAD FOOD

Service may just be one reason why an experience is poor. What do you remember most about a poor hospitality experience? Was it the service? Was it the decor? Was it the event, the room, or the food? Or was it a combination of these things? A common phrase is:

"Good service can make up for a bad food, but good food cannot make up for poor service."

With this in mind, consider the following two scenarios.

SCENARIO A

You are at a nice restaurant with a date. Your evening plans are for dinner and an evening show. You mention to the server that you have show tickets. The server says, "OK." You are unsure what that means, but continue to order a medium-rare steak. Your date orders the pasta special. Within a reasonable amount of time, the dinners arrive at the table. You cut into your steak and discover that it is overcooked to the point of almost being well done. You look around and cannot find your server. After a few minutes, you catch a glimpse of your server walking back into the kitchen. You spend the next few minutes trying to get the server's attention as he runs around tending to other guests. You are finally successful and able to explain the situation. The steak is returned to the kitchen and you are left with nothing in front of you while your date sits uncomfortably waiting for your new steak to arrive. Despite your requests for your date to begin eating, he or she feels awkward eating while you have no food. Your new steak eventually arrives. By that time, nearly 20 additional minutes have passed and you have to eat quickly, with no time to enjoy your food. You are nervous that you will be late for your show. You try to get the check as soon as you can, but spend the rest of the time anxious that you will be late for the show.

SCENARIO B

You are at a nice restaurant with a date before an evening show. You mention to the server that you have tickets. The server inquires whether the show is at the nearby theatre and confirms the time. The server then smiles, nods, and says "Very well. We will do our very best to ensure that you have a great experience and make the show in plenty of time." You order a medium-rare steak. Your date orders the pasta special. Within a reasonable amount of time, the dinners arrive at your table. You cut into your steak and discover that it is overcooked to the point of being well done. You look up and realize the server has remained at the table to address any issues. He immediately apologizes and rushes the steak back to the kitchen to correct the issue. He promptly returns with a complimentary appetizer so that you and your date can begin eating together. Before you know it, your new steak is delivered to the table. Again, the server stays to ensure that it is cooked to your liking. This time it is. You are delighted that it was solved so effortlessly. You are asked if there is anything he can get for you. Your response is no. At that point, your check is placed on the table and you are told that there is no rush but that it can be settled at any time that you would prefer. You finish your dinner pleasantly and arrive at your show in plenty of time.

Shortcomings will occasionally occur. When they do, good service can help to make them much more bearable. Remember that good service can make up for other problems, but those other items cannot make up for bad service. Even if the steak was prepared perfectly, the guest would have worried about making the show on time. No matter how great things are, good service must be present.

❧ COMPETITIVE ADVANTAGE OF SERVICE

While each business is slightly different, most hospitality businesses offer a generic product. Nearly every:

- hotel offers a bed in a private room with a bath.
- restaurant delivers a meal with seating.
- theatre has seats and a stage with performances.
- airline flies you from a gate at one city to the next.

Of course there are different styles, settings, shapes, and colors, but what really makes the difference is the specific service of the business or establishment. This idea can generally be applied to all businesses that offer guest individual service. The tangibles and logistics can be copyrighted but are quickly replicated. Employees and managers transfer among brands, and companies benchmark each others' ideas. What competitors have the most difficulty with is replicating the individual service experience.

The Interview

All businesses realize that they need to be nice to the guest and deliver quality guest service, but a few rise above the rest and actually consistently meet or exceed guests' expectations. Some boast of this as part of their brand marketing and use it as a competitive advantage. One such example is the Ritz Carlton Hotel chain. This company has based its strategy on providing exceptional customer service. As a result, it has twice won a prestigious Malcolm Baldrige Award for quality excellence. Much planning, training, and preparation resulted in standards that are copied throughout many industries. Most notable is their motto stating: "We are Ladies and Gentleman serving Ladies and Gentleman." This statement gives the employees a high status, leading them to take pride in their positions while treating the guests with the expected high standards.

They also have a credo telling the employees to "fulfill even the unexpressed wishes of our guests." The customers are referred to as "guests." The services provided are "wishes" that are fulfilled, and the employees should anticipate the needs above and beyond those verbalized.

Ritz Carlton also implements empowerment to a high degree. Their service values include statements such as: "I own and immediately solve guest problems." It does not matter who caused the issue or what department it is in, the employee owns the problem and will see to it that it is solved immediately.

The Ritz Carlton goes on to train their employees to think about the big picture. Another service value tells employees to, "build strong relationships and create Ritz Carlton guests for life."

The Ritz Carlton also trains its employees on the basics of service with the "Three Steps of Service," including:

1. *A warm and sincere greeting. Use the guest's name.*
2. *Anticipation and fulfillment of the guest's needs.*
3. *Fond farewell. Give a warm good-bye and use the guest's name (The Ritz-Carlton).*

✧ BAD NEWS TRAVELS FAST

Advertisements show happy customers and boast about award-winning service, but how convincing is that compared with the testimony of a friend sharing his or her personal experience? These experiences have an especially great impact when they are about bad service. When a customer goes away unhappy, they are far more likely to tell another about their experience.

> *A woman and her friend were finishing their meal at a small café when she asked the waitress if they had decaffeinated tea. The woman informed the waitress that, because of health reasons, she could not have caffeine. The waitress replied that she wasn't sure but would check to see. The waitress quickly returned to the table and informed the customer that they only had regular, caffeinated tea. The customer, prepared for this situation because she enjoys tea and cannot have caffeine, requested a cup of hot water and took a decaffeinated teabag out of her purse. A few minutes later the bill came and she saw a miscellaneous charge of $2.00 on her bill. The woman inquired about the miscellaneous charge to the waitress who replied that the manager assesses a $2.00 charge for hot water. This was verified after the manager came to the table. Despite the reasoning, the manager simply ignored her feelings regarding the matter. Granted, it was only a small charge, but it wasn't about the money. As it turns out, the customer was a group session counselor at the local Weight Watchers Center. She told everyone in her classes about the situation. She vented and they became worked up for her cause. Those people went home and told others, who told others, and so on. This small café was dependent on the population from the small community. They will likely see the result of this seemingly insignificant incident amounting to much more damage than $2.00.*

"Bad news travels quickly" is a common expression. A customer will tell people, and those people may tell other people, who may tell more people, and so on. By some accounts, *customers will share a bad experience with 8 to 10 people.* The actual number varies, but a commonly accepted notion is that a guest who has a poor experience will tell several others and the word will continue to spread Occasionally, someone receiving poor service has a large audience, as in the story above. Online ratings are especially important because of the potential audience size or "reach" of the postings.

There are reasons why bad news travels so quickly. Perhaps these customers weren't heard or they want revenge; other reasons come to mind. Below is a list of reasons why bad news travels quickly to help explain the reasoning behind this phenomenon:

1. *The customer still needed to vent.* Customers need to be afforded the chance to express themselves. Venting is a normal part of the customer service process. Customers will need to share if they believe they weren't given the opportunity to be heard or understood. As a result, they recount their experiences to anyone and everyone who will listen.

2. *Customers may seek revenge.* If customers believe they have been wronged, they want to get even. When people feel as though they haven't received what they had expected and paid for, they feel the need to level the playing field. They tell friends and write poor reviews or anything else that justifies their pain and loss.

3. *Customers remember unusual events.* Because we have so many experiences throughout life, we filter the mediocrity from our brains. Customers continually take in information and filter all but the most unusual, emotional, or important of information. They tend to forget usual, typical, or mediocre experiences. If the guest experience was just OK or even good, people are not as likely to share the experience because it is deemed insignificant by their memories and is quickly forgotten.

4. *People love to repeat extreme events.* Really great and really bad events are more interesting and therefore more worthy of sharing with others.

5. *People can relate to these incidences.* Everyone has been wronged at some time. Bad news is particularly worth sharing because it has a sense of wronging that others can easily connect to.

6. *Service organizations and employees appear impersonal.* Talking about people may be seen as gossip, and criticizing others may be seen as unforgiving and impolite. However, talking about businesses is fair game. Businesses appear as large, non-human entities. Employees can easily be lumped into this same, disconnected state. Since they have no human connection, they can be easily blamed and criticized. While humans may make mistakes, businesses are faceless. Hotels, casinos, restaurants, and their employees are not seen as real people with feelings.

Each service encounter is important. Every time a customer is wronged is an opportunity for bad news to travel quickly. Management and staff should keep this in mind in their daily operations by imparting this knowledge upon their employees through training, and then monitoring their performance to ensure the point is remembered.

THE VALUE OF A RETURNING CUSTOMER

Imagine running a small restaurant, with a loyal customer base of 800 who eat at your establishment once a week. Out of a small town and surrounding area totaling 100,000 people, you have successfully captured just under 1% of them. You don't need to market, because you already have all the customers you need. You and your staff quickly learn all of their names because they are all repeat customers and you don't need to attract anyone new. You know the likes and dislikes of these regulars, and can tailor the experience to precisely meet their needs. You know how many to staff for and how much food to prepare. You run at maximum efficiency and reap the rewards.

While this would be an ideal situation, the truth is, it is never that easy. Loyal, return customers are highly sought-after prizes. **Businesses spend infinite amounts of money attracting customers and then undervalue them as they arrive and experience the product**. They are often treated as if it is the first and last time they will ever be seen. A return customer costs far less to keep than obtaining a new one. Businesses should spend less money attracting customers and more effort retaining the ones that they have.

❦ HISTORY OF SERVICE IN THE UNITED STATES

Age of Service
The current age in the United States. As the United States lost its manufacturing jobs, they were replaced with service-related jobs.

The history of customer service is not very old, at least from a scientific management point of view. References discuss innkeepers being hospitable and tavern owners keeping people happy, but the application of scientific methods to the art of customer service has expanded into what it is now only within the past 100 years.

Within that time, the United States has seen ages of change advance relatively quickly. We have transitioned from an agrarian society to a service society in just about the past 100 years. It is unlikely that either agriculture or industry will ever return as it once was, so the **age of service** should be present for quite some time.

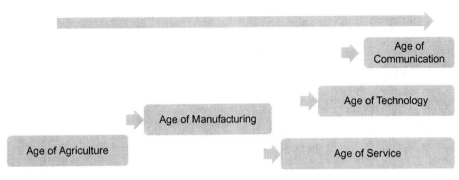

FIGURE 1.1   Ages of Change in the United States.

Age of manufacturing: Originally, the United States was largely an agricultural nation. It evolved into a thriving manufacturing nation but then quickly lost its dominance to other nations. A large portion of the management techniques used in the service industries have been adopted from manufacturing, which dominated the literature before the late 1900s.

Age of service: At present, the U.S. economy is comprised largely of service organizations. As the United States lost many of its manufacturing jobs to other countries, it began replacing them with service-related jobs.

Age of technology: Coupled with service, the United States also saw a boom in analog, then digital technology in the 1980s and 1990s. This heavily influenced the way that businesses operate. Business functions were expedited by computerization. Customers enjoyed the many new conveniences associated with technology.

Age of communication: While service continues to dominate the economy and employment of the United States, the advances and proliferation of technology spurred a new phenomenon of communication. Never before could so much information be so readily available so cheaply and easily. This spread of communication has forever changed the way that customer service operates in the United States and the world. Suppliers, businesses, and customers can now all communicate in real time and have the ability to access each other's records. A bad-service situation, such as an airline attendant berating fliers, a foodborne outbreak at a restaurant, or bedbugs in a hotel can now be seen around the world instantly. Customers' opinions can now be accessed by other potential customers, for better or worse.

Most Popular Sharing Websites

- Communicative
  - Facebook
  - Twitter
  - Blogs
  - YouTube
  - Wikis
  - Digital Pictures (Flickr, Picasa)

Age of Technology
Another recent age in the U.S. The increase and dominance of technology in U.S. culture and business operations.

Age of Communication
The service economy combined with proliferation technology created an age in which services can be communicated instantly, information can be accessed cheaply, and ratings can be found easily.

- Customer Engagement
  - Company websites
  - Fodor's
  - Google Alerts
  - Trip Advisor
  - Urbanspoon
  - Yelp
  - Google places
  - Four Square
  - QR Codes

Sporting events could poll their fans on their cell phones. Conference attendees could tweet by use of a hash tag. New hotel guests could be recognized and their preferences known before they utter a single word.

❦ BACKGROUND OF SERVICE

Until recently, a majority of people lived in relatively small neighborhoods where everyone knew each other. Traditionally, workers had a craft or trade. They took pride in their craft, so quality and service was natural. As a few businesses became larger, the smaller businesses could not compete with lower prices of the bigger businesses. The small craftsman went out of business. As more and more people began working for an hourly wage for big-businesses, craftsmen began to lose their sense of neighborhood and craft. **More and more, a job was simply a job, and only a means to earn money. The idea of a proud, neighborhood craftsman was lost**.

This forever changed the idea and tradition of service. Management also changed to reflect the progression. Rewards, motivations, standard operating procedures, and punishments reduced craftsman to a subhuman standards. Trust in employees dwindled and customer service suffered. Good economic times, coupled with an increase in disposable income, only made the situation worse. It wasn't until the 1950s and 1960s that management began to change and treat humans as a resource, spawning the now common phrase, "human resource."

Since the end of World War II in the late 1940s, Americans developed a "need for speed." The world began to want and need all things fast. This cultural phenomenon also changed the way that the hospitality service industry operated. This shift gave way to an explosion of fast food, fast travel, fast service, and fast communication. Customers could be impulsive, and expectations increased. Suddenly, speed was added to the list of quality, comfort, personalization, and price.

The past two decades have also spawned the recent increase in self-service. Has the replacement of computers in customer service really made things better, or are they worse? At present, we have self-service at many places that we now take for granted, including:

- check-ins, check-outs
- banks
- ticketing

- streaming entertainment
- toll booths
- coin redemption

Over time, customers have adapted and the playing field has changed. Consider the following service examples of just 20 years:

- Most all banking was done through bank tellers.
- Only a few ATMs existed, and many customers did not trust them.
- No Internet banking existed.
- Self check-outs did not exist, and bar-code technology was not yet standardized.
- Shopping was done in stores or through mail-order catalogs.
- Reviews were read in newspapers, magazines, and travel booklets.
- No smart phones or "apps" existed.
- People went to the movie theatre to see a new release.
- Air travel was booked only through airlines or a travel agent.
- Hotel reservations were booked through reservations agents or travel agents.

Things have certainly changed. The idea of self-service is now ubiquitous. It has provided the industry with both advantages and disadvantages. Below is a list of each.

Advantages

- Decreased labor
- Increased speed of service
- Increased processing
- Shorter lines
- Increased access

Disadvantages

- Loss of human interaction
- Subject to input error
- Difficulty fixing errors
- Unfamiliar with technology
- Unfamiliar with process
- Uncertainty of transaction

Despite the loss of the craftsman, the need for speed, and the increase in self-service, quality customer service remains the cornerstone of the hospitality industry. We seldom refer to total quality management or customer quality initiatives in recent times, but the techniques are still used to this day. Guest service has evolved but still continues to be an underlying assumption of the hospitality industry. It continues to set businesses apart from one another. Most businesses claim to have a passion for service, but only a few do it exceptionally well. When a business masters customer service, that service truly becomes a strategic advantage.

❧ LEGENDS IN SERVICE MANAGEMENT

Photo courtesy of
Dr. W. Edwards Deming

W. Edwards Deming: Total Quality Management

Dr. W. Edwards Deming, a talented statistician and management consultant, is considered to be a leader in the customer service movement because of his work with the total quality management (TQM) movement. While most of his earlier work was attributed to manufacturing, his efforts have been transferred to non-manufacturing, including the hospitality industry. TQM management is an effort geared toward promoting quality products through many methods, including suppliers, employees, and management working together.

Dr. Deming tried to lend his talents to the U.S. manufacturing industries but his advice went unheeded. After World War II, Deming approached the Japanese with his ideas of applying statistics to automotive manufacturing. They accepted and embraced his ideas. He helped the Japanese automakers implement "continuous process improvement." As a result, the 1980s saw Japanese cars dominate the U.S. market, while domestic cars were left suffering. Deming was very direct at involving the employees in the process. He showed them that management cared and that they should also care about the product. He later involved the customers in the process. As a result, the Japanese automotive industry went from last to first.

The TQM movement advanced and was re-popularized throughout the 1990s, but then lost steam as the economy improved and customer service had less of an impact because businesses did well regardless.

Dr. Deming was also popular for his Deming Cycle, most commonly referred to as the **Plan–Do–Check–Act (PDCA) Cycle**. This is a four-step process for implementing change, or, continuous improvement. It is useful for incremental or breakthrough improvement. It promotes the idea that a business can always improve.

PDCA

Plan–do–check–act cycle. A four-step process for instituting continuous improvement.

FIGURE 1.2 Plan–Do–Check–Act (PDCA) Cycle.

Instructions: Apply your change process to the following four-step process:
1. Plan
   - Determine the appropriate strategy.
   - Organize to conduct the change.
   - Form teams.
     - Define problem.
     - Collect and review data.
2. Do
   - Test the change.
     - Pilot test.
     - Observe.
     - Change as needed.
   - Implement the change.
3. Check
   - Measure the effects of the change.
4. Act
   - Take action according to the results.
     - Document.
     - Standardize and formalize.
     - Promote the change throughout.
5. Start back at step 1, making it a continuous process.

Joseph Juran

Joseph Juran was credited as being the Father of Quality Service. A friend and colleague of W. Edwards Deming, Dr. Juran also helped to introduce quality to the Japanese. He first spoke to Japanese managers in a series of 1954 lectures promoting quality. He was a lecturer and business consultant in over 40 different countries. He published the *Quality Control Handbook,* among other texts. He established the Juran Institute to help develop and test new quality assessment tools. Steve Jobs, founder of Apple Computers, credited Dr. Juran's "deep, deep contribution" to the advance of quality.

Philip Crosby

DRIFT
Doing it right the first time. A quest to reduce errors and inefficiencies so that you won't have to fix as many things and pay the price for producing a poor product.

Later in the Quality movement, Philip Cosby was originally a quality manager for International Telephone and Telegraph (ITT) before leaving and setting up his own consulting firm in 1979. He published a well-known book, *Quality is Free.* He was able to show that quality programs would save much more money than they cost. He is popularized for **DRIFT** (do it right the first time) and Zero Defects. DRIFT was originally derived from manufacturing. It is an idea that promoted processes and procedures that ran smoothly and efficiently, thus, doing it right the first time. This reduced wasted, repeats, comps, and the need for service recovery efforts. This followed with the notion that, "if you don't have time to do it right the first time, how will you ever have time to do it over?"

Tom Peters: Management by Walking Around (MBWA)

MBWA
Management by walking around. Idea that managers should "get in touch" with the employees and customers to learn what is really occurring.

Author of numerous books, including *In Search of Excellence,* and a presenter and business consultant, Dr. Peters was one of the first and most influential gurus of contemporary management. He has advocated for service excellence through practical means. **MBWA** is a simple but highly effective premise that managers should spontaneously walk around and talk to their staff and customers. Paperwork and other tasks prevented managers from walking around the department or property. MBWA promotes listening and qualitative assessment. The management can stay in touch with the staff and customers and identify problems and seek solutions more effectively than sitting in the office and looking at reports.

Peter Drucker

Commonly known as the Father of Modern Management, Peter Drucker was an author and management guru who advocated for the human side as opposed to the numbers. He was popular for ideas such as "management by objectives" and the "knowledge worker." He was very interested in the concept of permitting workers to think for themselves. He made many predictions, some of which came true. He, too, helped the Japanese and was also involved in helping General Motors.

PARADIGMS

A paradigm is a belief that is commonly accepted as being the proper way or method that something is to be done. This was popularized by Thomas Kuhn in 1962. This promoted "thinking outside the box," in which a paradigm was considered to be "the box." The idea of a paradigm shift became very popular with the quality movement. The cliché of thinking outside the box is still very popular today. For example, fast-food giant Taco Bell has a mainstream advertising campaign encouraging customers to "think outside the bun," imparting the idea that fast food doesn't have to be burgers.

MOMENT OF TRUTH

Moment of Truth
A point of service at which customer service is either made or lost.

The concept of the moment of truth was first popularized by Jan Carlzon of SAS Airlines. Jan theorized that a service experience is comprised of many different moments of truth at which customer service is either made or lost. Different situations have varying amounts of **moments of truth**. For example, a quick-service restaurant may have three to five, but a resort hotel may have several hundred. In breaking down the experience into moments of truth, management and employees can better analyze, realize, and monitor the crucial points in the process.

Service Insight

Paradigm Shift

In 1967, technology for the quartz watch was presented to the world at a watch trade show. The Swiss, who had led fine watch-making for decades, dismissed the idea as being insignificant because they believed that it wasn't how watches were supposed to be made. Despite being cheaper and having fewer mechanical parts, it went against the watch-making belief, or paradigm. The Japanese saw the quartz technology as a new way to make watches; they saw the potential. They saw it as a new way of making watches, or a paradigm shift, and embraced it. Two years later, in 1969, Seiko introduced the first commercially available quartz watch. It caught on so well that the Swiss forever lost their hold on the traditional watch market.

The public—the most important people in our business. They are not dependent on us— we are dependent on them. They are not an interruption of our work. They are the purpose of it. We are not doing them a favor by serving them—they are doing us a favor by giving us an opportunity to serve them. They are not outsiders in our business—they are our business! They are not a cold statistic—they are flesh and blood, human beings with feelings and emotions, likes and dislikes. They are not there to argue with or match wits with, or try to outsmart. No one ever wins an argument with the public. The public— people who bring us their wants. It is our job to handle their requirements so pleasantly and so helpfully that they return again and again.

—Gold, C. 1983. *SOLID GOLD CUSTOMER RELATIONS.*
New York: Prentice Hall.

CHAPTER REVIEW QUESTIONS

1. What is the definition of *quality guest service*?
2. Why do some customers choose not to complain?
3. What "Age of Change" are we currently in?
4. List five examples of self-service that you have used in the past week.
5. How did Deming help the Japanese?
6. Why do we tend to forget certain events while remembering others?
7. When did the need for speed become popular in the United States?
8. Why does bad service still exist?
9. Who is the Father of Quality Service?
10. Who is the Father of Modern Management?

CASE STUDIES

A Loyal Following

A loyal following is very important. Giving customers what they want, when they want it, and how they want it can produce a great following. This has been extremely evident in the following performances. DJs, niche bands, and other events have struck a chord with the public to produce overwhelming results.

An example of this was the band the Grateful Dead. Led by Jerry Garcia, the Grateful Dead formed in 1965 and played over 2300 concerts until Garcia's death in 1995. The legend of their music was much more than a performance. It gave society what it needed at a crucial time in California. They were part of the hippie movement of peace and performed more free concerts than any other band in history. It struck such a chord in society that few bands are even close to having the same impact on their fan base. Loyal followers, or Dead Heads, as they were called, would follow the band anywhere they performed. They were easily spotted by their tie-dyed shirts and famous dead art, including dancing bears, Uncle Sam skeletons, and a Red, White, and Blue "Stealie Skull" with a lightning bolt going through it. People would camp out for days before a concert and follow the band for lengthy periods. Networks were established. Fans traded and exchanged information regarding performances and band news like no other band at that time. All of this happened before Twitter, texting, and Facebook. There were crowds of tens of thousands at nearly every performance. Tickets were difficult to obtain, no matter what the going rate. People weren't just entertained by the Grateful Dead; they knew and loved the band, its members, and its music. For most of the fans, it was a lifestyle.

1. List the customer traits of a Dead Head.
2. How did the band differentiate itself from the competition?
3. What did the band do to produce such a loyal following before the age of communication?

❦ CASE STUDIES continued

Club Me

Club Me is a new dance club in a downtown area, in close proximity to a three colleges. It is located in an old factory building. It has a loft, balcony, and many cool private areas around the sides of the dance floor. Its main target market is the students attending the three local colleges. Dance clubs are a very competitive market in this area. Loyalty does not exist. The students can decide to go to one club or another within an instant and the whole scene changes.

Club Me was off to a great start. It was new and fresh and fun and had a mass of people waiting to get in, which only made more people want to get in. They had a great line-up of DJs and regularly held contests with giveaways. It was packed every night of the week, and Club Me became more and more crowded. At first, it was a fun, packed atmosphere. As time passed and crowds continued to grow, it became apparent that Club Me couldn't adequately handle the crowd. This became apparent when a fight broke out in one of the private areas, when one woman attacked another. Security was stationed at the door, the dance floor, and the bar, but had little notice of the secluded areas, which were largely ignored. When a security guard was told there was a fight between two women, he smirked and said, "Cool, a chick fight." He did not call for back up, thinking it was just an argument. By the time he responded, a woman was beaten to the point of unconsciousness while others just watched. She had to be taken out in an ambulance and remained in critical condition. The club had failed to react to the incident to the point of neglect.

Club Me quickly hired more trained security, but the crowds stopped coming. This news had spread throughout the club scene. Females didn't feel safe. When the females stopped coming, so did the males. They felt unprotected against attacks and they stopped going to Club Me.

1. Why did large crowds go to Club Me?
2. How had Club Me met customer expectations?
3. How had Club Me failed to meet customer expectations?
4. How can Club Me change the attitudes of their target market?

Chivo's Banquet Hall

Chivo's Banquet Hall is a landmark. It is a family-owned establishment that boasts the offerings of the Chivo family. Nearly everyone in the immediate and extended family can be found there during an event. The Chivos are very proud of their establishment. Mama Chivo, as she is called, can be found running the front-of-the-house operations. It is not uncommon to find her giving orders to her staff, hugging and kissing repeat guests, and even offering advice to attendees. She is a true old-style Mama.

Mr. Chivo runs the food. He is a proud chef. He is very passionate about his work. Occasionally he and Mama will have an argument over the best way to serve an event. Mama usually wins and Chef Chivo retreats into the kitchen.

Chef Chivo's way of ensuring customer satisfaction is by walking around the room in his chef's attire. After the food has been served, Chef Chivo works the room and stops by every table. He asks everyone at each table if they liked the event and the food. Everyone always says that everything is great. He looks at everyone's plates. If it is empty, he directly asks them if they would like more. If it has food on it he asks them what was wrong with it. He puts people directly on the spot. People almost always tell him there is no problem at all. He looks at them suspiciously and shakes his head letting them know that he is offended. Sometimes he will tell them that they need to eat more and that they look thin, even if they are not.

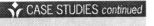

CASE STUDIES *continued*

1. Describe the tone of guest service at Chivo's Banquet Hall.
2. Critique Chef Chivo's unique style of customer service.
3. What are some likely reasons why the Chivos seldom hear complaints?
4. If you could give the Chivos advice regarding customer service, what would it be?

Mount Will

Mount Will is a small, steep mountain. It features skiing and snowboarding in the winter and offers other extreme opportunities throughout the rest of the year. It is known for having the most extreme offerings to make up for its small size. Its motto is "Little mountain, big adrenaline." Mount Will attracts many visitors who want a special challenge in a mountain experience. Luckily, it's located beside a major highway and is highly visible to people traveling through the area. The managers try to change the options every year to keep it fresh. This year, they have arranged for a company to bring in a large crane to allow bungee jumping right next to the highway. Everyone passing by could watch the falls, and it would be great for publicity. They negotiated a great price with the subcontractor and are pleased to offer this attraction.

Unfortunately, Mount Will has not been very successful this year. Very few people have dared to brave the bungee jump, and their overall attendance is down for the season. Feeling the pressure in the loss of revenue, Scott, the Mountain Manager, decides to set up a small booth at a local grocery store to promote the event and hand out coupons. People are typically polite but he doesn't count it a success.

He decides to go out front to the crane by the road to discuss this matter with them. What he sees amazes him. There is a different view from the highway. The front of the contractor's crane looks dingy and dull. The cables appear rusty. The staff are unshaven and dressed poorly. Upon mentioning it, he is told that the cables are more than adequate and that it is only surface rust. The crane was inspected by the state and it passed the quality tests. Still, Scott is concerned with the image. He now realizes the issue.

1. As a customer, list your expectations of a bungee-jumping crew and equipment.
2. What are the thoughts of potential customers passing by on the highway?
3. How could the expectations of the potential customers best be met?

Chapter 6

Recruitment, Selection, and Orientation

Overview

The Labor Market

Determining Labor Needs

Recruiting

Selecting the Right Person

Negligent Hiring

Orientation

You've run an ad in the Sunday paper for a weekend housekeeper, but the only person to put in an application is a high school student looking for her first job. You interview her, and you look at the housekeeper's work schedule and realize that if you don't hire her today, you'll have to spend the weekend doing housekeeper duties yourself. So you hire her and the next day, when she starts, you ask an experienced (but not very friendly) housekeeper to get the new hire started. By next Saturday, she has quit, so you put another ad in the Sunday paper and you think, "There's got to be a better way."

How do you find the people you need? How can you choose people who will stay beyond the first week, do a good job, and be worth the money you pay them? Does it always have to be the way it is today? No, it doesn't.

There is no foolproof system: Human beings are unpredictable, and so is the day-to-day situation in the typical hospitality operation. But the knowledge and experience of people who have faced and studied these problems can be helpful to you, even though you must adapt it to your own situation.

In this chapter, we examine the processes and problems of recruiting and selecting hourly employees for hospitality operations. After completion of this chapter, you should be able to:

■ **Describe the typical characteristics of entry-level jobs in the hospitality industry.**
■ **Identify common sources of workers for the hospitality industry.**

167

- Define a job's qualifications.
- List factors that affect forecasts of personal needs.
- Identify and avoid discriminatory language and practices in recruiting, interviewing, and selecting.
- Describe the most-used methods of recruiting and evaluate their usefulness.
- Discuss and evaluate the standard tools and practices for screening people and selecting the best person for the job.

The Labor Market

labor market
In a given area, the workers who are looking for jobs (the labor supply) and the jobs that are available (the demand for labor).

The term *labor market* refers to (1) the supply of people looking for jobs as well as (2) the jobs available in a given area. When you need people to fill certain jobs, you are looking for people with certain characteristics—knowledge, abilities, skills, personal qualities—and you have a certain price you are willing or able to pay for the work you expect them to do. The people who are in the market for a job are looking for jobs with certain characteristics—work they are qualified to do or are able to learn, a place they can get to easily, certain days and hours off, a pleasant work environment, people they are comfortable working with and for, and a certain rate of pay (usually, the most they can get). The trick is to get a good match between people and jobs. Recruiting and retaining employees has become much less difficult for restaurant and hospitality operators as the industry continues to reel from the effects of the recession.[1]

A challenge in the best of times, recruiting and retention has again emerged as one of the most critical issues facing the hospitality industry. The average U.S. unemployment rate fluctuates; it was close to 9 percent in the first quarter of 2011, but has averaged 5.7 percent from 1943 to 2010. The National Restaurant Association estimates that the number of jobs in the industry will grow by 15 percent over the next decade.[2] Operators across the country are offering higher hourly wages, and may have to offer benefits like healthcare.

When jobs are plentiful and few people are unemployed, employers have a harder time finding the people they want, and workers are more particular about the jobs they will accept. When many people are looking for jobs and jobs are scarce, employers have a better choice and workers will settle for less. The number of employers looking for the same kinds of people also affects the labor market. You are always in competition with hospitality operations like your own, as well as retail stores, which also offer many part-time, entry-level jobs.

Hospitality companies identify where they are in the marketplace for employees, meaning the Ritz-Carlton will likely attract a different person than a Motel 6. Companies assess the need for additional employees for a brief period of a "full house" versus some overtime being worked by existing staff.

The following comment from Jim Sullivan, a seasoned hospitality consultant, gives us something to discuss: "Human resource professionals and supervisors spend too much time on dealing with difficult employees. If you do not terminate people who are not working out, you increase the possibility of having to let go of the people who are."[3]

✳ JOBS TO BE FILLED

Many of the jobs in food and lodging operations demand hard physical labor. People are often on their feet all day doing work that is physically exhausting. About the only people who sit down are telephone operators, cashiers, reservationists, and many clerical employees. Kitchens are hot and filled with safety hazards. At busy times, pressure is intense and tension is high. Many jobs are uninteresting and monotonous—eight hours of pushing a vacuum cleaner, making up guest rooms, polishing silver, setting up function rooms, washing vegetables, spreading mayonnaise on bread, placing food on plates, washing dishes.

In many of these jobs the pay is entry level, but there is the possibility of promotion. It is not surprising that the duller and more demanding a job is, the harder it is to fill it with a good employee and the more often you have to fill it. The main attraction of such jobs is that they are available, and you are willing to take people with no experience and no skills. For example, operators may offer starting positions to employees whose English communication skills need improving.

These individuals can, once they are more proficient in English, advance to other positions within the operation. Examples of this in a hotel would be in housekeeping and stewarding. For certain jobs you must look for specific skills and abilities. Front desk clerks, servers, and bartenders must have several kinds of skills: verbal and manual skills and skill in dealing with guests. Cooks must have technical skills, varying in complexity with the station and the menu. All these jobs require people who can function well under pressure. The rate of pay goes up for skilled employees, except for servers, who are usually paid minimum wage or less and make most of their money in tips.

✳ DAYS AND HOURS OF WORK

In the hospitality industry, there is a pattern of daily peaks and valleys, with the peaks forming around mealtimes and the valleys falling between. This makes for some difficulty in offering the regular eight-hour day that many people are looking for. You also have some very early hours if you serve breakfast, evening hours if you serve dinner, and late-night hours if you operate a bar or feature entertainment or serve an after-theater clientele.

This irregular kind of need encourages split shifts, part-time jobs, and unusual hours, which can work both for you and against you in finding employees. Sometimes you cannot guarantee a certain number of hours of work per week: employees are put on a call-in schedule and must simply take their chances of getting as many hours as they want. But if they cannot count on you, you may not be able to count on them.

You also have varying needs according to days of the week. These form a fairly predictable pattern, predictable enough for you to plan your hiring and scheduling. In restaurants, staff needs are lighter during the week and heavy on weekends, which closes your doors to people looking for a Monday-to-Friday week. In business hotels the pattern is the reverse, heavy during the week and light on weekends; however, resorts are busier on weekends.

Restaurant employees typically work when other people are playing—evenings, weekends, and holidays—which complicates finding people to fill your jobs. Restaurants may also have urgent temporary needs for parties and promotions and emergencies when regular employees are out sick or leave without warning. This requires a banquet server call-in system or overtime for regular employees.

In some facets of the foodservice industry, the timing of people needs is regular and predictable. In hospitals and nursing homes, the population is generally steady seven days a week, and the only variation in need comes with the daily peaks and valleys of mealtimes. Schools have steady Monday-to-Friday patterns, with short days built around lunch, and they follow the school calendar, closing down for vacations, when they lose many people. Business and industry feeding follows the workweek of the business or plant.

In hotels the pattern of need is likely to be irregular but fairly predictable. Reservations are typically made ahead except in the restaurants, and need is generally geared to coming events in the community or in the hotel itself, or to predictable vacation and travel trends. Often, a hotel will require large numbers of temporary workers for single events such as conventions and conferences. Temporary extra help is often supplemented by having regulars work overtime. Where needs vary widely and frequently, leaders can spend a great deal of time on staffing and scheduling alone. Hospitality operators normally have a number of "on-call employees" who are called on to work banquets and catering functions as required.

The types of jobs, unusual working hours and days, minimum wages, and the up-and-down character of the need for workers limits the appeal of hotel and foodservice jobs to people who can fit this pattern or can slip in and out of it easily. Accordingly, it attracts people who are looking for short-term jobs, part-time work, or jobs requiring no skills or previous experience. Some people deliberately seek the unusual hours to fit their own personal schedule: people going to school, moonlighters, parents who must be at home to take care of the kids. Many people are looking for temporary work and have no interest in long-term employment or a career in the industry. "I am only working here until I can find a *real* job" is a common attitude.

❊ SOURCES OF EMPLOYEES

The source of workers continues to change as the composition of the U.S. labor force changes. The majority of new workers entering the hospitality workforce are women, minorities, and immigrants. Why is this? It is due to the combination of a shrinking, older, white U.S. population; a younger, growing minority population; recent easing of immigration restrictions; and increasing numbers of women entering or returning to work.

If the job you need to fill is anything above the lowest level in terms of pay, interesting work, and decent hours, *the first place to look for someone to fill it is inside your own operation*. Upgrading someone whose attitudes and performance you already know is far less risky than hiring someone new and will probably assure you of a good, loyal worker. You will spend less time in training, and the adjustment will be smoother all around.

Social media have become free and increasingly popular ways for hospitality companies to advertise and recruit employees. Operators are using marketing companies such as Facebook, Twitter, LinkedIn, and YouTube.

The top nine recruiting methods are:[4]

1. In-house job referral
2. Company website
3. Social media
4. Newspaper/magazine
5. Job fairs
6. Online résumés
7. Schools
8. Employment agencies
9. Professional/industry association

Consider also how people would feel if you brought someone in from outside to fill a job or a shift they would like to have. It is important for morale to give your workers first chance, even when you might find it easier to fill the vacant job from outside than to fill the job your current employee will vacate. It is part of being a good leader to consider your own people first and to move them along and develop their capabilities for better jobs.

As an industry, we are always looking for people, and we are among the few employers who will hire people without experience. Usually, first-timers want the jobs for the money, the experience of working, and the advantage it gives them in getting their next job. A few, but not many, apply because they think the work will be interesting. Often, they choose a particular place because a friend is working there or because it is close to home.

Many are looking for part-time work because they are students. Many are working *until*—until school starts or until they get enough money to buy a car. Some hospitality companies are now helping new employees with English classes so they can become more valuable employees. One hotel even offered a quick course overview of the hotel to recently graduated but unemployed former high school students and ended up hiring several of them to work at the resort.

Another group of potential hospitality employees is *women* who want to go to work to supplement the family income or simply to get out of the house. A woman with children may be very happy with part-time work, three or four hours spanning the lunch period while the kids are at school, or an evening shift when her husband can take care of the children.

Another group of part-time employees is interested in evening work: *the moonlighters*, people looking for a second job. This is not ideal for either you or them, since they are often tired from working their first job. However, students and homemakers also carry a double load, so perhaps moonlighting is no more difficult.

Another source of employees is the *unemployed*. If they have worked in an operation like yours, they may have skills and experience useful to you. If they were in another line of work, you may be competing with unemployment compensation, which is often more than the wages you pay. Workers from the automobile industry, for example, may have been making $52 an hour in wages and benefits, and although their unemployment compensation is not as high as that, it is still above hospitality wages.

If compensation runs out and they go to work in a hotel or restaurant, workers from higher-paying industries rarely find satisfaction in their jobs. They are likely to see both the pay and the work as a step down from the jobs they lost. They are truly *until*-type employees. Yet, some welfare-to-work programs are having successes with companies such as Marriott.

Some people seek work in hotels or restaurants just to get away from what they have been doing. Sometimes, recent college graduates find that they are not happy with the jobs they have taken or the field they prepared for, and they just want to get out. Sometimes these people just want a breather, some time to think things over and make new plans. Sometimes they are thinking of switching to the hotel or restaurant field and want to experience it from the inside before they make up their minds. A number of people today are interested in learning professional cooking because the pay at the top is high and a certain glamour goes with it.

Hiring *retired people* is becoming more commonplace, although the number of retired people who do return to work is still quite small. The over-65 group is growing and will increase to 20 percent of the population in 2030. Retirees often want to work to fill some empty time or perhaps to supplement their income. Although some

Some first-time job hunters apply for lodging and foodservice jobs because the jobs are available.

Photo courtesy of the author.

of our jobs are not suitable because of physical demands and odd hours, this is not a labor source you should dismiss routinely. Not only is it against the law to discriminate based on age but also, older workers often have stability and an inner motivation that younger people may have not yet developed.

One national fast-food chain has made a special effort to develop jobs and hours that fit the availability and skills and talents of the retired. It has found this group to be an excellent source of employees: they are dependable, work-oriented people who are happy to have the jobs. In general, retirees have proven to be loyal, willing, and service-oriented workers. They come to work on time, have much prior work experience on which to draw, and do their jobs well.

Another group of people who might be interested in working in the hospitality industry is the *disabled*. A disabled person has a physical, mental, or developmental impairment that limits one or more of life's major activities. For example, a disabled person may have a visual or hearing impairment or may be disabled. Although you may spend more time training some disabled employees, they tend to be loyal, enthusiastic, hardworking, and dependable.

There are disabled employees doing many different hospitality jobs. For instance, a cashier or payroll clerk can work from a wheelchair, a hearing-impaired person can do some food preparation tasks, or a person with mental development disabilities can wash dishes and pots. It is illegal not to hire a disabled worker unless the disability would interfere with the person's ability to perform the work.

As a leader, you need to be aware of the fact that your employees may be reluctant to work with a disabled person. This is usually due to a fear of the unknown; most of your employees probably don't know what it is like to interact and work with someone who is disabled. It is your job to build a supportive environment in which the disabled employee, and your other employees, will work well together. Discussing with your employees ahead of time what the new employee will be doing and what to expect can do this. Encourage your employees to talk honestly about how they feel and about their concerns. Be positive about the placement of disabled people in the workplace and what they can accomplish.

Often, we set up qualifications for jobs we want to fill that are totally unrealistic (and quite possibly illegal), and if we get what we say we are looking for we will have overqualified and unhappy people. We do not need high school graduates to make beds, bus tables, cook hamburgers, wash vegetables, push vacuum cleaners, or wash pots or floors. Setting such requirements, in fact, can be interpreted as discriminatory. For some jobs, people do not even need to be able to read and write. All they need is the ability to perform the required tasks. The requirements we set up for a job must be based on the requirements of the work.

Christine Le Fave offers these suggestions to operators for hiring:[5] First, say operators, a concept must consider carefully its brand and its work culture in crafting a message that will stand out from a crowd of hiring notices. Second, target potential talent where they spend their spare time—in person and online. Motivated job seekers, especially those in generations X and Y, respond well to employers who can showcase flexibility, a sense of humor, and a commitment to social values such as sustainability and community involvement.[6]

Some operators do not accept applications; they direct job seekers to the Internet, where their applications are automatically assessed for attitude and availability. Supervisors and managers can then focus only on those candidates who are highly rated and predetermined to be a good fit.[7]

Being green is important to an increasing number of applicants. Dan McGowan, president of the Chicago-based pan-Asian chain Big Bowl, had a group of ten applicants, eight of whom applied because they had read about some of the chain's green efforts.[8]

Check Your Knowledge

1. To what does labor market refer?
2. Compare and contrast the need for staff in a restaurant and in a hotel.

✳ CHARACTERISTICS OF YOUR LABOR AREA

You will find it helpful to know something about the labor market in your own area: such things as prevailing wages for various kinds of jobs, unemployment rates for various types of workers, the makeup of the labor force, and the kinds of enterprises that are competing with you for workers, both in and out of your own industry.

demographics
Characteristics of a given area in terms of the data about the people who live there.

You should know something of the *demographics* of your area: ethnic groups, income levels, education levels, and where in your area different groups live. Where do low-income workers, young married, immigrants, and the employable retired typically live? Employers sometimes note the zip code of the area in which the majority of their employees live to know where to do community advertising.

There are other useful things to know about your community. Where are the high schools and colleges that can provide you with student workers? What agencies will work with you to find suitable disabled workers? What are the transportation patterns in your area? Are there buses from where your potential workers live that run at hours to fit your needs? Can workers drive from their homes in a reasonable length of time?

Operations such as airports or in-plant cafeterias in outlying areas often find transportation the greatest single problem in finding employees. In a large organization your human resource department may have such information. In fact, they often take care of much of the routine of recruiting. But the more you participate and the better you know the labor resources of the area, the more likely you are to know how to attract and hold the kind of people you want.

Determining Labor Needs

If you are a busy hospitality leader and you see a heading like this, your first reaction may be to laugh. What the heck, you need people all the time. You've got no time to make out lists, you need whoever walks in the door, and you are just afraid nobody will walk in.

But what if you could turn things around and avoid panic and crisis by hiring employees who are right for the job and will not walk off and leave you in the lurch? And do you realize the hidden costs when you hire unqualified people or people who are wrong for the jobs you ask them to do?

Hiring such employees is worse than useless. Either you will keep those employees and suffer their shortcomings, or you will have to fire them and start all over—and perhaps make the same mistakes. If you train those workers and the ones you replace them with, your training costs will skyrocket and the work will suffer until you get them trained. If you do not train them, they will not do their jobs right and they will waste things and break things and turn out inferior products and give inferior service.

If they are unhappy or incompetent, they will be absent or late a lot, and their morale will be poor and so will everyone else's. They will not get the work done on time, and you will have to pay overtime. They will give poor service and drive customers away, and your sales will dwindle. When you finally do fire them, your unemployment compensation costs will go up and you will have to hire people to take their places: and the next people you hire may be even worse. It is a very, very costly way to choose people, and in time it could cost you your reputation as a good employer, your job, or your business. There are better ways to go about hiring people based on the thinking and experience of experts, and the place to start is to figure out exactly what to look for.

✳ DEFINING JOB QUALIFICATIONS

job specification
A list of the qualifications needed to perform a given job.

To define a job's qualifications, you need to list the knowledge, skills and abilities, work experience, and education and training required. This is known as a *job specification*. Figure 6.1 shows a sample job specification. Note that there is a heading "Preferred Qualifications"—the reason for this is to avoid any problems with affirmative action. If some applicants do not have the preferred qualifications then they are not as qualified for the position as those who do have the preferred qualifications. Training and certifications may also be added to the specification.

Knowledge consists of the information needed to perform job duties. For example, a cook must know that one cup holds eight ounces, and other measurements, just as the dietary manager in a hospital kitchen must know which foods are not allowed on modified diets. You can use verbs such as *knows, defines, lists,* or *explains* to begin a knowledge statement.

Skills and abilities refer to competence in performing a task or behaving in a certain manner. Must a person be able to lift 100-pound bags and boxes? Add and subtract and multiply? Convert recipes? Mix *x* number of drinks per hour? Cook eggs to order at a certain rate? Have a responsive, outgoing approach to people? Be as specific as possible.

Performance standards, if you have them, will tell you the specific skills you are looking for. You must decide whether to buy these skills or do your own skills training. If you plan to train, you need to define the qualities that will make people trainable for a given job. A bartender, for example, needs manual dexterity. Desk clerks and serving personnel need verbal skills.

The qualifications that you list in your job specification must not discriminate in any way on the basis of race, national origin, gender, age, marital or family status, religion, or disability. The place to begin in avoiding discrimination is with your job specifications. It is important that you phrase them in concrete terms of what each job requires and that you think in these terms as well. According to OfficeTeam of Menlo Park, California, interviews and reference checks are the most effective tools for

---

Job Specification: Server

Department: Dining Room

Grade   6

Job Qualifications:

KNOWLEDGE   Basic knowledge of food and cooking.

SKILLS AND ABILITIES   Present a good appearance—neat and well-groomed, interact with guests in a courteous and helpful manner, work well with other personnel, write neatly, perform basic mathematical functions (addition, subtraction, multiplication, and division), set tables, serve and clear.

WORK EXPERIENCE   Six months satisfactory experience as a server required. One year preferred.

EDUCATION AND TRAINING   High school graduate and/or service training preferred.

PREFERRED QUALIFICATIONS   a) 1 year in a fine dining restaurant environment. b) must be able to work on weekends.

FIGURE 6.1:   Job specification.

identifying top performers. Interviewers look for motivation, versatility, and a proactive approach. Other qualities to consider:[9]

1. Passion
2. Favorites
3. Optimism
4. Expectations
5. Tone

✳ FORECASTING STAFFING NEEDS

Anticipating your needs for staff will give you time to look for the right people. If you need extra people for holiday and vacation periods, hire them ahead of time or else your competitors will beat you to the best people. Records of past sales or occupancy or special events may indicate trends in people needs. Look ahead to changes in your business: Is your employer planning to expand? And how will it affect your department's need for people?

scheduling
Determining how many people are needed when, and assigning days and hours of work accordingly.

Scheduling is a key factor. Your work schedules form a day-to-day forecast of the people you need at each hour of the day. Plan them in advance. Make sure that your workers are aware of any changes you make, and make sure that they tell you well in advance of any changes that they have in mind.

Employees need an environment that motivates them and offers benefits. Let employees know that you value their opinion. If at all possible, allow schedules to be flexible. This gives employees a feeling of control and the comfort of knowing that if something comes up, they will not be criticized. Today, more people are demanding that their personal lives be taken as seriously as their work lives. People want to be taken seriously; they are concerned about pursuing their own personal goals. Your employees need to feel respected by you.[10]

As an employer it is important that you try to meet the needs of both your employees and the company. Examine your scheduling as a whole. First, does it provide efficiently for your needs? Second, are there ways of organizing the shifts that would be more attractive to the type of person you would like to hire? Do you ask people to work short shifts at unattractive hours, such as early in the morning or late at night? A country club advertised a split shift of 11 to 3 and 5 to 11, three days a week—who is that likely to appeal to? That's a 10-hour day with hardly enough time between shifts to go home, yet it is not a full 40-hour week.

Scheduling is an important task, which, when done well, helps ensure a smooth-running operation.
Photo courtesy of the author.

Consider revamping your schedules with people's needs and desires in mind. Look at the hours from their point of view. How far do they have to travel? How much useful personal time does your schedule leave them? How much money do they make for the time involved in working for you, including travel times? Ask your workers how they feel about their days and hours, and try to devise schedules that will not only fill your needs but will be attractive to new people as well.

Your employees will appreciate it if you give them a chance to move to a shift they like better before you hire someone new to fill a vacancy. Often, before making decisions it is important to implement new plans or policies with the staff. Include staff in the decision-making process and find out how they feel on certain policies; you may be surprised at what they have to say.

Another key factor in forecasting employee needs is *downtime*, the length of time that a position is vacant until a new employee who can fully perform the job fills it. Let's consider how long downtime might normally be: An employee resigns and gives you only two days' notice. It's not unusual, particularly if you don't make a point of requiring proper notice (usually two weeks) and withhold something of value to the employee, such as accrued vacation time, if proper notice is not given.

Once the employee resigns, depending on your employer's procedures, you might have to fill out an ***employment requisition form*** (see Figure 6.2). A requisition is something like a purchase order that must be signed by the appropriate person before you can begin the recruiting process.

employment requisition form
A standard form used by departments to obtain approval to fill positions and to notify the recruiter that a position needs, or will need, to be filled.

Let's say that this takes one week. If you want to advertise the job, you will probably have to wait another week before the ad appears and you get responses. Now you can probably plan on one to two weeks to screen applicants, interview and test applicants, check references, and make a final selection. Often, the person you hire must give his or her current employer two weeks' notice, so you wait a little more.

Now if you believe in magic, when the new employee shows up for the first day of work, you will think your problems are over and put the new employee right to work. Wrong! Now it will take at least one week, probably more, before your new employee gets up to speed in the new position. It has now been about six to seven weeks since your former employee resigned. One way to help reduce downtime is to forecast your personnel needs periodically. Figure 6.3 shows a staffing guide form that can be used every two months to help determine when to hire new employees so that downtime is minimized. Staffing guides are based on the budget and expected volume of business.

❋ TRAINING VERSUS BUYING SKILLS

In determining your staffing needs, you must decide whether to buy skills or to train new people yourself. Most managers will tell you they simply don't have time to train people—they are too busy with the work itself. They look for people who have experience in the jobs they are hiring for, even when they have to pay a higher wage.

There is no security in hiring experience, however. You might pay more to break someone of five years of forming bad habits than it would cost you to train an inexperienced person from scratch. For exactly this reason, a number of corporations hire only people with no experience for certain jobs. If you do hire experience, it is important to verify it by checking references and to evaluate it by testing performance.

Employment Requisition

Department: _____

Position: _____

Reason for vacancy: _____ Incumbent leaving the company

Name: _____

Separation Date: _____

_____ New Position

Is position budgeted? _____ Yes _____ No

Is position temporary _____ or permanent _____?

Is position full-time _____ or part-time _____?

Hours of position/days off: _____

When needed? _____

Job qualifications: _____

_____

_____

_____

_____

Approvals   Department Head _____

General Manager _____

Director, Human Resources _____

FIGURE 6.2: An employment requisition is completed by the department head and given to HR either electronically or by hard copy.

Check Your Knowledge

1. Discuss why it is important to know the characteristics of your labor needs.
2. Explain what is known as job qualification.

Training takes the time of both trainer and trainee, and that is expensive. But putting people in jobs without enough training is likely to be more costly in the end. The worker does not perform well and is not happy, the customer suffers and is not happy, and you will suffer, too, and you will not be happy. You really don't have time not to train people. There is more on this subject in Chapter 10.

STAFFING GUIDE

Department: _____ Date: _____

Positions	Number Full Staff	Staff on Hand	Current Openings	Anticipated Openings	Total to Be Hired	Time Required to Recruit and Train

FIGURE 6.3: Staffing guides help supervisors determine when to hire new employees.

Recruiting

Recruiting is finding the most suitable employee for an available position. The process begins with announcing the opportunity; sometimes this is done first within the organization, then outside. Applications are received from a variety of sources: internal promotion, employee referrals, applicants filed from people who have sent in résumés, online applicants, company website applicants, transfers within the company, advertising, colleges and universities, and government-sponsored employment services.

✳ GENERAL RECRUITING PRINCIPLES

Since the legal aspects of recruiting and selection were covered in Chapter 5, we will move on to recruiting. *Recruiting*—looking actively for people to fill jobs—is a form of marketing. You are in the labor market to sell jobs to people who might want them. Because your need is constant and urgent, because you have many competitors, and because many of your jobs are not the most exciting ways of making a living, you really need to work at making your recruiting effective.

The first word to keep in mind is *appropriate*. You must put out your message in appropriate places and aim it toward people you would like to hire. Use techniques appropriate to your image and to the kinds of people you want to attract. A help-wanted sign in a dirty and fly-specked window is going to reach only people who pass by and attract only people who reflect that image themselves—if it attracts anyone at all.

"Now Hiring" hanging in a clean window is only one step up. Take a look at some of the classified ads found in Figure 6.4. Which one might you respond to? Can you decipher what all the abbreviations mean? Which advertisement tells you the most about the restaurant and the nature of the jobs available? If you project an image of being a desirable employer through your advertisements, you are probably going to attract desirable applicants.

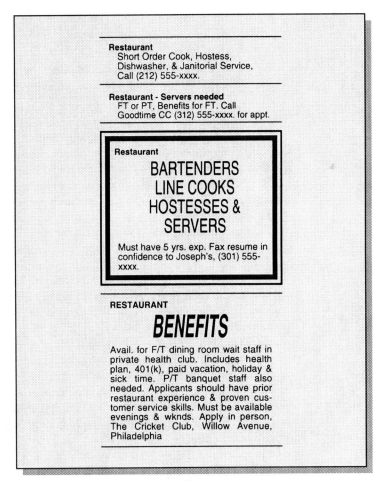

FIGURE 6.4: Classified advertisements.

Recruiting excellent candidates is requisite to ensuring excellent morale and guest satisfaction.
Photo courtesy of the author.

Your message must be appropriate: Tell them what they want to know. They want to know (1) what the job is, (2) where you are, (3) what the hours are, (4) what qualifications are needed, and (5) how to apply. "Bartender Wanted" and a phone number will not pull them in until after they have tried everyone else. They are also interested in (6) attractive features of the job, such as good wages and benefits.

It is also essential to use channels of communication appropriate to the people you want to reach, the same channels that they are using to look for jobs. You must get the message to the areas where they live and use the media of communication they see and hear.

The second word to keep in mind is *competitive*. You are competing with every other hotel and foodservice operation in your area for the same types of people. For unskilled labor you are competing with other types of operations as well: retail stores, light industry, and so on. You must sell your jobs and your company at least as well as your competitors sell theirs, if not better.

The third word to remember is *constant*. It is a good practice to be on the lookout for potential employees all the time, even when you have no vacancies. Even the best and luckiest of employers in your field will probably replace at least 6 out of every 10 employees in a year's time, and many operations run far higher than that. Keep a file of the records of promising people who apply each time you fill a job, and look through them the next time you need to hire.

You will also have drop-in applicants from time to time. Pay attention to them; they have taken the initiative to seek you out. Ask for a résumé and let them know that you will add it to the talent bank. Give them a tentative date to call back, and be cordial. They should leave with a feeling of wanting to work for you; remember that you are marketing yourself as a good employer, and you may need them tomorrow.

✳ ONLINE APPLICANTS AND SELECTION TESTS

Today, many hospitality companies have a space for employment opportunities on their websites. This free advertising is attracting an increasing number of applicants. Applications can be completed online, saving both time and money. Applicants may be asked to complete selection tests online. Here are some examples:

- *Cognitive ability tests* measure intelligence.
- *Aptitude tests* measure the ability of an individual to learn or acquire new skills.
- *Personality tests* measure an individual's basic characteristics, such as her or his attitudes, emotional adjustment, interests, interpersonal relationships, and motivation.
- *Honesty/integrity tests* are designed to measure an applicant's propensity toward undesirable behaviors such as lying, stealing, and taking drugs or abusing alcohol.
- *Substance abuse tests* are intended to ensure a drug-free workplace. Concern about workplace safety issues, alcohol, and illegal and unsafe drug use in the workplace has prompted many employers to require employees and applicants to submit to substance abuse testing.

There are some who do not agree with applicant/employee testing. However, if employers keep selection tests in context and perspective, and if they are used in their proper job-related manner and are nondiscriminatory to protected-class members, then they are permitted under the law in your state, county, and city.[11] Employment testing is discussed later in this chapter.

The final words of wisdom are: *Use multiple approaches.* Do not depend on a single resource or channel; try a variety of methods to attract people. There are many channels: social media, craigslist, schools and colleges giving hotel and foodservice and bartending courses, well-chosen word-of-mouth channels such as current employees, notices on the right bulletin boards (the student union, the school financial aid office), newspaper and radio ads, online job resources, trade unions, employment agencies, community organizations, summer job fairs, and organizations working to place certain groups of people such as refugees or minorities or disabled persons. You can also go out into the field and recruit workers directly wherever they are.

Let us look at some of these resources and channels in more detail.

✳ INTERNAL RECRUITING

internal recruiting
Searching for job applicants from within an operation.

promoting from within
A policy in which it is preferable to promote existing employees rather than filling the position with an outsider.

Internal recruiting is the process of letting your own employees know about job openings so that they may apply for them. Often, the most successful placements occur through people who already work for you. Internal recruiting often results in *promoting from within*, a practice in which current employees are given preference for promotions over outside applicants with similar backgrounds. Promoting from within has several

Courtesy of
Sharon Morris.

As a restaurant supervisor, when recruiting I always prepare myself by reviewing the applications of candidates selected for interview. Our restaurant requires all applicants to go online and complete a talent assessment questionnaire to assess their aptitude for a service position, back or front of the house.

I use a structured format with some flexibility. For example, if I ask about a success the candidate had at a previous job, the applicant's response might lead to a follow-up question. But always the same questions are asked of each candidate. A skills test is also given in the relevant job area. If it's in the kitchen, then a kitchen-related skills test is given—the applicant is asked to prepare a certain food item on the menu.

Before offering applicants a position we must do a background check. We use an outside company and request them to do as extensive a background check as the law permits and the results of a drug test—the reason being that we do not want to be held liable for negligent hiring—meaning, if an employee were hired and does something serious to a guest or another employee, then we could be held liable. Finally, we need to ensure that applicants can do the job description that they were hired to do. We get their signature on the job description saying that they can do the job.

advantages: It rewards employees for doing a good job, it motivates employees and gives them something to work toward, and it maintains consistency within the enterprise.

Now how can you be sure of letting all employees know about open positions? Using a practice called *job posting*, a representative (usually from the human resources department) posts lists of open positions (see Figure 6.5) in specific locations where employees are most likely to see them, including the company website.

Usually, employees are given a certain period of time, such as five days, in which to apply before applicants from the outside will be evaluated. In most cases, employees must meet certain conditions before responding to a job posting. For instance, the employee may be required to have a satisfactory rating on his or her last evaluation and have been in his or her current position for at least six months. These conditions prevent employees from jumping around too often to different jobs, a practice that benefits neither the employee nor the employer.

When you can't find a current employee to fill an open position, your employees may refer their friends and acquaintances to you. Some employers give a cash or merchandise reward to employees who bring in somebody who works for at least a certain time, such as 90 days. Many employers trying to draw in new employees have used these types of programs, called *employee referral programs,* very successfully. Employees who refer applicants are usually asked to fill out a referral form or card that may be handed in with the applicant's application form.

The idea behind this type of program is that if your current employees are good workers and are happy working for you, they are not likely to bring in someone who won't suit you or who won't fit into the work group. Bringing a total stranger into a group of workers can be very disruptive. Sometimes employees bring in relatives.

job posting
A policy of making employees aware of available positions within a company.

employee referral program
A program under which employees suggests to others that they apply for a job in their company. If a person referred gets a job, the employee often receives recompense.

Date: Monday, September 25

Department: Food and Nutrition Services

Job Title: Food Service Worker

Job Code: 600026

Reports to: Operations Supervisor

Job Qualifications:

1. Six months experience in a health care facility.
2. High school graduate.
3. Courtesy and diplomacy in dealing with patients, hospital staff, fellow workers, and the department's management team.
4. Ability to consistently demonstrate the values of Sarasota Memorial Health Care System.
5. Communication skills, verbal and reading: required to read and understand written instructions, recipes, and labels.

Mental/Physical Demands:

1. Adaptability to routine work involving short-cycle repetitive duties under specific instructions.
2. Demonstration of good judgment consistently showing insight into problems.
3. Continuous physical activity involves standing, walking, bending, and stooping. Amount of weight lifted is routinely 25–30 pounds, and up to 50 pounds. Must be able to push carts weighing to 400 pounds.
4. Talking, hearing, and visual acuity essential.
5. Versatility required to adapt to frequently changing conditions in job duties covering a broad range of food service and production activities.
6. Finger and manual dexterity and motor coordination as required to manipulate kitchen utensils and food service supplies skillfully.

FIGURE 6.5: Job posting.

Among employers, there are two schools of thought about this: Some say that it is an absolute disaster, whereas others find that it works out well. It probably depends on the particular set of relatives. If a family fights all the time, you do not want them working for you. Some people point out that if one family member leaves or is terminated, the other will probably quit, too, and then you will have two jobs to fill. You have a similar problem if there is a family emergency; you will be short both employees.

Other internal recruiting methods include speaking with applicants who walk in, call in, or write in. These applicants should be asked to fill out an application form and should be interviewed when possible.

✳ EXTERNAL RECRUITING

external recruiting
Looking for job applicants outside the operation.

The remaining recruiting methods are all considered *external recruiting*, that is, seeking applicants from outside the operation. An advantage of bringing in outsiders is that they tend to bring in new ideas and a fresh perspective.

Today, hospitality companies use their own Web page as a recruiting tool. By having an icon for employment opportunities, they can save money by driving would-be applicants to their Web page, thus avoiding costly charges made by various *job search engines.*

In recent years, some hospitality companies have teamed with job search engines such as Monster.com and others to help find suitable applicants for their available positions.

Advertising

The classified ad section of the weekend paper is one common meeting place for job seekers and employers. It is also the best source for reaching large numbers of applicants, although it is expensive and does not necessarily bring in the best candidates. Due to the high cost of newspaper advertising, an increasingly smaller percentage of employers looking for non–college-educated employees advertise in newspapers; most use their own website or employee referrals.

There are two types of ads: *classified* and *display*. Because they take up less space, classified ads are less costly than display ads. However, display ads using the company's logo attract more attention and set your ad apart from others (Figure 6.6). Due to their higher cost, they are used for more senior positions. Regardless of the type of ad, be sure to include information on (1) what the job is, (2) where you are, (3) what the hours are, (4) what qualifications are needed, and (5) how to apply.

Regarding how to apply, there are two types of ads: *open*, which give your company name and address, and *blind*, which do not reveal company identity, but instead, give a box number for responses. Blind ads pull in fewer responses than open ads because readers don't know who the company is (it could even be their current employer). The open ad brings in larger numbers of applicants, or it can screen applicants by listing job requirements in detail.

Another way to screen is to include a specific instruction such as "Call Joe 9–11 A.M." The people who call Joe at 2 P.M. obviously do not follow written instructions, so if the job requires following written instructions, you can eliminate these callers (unless nobody calls between 9 and 11 and you are in a panic). Your company name and address will screen out people who do not want to work there for whatever reason.

When you are writing job advertisements, avoid terms that could be perceived as discriminatory, such as *busboy* or *hostess*. These terms indicate that the applicants should be male in the case of the busboy, or female in the case of the hostess. This is discriminatory, and therefore illegal, but you see it frequently in the newspapers. Also, avoid references to age, such as "young" or "recent high school graduate."

JW Restaurants has a career for you

RESTAURANT MANAGERS
&
ASSISTANT RESTAURANT MANAGERS

We are a high-quality tablecloth restaurant company based in Chicago and Atlanta with 24 restaurants, expanding to 28 this year. We are looking for outstanding individuals to join our team.

We offer:

> Moving and relocating expenses

> A $3000 signing bonus

> An exciting work environment

> Paid medical, dental, and optical insurance

> Paid vacation

> A 401(k) plan

> Career development, training, and seminars

> Exceptional salary and bonus package

• VIEW OUR WEB SITE AT **JWRESTAURANTS.COM** •

Email or send your résumé to: Jwrestaurants.com
1000 Restaurant Way
CHIGAGO, IL 12345

FIGURE 6.6: Display ads attract more attention and can give more information than classified ads.

The number of applicants an ad pulls will vary greatly with the state of the economy. In good times, even an enticing ad may pull fewer responses than you would like. But when unemployment is high, even your most careful attempts to screen will not keep the numbers down. People who need that job are going to apply for it no matter what your ad says. You might have 250 applicants for one pot-washing job.

If you are going to advertise in the paper, it is well worth studying the ad pages to see what your competition is doing. Read all the ads with the mind-set of a job seeker, and then write one that will top them all. Display ads such as those in Figure 6.6 attract attention and project a good image. Many ads mention incentives such as benefits, equal opportunity, job training, career growth, and other attractions. Usually, such ads are for large numbers of jobs (hotel openings, new units of chains, and so on) or for skilled labor or management jobs. If you are only looking for one pot washer, you may not want to go all out in your ad, but if you want a competitive pot washer, run a good-looking, competitive ad. Some employers and job seekers use the services of companies such as CareerBuilder.com to list their vacancy or résumé.

Some companies advertise all the time. There are two types: the third-rate place whose third-rate ad isn't pulling anyone in ("Needed: intelligent, well-groomed person for nightclub work; call Pete") and the large corporation that runs a two-line ad to keep its name in the job seeker's consciousness ("TGI Friday's, have a nice day!" or "Plaza of the Americas Hotel is the finest").

Today, most hospitality operators avoid expensive advertising in the major area paper; instead, they are running ads in places where potential workers will see them. Many cities have special area newspapers and shopping guides. Place your ads in those areas where your target employees live—people within commuting distance who may be candidates for your types of jobs.

For instance, if many of the potential employees in your area speak Spanish, consider running an ad in Spanish-language local newspapers. Other special places are the schools and colleges in your area. There are also websites that list job openings in the same ways as newspapers. Tommy Bahamas in Sarasota uses craigslist, for example.

Many employers use their own website to advertise for jobs. A low-cost place to advertise is right in your operation. You can use any of the following to bring in applicants: placemats, indoor or outdoor signs (if done professionally), receipts, or table tents, to name just a few. Finally, you can advertise open jobs by posting notices in supermarkets, libraries, churches, synagogues, community centers, and health clubs. Some restaurants even put a sign in the window: "Now hiring smiling faces."

Employment Agencies

employment agencies Organizations that try to place persons into jobs. **Private employment agencies**: privately owned agencies that normally charge a fee when an applicant is placed. **Temporary agencies**: agencies that place temporary employees into businesses and charge by the hour.

Employment agencies are a resource you should look into under certain circumstances. We will look at three common types of agencies: private, temporary, and government. *Private employment agencies* normally charge a fee, which is not collected until they successfully place an applicant with you. In most cases, if this person does not stay with the company for a specified period of time, the agency must find a suitable replacement or return the fee. The fee is often 10 percent of the employee's first-year salary. These types of agencies most often handle management or high-skills jobs and should be used only if they specialize in your field.

Temporary agencies have grown in size and importance, and now a small number specialize in filling positions, including entry-level positions, for hotels, restaurants, and caterers. Temporary agencies charge by the hour for personnel who work anywhere from one day to as long as needed.

Using temporary employees is advantageous during peak business periods or other times when emergency fill-in personnel are needed. However, you can't expect a temporary employee to walk into your operation and go straight to work. You must be willing and able to spend time and money to orient and train these employees.

Another source of employees, at no cost, is the U.S. Employment Service, a federal and state system of employment offices called *job service centers.* Your local job service center will screen and provide applicants for entry-level jobs. The centers have many unemployed people on their books who are looking for jobs. It is a question of whether they are well enough staffed to be able to sift through the people and send you suitable applicants who will not waste your time.

job service center
An office of the U.S. Employment Service.

Direct Recruiting

Direct recruiting, going where the job seekers are, is practiced primarily by large organizations seeking management talent or top-level culinary skills.

Such organizations send recruiters to colleges that teach hospitality management or culinary skills to interview interested candidates. There are also certain situations in which direct recruiting is appropriate for entry-level and semiskilled personnel.

direct recruiting
On-the-scene recruiting where job seekers are, such as at schools and colleges.

For example, when a hotel or restaurant closes, you might arrange to interview its employees. A large layoff at a local factory might be another such situation. It might be worthwhile to interview foodservice students in secondary or vocational schools. Some large cities hold job fairs in early summer to help high school students find summer work. This would be an appropriate place for direct recruiting. Summer employees, if they like the way they are treated, can also become part-time or occasional employees during the school year that follows.

One of the advantages of direct recruiting is that you might get better employees than you would by waiting for them to drop around or to answer your ad in the Sunday paper. Another advantage is the image-building possibilities of direct recruiting. You are not only hiring for the present; you are creating a good image of your company as a place of future employment. Some companies also have internal job fairs where managers are available to talk with employees about their jobs so they have a better idea of what it takes to be a manager. It shows the companies' willingness to promote from within.

Additional External Recruiting Sources

Organizations that are involved with minorities, women, disabled workers, immigrants, or other special groups will usually be very cooperative and eager to place their candidates. Examples of such organizations include the National Association for the Advancement of Colored People, the National Organization of Women, and the American Association for Retired Persons.

Since these organizations do not work only in hospitality, they may not be familiar with the demands of your jobs, and it is absolutely necessary that you be very clear and open and honest about what each job entails. Here again, your detailed job descriptions and performance standards are available. In addition, community organizations such as church groups, Girl Scouts, and Boy Scouts can be sources of employees.

It is a good idea to tell people with whom you do business when you are trying to fill a job. Many of the salespersons you deal with, for example, have wide contacts in the field, and they have good reason to help you out if you are a customer.

Sometimes friends and acquaintances in other fields know of someone who needs a job. Clergy or priests may be able to send people looking for work to you. Sometimes parents are looking for jobs for their children. Through individual contacts, you often reach people who are not yet actively looking for jobs but intend to start soon.

Many people say that one person's telling another that yours is a good place to work is the best advertising there is, and that it will provide you with a steady stream of applicants. Whether the stream of applicants appears or not, there is no guarantee that it will send you the people you want. You are more likely to get the type of people you are looking for through a systematic marketing plan to reach your target groups. But one thing is true: If yours is a good place to work, you will not need as many applicants because they will stay with you longer.

In the never-ending search for talent, some restaurant companies are considering podcasting as a way to attract young employees. Chris Russell recently launched JobsinPods.com, a website that allows employers to create online audio messages about their businesses for potential job applicants to download to their MP3 players or iPods.[12]

✳ EVALUATING YOUR RECRUITING

To determine which sources give you the best workers, you need to evaluate the results over a period of time. What is your successful rate of hire from each source? What is the cost, not only the cash paid out for ads but the hire ratio to numbers interviewed from each source? Interviewing is time consuming, and if interviewing people from a certain source is just an exercise in frustration, that is not a good source.

What is the tenure of people from each source: How long, on average, have they stayed? How many have stayed more than 30 days or three months? How good is their performance? If you find that you are getting poor workers from a particular source, you should drop that source. If you are getting good people from a certain source, stick with it.

You should also evaluate your own recruiting efforts. Are you staying competitive? Do you explain the job clearly and completely and honestly, or do you oversell the job? Do you project a good image for your enterprise, or do you oversell the company? If you oversell, your mistakes will come back to haunt you.

Check Your Knowledge

1. What is negligent hiring? As a supervisor, what responsibilities should you have to take into consideration?
2. Discuss briefly the principles for recruiting.
3. What are internal recruiting and external recruiting?

Do You Know?

How would you review a group of five applicants for a cook's position?

Selecting the Right Person

Let us suppose that you now have a number of applicants for a job you want to fill. Ten applicants for one job is considered by experts to be a good ratio, but that number will vary. Up to a point, the more you have to choose from, the better your chances are of finding someone who is right for the job. But even if you have only one applicant, you should go through the entire selection procedure. It may save you from a terrible mistake.

It is critical to select the right person for the open position. Companies such as Ritz-Carlton arrange for final applicants to complete a "talent" interview to determine if the candidate will fit with the Ritz-Carlton culture and be able to provide genuine caring service to guests. The most successful person is not always the most experienced person—natural talent plus a really positive attitude and desire to be a team player and to learn more every day will frequently be a better person for hospitality companies.

Other positive signs of a good candidate are things like—do they smile in the first few seconds, and what feeling do I get from them, and do they exhibit a passion for the hospitality business?[13] Some companies use current employees on a selection committee because they will be working with the new hire.

We all know that the hospitality industry has a high turnover rate, and much of this high turnover is due to poor selection. The cost of replacing employees is about $8,000 in a high-end hospitality business. This sounds like a lot, but by the time you add up all the costs involved with every stage of the process—position announcements, advertising, recruiting, selection, interviewing, testing, drug screening, talent interview, background checks, and job offers—you can see that this is no overstatement.[14] For line employees in mid-market hospitality organizations, the typical cost of turnover is about $5,000 per position. However, the payoff is more than offset in reduced turnover that can occur with effective and efficient selection.

So, if you want friendly, courteous service, you must hire friendly, courteous people. Hiring employees is like casting stars for a movie—if we do the job well, people will believe that the actor is actually the person they are portraying. Walt Disney World allows its best employees, known as star "cast members," to select future cast members.

Disney gives these star cast members three weeks of training in the selection process before they join the selection team. When screening, it is important to strike a balance. Extensive screening of potential and existing staff risks falling foul of the law, failing to respect individuals' rights and treating people in a discriminatory manner. Conversely, organizations could miss out on people who could be a highly valuable asset. Tread carefully.[15]

Assuming that you have already established job specifications and have done some preliminary screening through your ads or on the phone, the selection procedure from here on has five elements:

1. The application form
2. The interview and evaluation
3. Testing
4. The reference check
5. Making the choice

According to Jim Sullivan, people like to work with those who like them and are like them but, when hiring key employees, there are two qualities to look for: *judgment and honesty*. Almost everything else can be bought by the yard. Remember, there are two kinds of people who never succeed: Those who cannot do what they are told and those who cannot do anything unless they are told.[16]

✳ APPLICATION FORM

An application form is a fact-finding sheet for each applicant. It is a standard form (see Figure 6.7) that asks relevant and job-related questions such as name, address, and phone number, type of job wanted, work history, education, references, and how the applicant heard about the job. As explained in Chapter 5, questions that can be viewed

IF MORE THAN THREE PREVIOUS EMPLOYERS, PLEASE LIST OTHERS HERE

Employment Dates		Company and Address	Position or Type of Work	Salary or Wage	Reason for Leaving
From	To				

Please indicate if you were employed under a different name from the one shown on the first page of this application in any of your previous positions.

Employer	Name Used

U.S. MILITARY RECORD (If related to the job you are applying for)

Branch of Service _____

Active Duty _____ From _____ To _____

Nature of Duties _____

_____

_____

CONVICTIONS/COURT RECORD

Have you been convicted of a crime within the last 7 years?

_____ Yes   _____ No   The existence of a record of convictions for criminal offenses is not considered an automatic bar to employment.

Date of Conviction _____   Describe circumstances: _____

_____

_____

ACKNOWLEDGMENT

I understand that this employment application and any other Company documents are not contracts of employment and that any individual who is hired may voluntarily leave employment upon proper notice and may be terminated by the Company at any time and for any reason. I understand that no employee of the Company has the authority to make any agreement to the contrary and I acknowledge that any oral or written statements to the contrary are hereby expressly disavowed and should not be relied upon by any prospective employee.

I hereby grant permission for the authorities of the Company, or its agents, to investigate my references, and I release the Company and all previous employers, educational institutions, persons, and law enforcement agencies from any and all liability resulting from such an investigation. Upon my termination, I authorize the release of information in connection with my employment.

I certify that the statements made on this application are true and correct, and thereby grant the Company permission to verify the information contained herein.

I understand that giving false information or the failure to give complete information requested herein shall constitute grounds, among others, for rejection of my application or my dismissal in the event of my employment by the Company.

DATE:_____   SIGNATURE OF APPLICANT: _____

FIGURE 6.7:   Application for employment.

APPLICATION FOR EMPLOYMENT
PLEASE PRINT ALL INFORMATION

Date

| Month | Day | Year |

Equal Opportunity Employer

The Company will not discriminate against an applicant or employee because of race, sex, age, religious creed, political affiliation, national origin, sexual preference, disability, or any veteran status.

| Last Name | First | Middle Initial | Social Security Number |

| Present Address (Street & Number) | City | State | Zip Code | Home Phone Number ( ) |

| Address where you may be contacted if different from present address | Alternate Phone Number ( ) |

Are you 16 years of age or older?   ☐ YES ☐ NO

U.S. Citizen or Resident Alien?   ☐ YES ☐ NO

If no, indicate type of Visa:

JOB INTEREST

Position you are applying for:

Type of position you eventually desire:

Available for:
☐ Full-Time ☐ Day Shift ☐ Weekends
☐ Part-Time ☐ Evening Shift ☐ Other _____
☐ Per Diem ☐ Night Shift

When would you be available to begin work?

Have you previously been employed by us?
☐ Yes ☐ No If yes, when

Previous Position(s)

Have you previously submitted an application to us?
☐ Yes ☐ No If yes, when

How were you referred to the Company?   ☐ Employment Agency   ☐ Your Own Initiative
☐ Advertisement—Publication _____   ☐ Employee Referral—Name _____

EDUCATION

School	Name and Address	Circle Highest Year Completed	Type of Degree	Major Subject
High School Last Attended		1 2 3 4		
College, University, or Technical School		1 2 3 4		
College, University, or Technical School		1 2 3 4		
Other (Specify)				

FIGURE 6.7: *(continued)*

PREVIOUS EMPLOYMENT—BEGIN WITH PRESENT OR MOST RECENT POSITION

1. Employer _____

Employed _____ to _____

Address (include Street, City, and Zip Code) _____

May we contact? ☐ Yes   ☐ No

Telephone Number (_____)

Starting Position _____

Salary _____

Last Position _____

Salary _____

Name and Title of Last Supervisor _____

Telephone Number (_____)

Brief Description of Duties: _____

Reason for Leaving: _____

Disadvantages of Last Position: _____

2. Employer _____

Employed _____ to _____

Address (include Street, City, and Zip Code) _____

May we contact? ☐ Yes   ☐ No

Telephone Number (_____)

Starting Position _____

Salary _____

Last Position _____

Salary _____

Name and Title of Last Supervisor _____

Telephone Number (_____)

Brief Description of Duties: _____

Reason for Leaving: _____

Disadvantages of Last Position: _____

3. Employer _____

Employed _____ to _____

Address (include Street, City, and Zip Code) _____

May we contact? ☐ Yes   ☐ No

Telephone Number (_____)

Starting Position _____

Salary _____

Last Position _____

Salary _____

Name and Title of Last Supervisor _____

Telephone Number (_____)

Brief Description of Duties: _____

Reason for Leaving: _____

Disadvantages of Last Position: _____

FIGURE 6.7: *(continued)*

as discriminatory are not allowed (refer to Figure 5.2). You should instruct applicants to complete everything, especially the work history, including places and dates of employment, and names of supervisors.

Before you interview an applicant, you should familiarize yourself with the material on the application and jot down questions. What about gaps in employment? Unanswered questions? The way applicants fill out applications can also be very revealing. Do they follow instructions? Can they read and write? Do they understand the questions? Are they neat or messy? Is their handwriting legible? Did they complete everything? Such things may relate to the job requirements. Did they sign the application form—because if they didn't, and you later find out that they had been convicted of a crime, they can always say, "I didn't sign the application form."

✻ THE INTERVIEW

The first essential for a good interview is a quiet place free of distractions and interruptions, and the first task is to put the candidate at ease. You can tell how they feel by looking for nonverbal clues: a worried look on the face, tensed posture. It is important to remember that people get nervous about interviews. If you can make them feel comfortable and unthreatened, they are more likely to open up and be themselves, and this is what you are after. Listen attentively; this calls for your best listening skills. Remember that you want to impress them favorably on behalf of your organization. A careless mistake in the beginning can ruin the entire interview.

Prepare a list of questions based on the job description—this underlines the importance of a good job description. The best interview questions employers use start with *how, what,* and *why*. When employers use those words, they give the interviewee a chance to explain what they have done and why they did it.[17] With lower-level jobs, it is best to follow a preplanned pattern for the interview, so that you cover the same territory with every applicant. You can start off with general information about the job and the company. The interview involves a two-way exchange of information: You want to know about the applicant, and the applicant wants to know about the job.

Some employers use a highly structured type of interview known as a ***patterned interview***, in which the interviewer asks each applicant a predetermined list of questions. It is important to ask the same questions of all candidates. There may also be additional questions on the interviewer's form that are not asked of the applicant but are provided to help the interviewer interpret the applicant's responses. The training required for a patterned interview is minimal compared to other methods, and the standardized questions help to avoid possible charges of discrimination.

You are after two kinds of information about the applicant: hard data on skills and experience and personal qualities important to the job. As you go over the application in the interview, fill in all details that the applicant left unanswered and ask questions about gaps of 30 days or more on the employment record.

Often, people will not list jobs on which they had problems. If they have something to hide, they will hide it, and these are exactly the things you need to find out. Don't hesitate to probe if you are not satisfied with either the applicant or his or her answers to your questions. Take care to avoid questions that could be considered discriminatory.

patterned interview
A highly structured interview in which the interviewer uses a predetermined list of questions to ask each applicant.

As to personal qualities, you might never really know what they are like until you put them to work. If you can get them talking, you can judge such traits as verbal skills or ease with people. But you will not be able to tell anything about motivation, temperament, absenteeism, honesty, reliability, and all the other things you are looking for.

Getting people to talk may be agonizing the first time you interview. The best method is to avoid questions that have yes or no answers. Ask: "What did you do at . . . ?" "What did you like best about . . . ?" "Tell me why. . . ." One owner always asked server applicants about the funniest thing that ever happened to them on the job. He would not hire people who said that nothing funny had ever happened to them because he believed that they could not deal with people effectively if they couldn't see the funny side of things. You should talk only about 20 percent of the time, with the candidate filling in the remaining 80 percent.

Other good work-related questions to ask are: Tell me about the strengths you bring to this job. This position requires good organizational skills; tell me about how organized you are. You can ask how the applicant would handle a situation that relates to your industry:

- A guest was unhappy with the room.
- A guest has eaten most of an entree and then says, "I don't like it."

Getting applicants to talk takes practice.
Courtesy of Digital Vision.

- A theme-park visitor says, "Why do I have to stand in line for two hours, just to go on one ride?"
- A patient says, "You forgot my dinner," to the hospitality server in a hospital room.

Avoid asking about what the applicant likes to do for fun. What if the answer is, "On Wednesday night, I have Bible study," and he or she doesn't get the job? The applicant could claim that you discriminated on religious grounds. If it doesn't pertain to the job, don't ask it.[18]

Ask if you may make notes (but not on the application form because it goes in the applicant's file and can later be used as evidence in a legal case, and your comments may come back to haunt you). You can do this during the interview if it does not inhibit the applicant; otherwise, do it immediately after, lest you forget. Avoid writing down subjective opinions or impressions; instead, write down specific job-related facts and direct observations.

Be objective, factual, and clear. Evaluate the applicant immediately on your list of specifications for the job, using a rating system that is meaningful to you, such as a point system or a descriptive ranking: (1) exceptional, hire immediately; (2) well qualified; (3) qualified with reservations; (4) not qualified. Some large companies have evaluation forms or systems to use.

Look at the applicants from the perspective of what they can do and what they will do. *Can-do factors* include the applicant's job knowledge, past experience, and education—in other words, whether the applicant can perform the job. *Will-do factors* examine an applicant's willingness, desire, and attitude toward performing the job. You want the person whom you hire to be both technically capable to do the job (or be trainable) and willing to do the job. Without one or the other, you are creating a problem situation and possibly a problem employee.

Evaluation is a subjective business; it is based primarily on feelings and emotions. People turn you off or they turn you on; you like them or you don't. You will make your decision to hire or not to hire primarily on this interview, whether your judgment is valid or not. Studies have shown that there is very little correlation between interview evaluation and success on the job. They also show that interviewers make up their minds in the first four minutes.

Yet you would not dare skip the interview. So how can you get the most value out of it? If you are aware of what is going on in your head and in the other person's behavior, it will help you to evaluate applicants more objectively.

One thing that is happening is that applicants are giving you the answers they think you want to hear and projecting the image they think you are looking for, and they may not be like that at all in real life. Yet often, they let their guard down when the interview is just about over and reveal their true selves in the last few minutes. If you are aware of this, perhaps you can exchange the first four minutes with the last few in making your evaluations.

It is very easy, in that first four minutes, to be influenced by one or two characteristics and extend them into an overall impression of a person. This is known as the *halo effect* or *overgeneralization*. You may be so impressed with someone who is articulate and well dressed that you jump to the conclusion that this applicant will make a great

can-do factors
An applicant's or employee's job knowledge, skills, and abilities.

will-do factors
An applicant's or employee's willingness, desire, and attitude toward performing a job.

halo effect or overgeneralization
The tendency to extend the perception of a single outstanding personality trait to a perception of the entire personality.

bartender. The first day on the job, this impressive person has drunk half a bottle of bourbon two hours into the shift.

A negative impression may be just as misleading. One restaurant manager interviewed a man for a dishwasher job and was so shaken by what he perceived as a wild look in the man's eyes that he was literally afraid to have the man in the place at all. So in the usual panic and crisis, he hired a young kid. He told a friend in the business about the wild-looking man, and the friend said, "You have just turned down the only absolutely professional dishwasher in this entire city." So after the young kid quit two days later, the manager got in touch with the wild-looking man, who accepted the position, stayed 15 years, never was absent, never was late, never broke anything, kept the dish room spotless, polished the dish machine every day, and retired on a company pension.

Another form of overgeneralization is to assume that all applicants from a certain school or all people your pot washer knows personally and says are okay are going to be good workers. This is not necessarily so; it is a generalization about personality rather than knowledge or skill.

Another thing that happens easily is to let *expectations* blind you to reality. If someone has sent you an applicant with a glowing recommendation, you will tend to see that applicant in those terms, whether or not they are accurate.

Still another thing that is easy to do is to see some facet of yourself in someone else and to assume that this person is exactly like you. You discover that this person grew up in your old neighborhood, went to the same school that you did, had some of the same teachers, and knows people you know.

A spark is kindled and you think, "Hallelujah, this person has got to be great!" This reaction is known as *projection*—you project your own qualities onto that person. Furthermore, you are so excited about finding someone exactly like you (you think) that you may even forget what that has to do with the job for which you are interviewing this person.

projection
In interviewing and evaluation, putting your own qualities on the applicant based on a perceived similarity.

What it all comes down to is that in interviewing and evaluating, you need to stick closely to the personal qualities needed *on the job* and to be on guard against your subjective reactions and judgments. Do not make snap judgments and do not set standards that are higher than necessary. Not all positions require people who are enthusiastic, articulate, or well educated, so don't be turned off by a quiet school dropout who can't put six words together to make a sentence.

When it comes to telling applicants about a job, you should be open and honest and completely frank. If they will have to work Sundays and holidays, tell them so. One supervisor told an applicant she would work a five-day week. The applicant assumed that it was Monday through Friday, and that was fine. But when she reported for work and they told her it was Wednesday through Sunday, she quit then and there. She felt that the supervisor had cheated, and from that point on the trust was gone.

truth in hiring
Telling an applicant the entire story about a job, including the drawbacks.

Be frank about days and hours, overtime, pay and tips, uniforms, meals, and all the rest, so the new employee will start the job with no unpleasant surprises. You might call this *truth in hiring*. Sure, you want to sell your jobs, but overselling will catch up with you.

Explain your pay scale and your promotion policy: "This is what you start at, this is what you can make with overtime, this is what you can realistically expect in tips, this is what you will take home, this is as high as you can go in this job, these are the jobs you can eventually work up to, these are your chances of that happening."

Give them a chance to ask questions, and then end the interview. Tell them when you will make your decision and ask them to call you the day after that if they have not heard from you. Altogether, it should take you 20 to 30 minutes to interview an applicant for an entry-level job and up to 60 minutes for a supervisory position. Tips for interviewing are summarized in Figure 6.8.

1. Be nonjudgmental during the entire interview process. Do not jump to conclusions. A poor interviewer reaches a decision in the first 5 minutes.
2. Recognize your personal biases and try not to let them influence you. Be objective. Do not look for clones of yourself. Do not let an applicant's age, gender, attractiveness, or verbal fluency influence your opinions.
3. Spend most of your time listening attentively. Allow the candidate to do at least 70 to 80 percent of the talking. Listen to each answer before deciding on the next question. Do not interrupt.
4. Make notes so that vital information is not forgotten.
5. Repeat or paraphrase the applicant's statements to make sure that you understand the applicant and perhaps get more information, or you may repeat the last few words the applicant just said with a questioning inflection. Also, summarize the applicant's statements periodically to clarify points and to bring information together. A summary statement may begin with, "Let's state the major points up to now. . . ." In this manner, the applicant can confirm or clarify what has been discussed.
6. Another technique to get a quiet applicant to talk and show interest is to ask open-ended questions (questions without a yes or no answer) and use pauses. Pauses allow the applicant to sense that more information is desired and hopefully, the interviewee will feel compelled to fill the silence.
7. Use body language to show interest and elicit information. Use direct eye contact, nod, smile, and lean forward slightly.
8. Do not be bashful about probing for more information when it is needed.
9. Instead of asking about an applicant's "weaknesses," refer to areas of improvement.
10. Paint a realistic picture of the job. Be honest.
11. Always be sincere, respectful, courteous, friendly, and treat all applicants in the same way.
12. Allow the applicant to ask questions of you.

FIGURE 6.8:   Tips for Interviewing.

During the interview, clarify the important aspects of the job. For instance: "This job requires that you work Tuesday to Saturday; are you able to do that?" or "This position requires you to work evenings and weekends; are you able to do that?" Or, "This position requires you to lift up to 50 pounds. Can you do that?"

✳ TESTING

Some companies use tests as an additional method of evaluating applicants. Sometimes tests are given before the interview to screen out candidates. Sometimes they are given after interviews to the small group of candidates still in the running, to add objective data to subjective evaluations. Various kinds of tests are used:

1. Skills tests measure specific skills.
2. Aptitude tests are intended to measure ability to learn a particular job or skill. Manual dexterity tests are a form of aptitude test and measure manipulative ability.
3. Psychological tests are designed to measure personality traits; large companies often use them in hiring management personnel.
4. Medical examinations measure physical fitness.

Except for medical examinations and skills tests, most hospitality enterprises do not use tests for nonmanagement jobs. There are several reasons for this. One is the time it takes to give tests and score them. Another is that many of the tests available have little relevance to the requirements of nonmanagement jobs. A third is that many tests, having been constructed for populations of a certain background and education, discriminate against applicants who do not have that background and education. It is illegal to use such tests either in hiring or in promotion.

To be usable, a test must be valid, reliable, and relevant to the job. To be valid, it must actually measure what it is designed to measure. To be reliable, it must be consistent in its measurement, that is, give the same result each time a given person takes it. To be relevant, it must relate to the specific job for which it is given. The user of any test must determine that it meets these criteria and must use it properly as its publisher designed it to be used.

All in all, the complications of testing, the risks of discrimination, and the possibilities for error at the hands of an untrained user make most tests more trouble than they are worth. Skills tests and specific aptitude tests such as manual dexterity tests are the exceptions. Your best bet, and the one most closely geared to your job needs, is a set of skills tests derived from your performance standards.

They must be adapted somewhat since the applicant will not know all the ins and outs of your special house procedures, but this can be done. It will give you an objective measure of an applicant's ability to perform on the job and an indication of how much additional training is needed.

Psychological tests are used to test for honesty and even broader qualities such as integrity. These tests are based on the assumption that honest and dishonest people have different values and see the world differently. Some employers use honesty tests

Employee Polygraph Protection Act of 1988
A federal law that prohibits the use of lie detectors in the screening of job applicants.

in the hopes of providing a secure workplace for their employees. Using honesty tests properly requires some work.

First, some states and localities do not allow such testing, so check the regulations. Next, you need to examine independent reviews and validity tests (provided that the instrument actually tests what it is supposed to test) of the instrument you want to use. Even if you find a good instrument, and it is legal in your location, don't forget that testing also requires money and time and that the results are not a substitute for any of the other selection steps you take, such as interviewing or making reference checks.

A medical examination can be required only after a job offer has been made to the applicant. When a job offer is made prior to the medical exam, it is considered a conditional job offer because if the applicant does not pass the medical exam, the job offer is normally revoked.

The *Employee Polygraph Protection Act of 1988* prohibits the use of lie detectors in the screening of job applicants. Although lie detectors have been used in the past in some states, they are now illegal to use in the employment process.

Check Your Knowledge

1. What are the elements that the selection process includes?
2. Give a tip that is useful when interviewing.
3. What does the Employee Polygraph Protection Act of 1988 prohibit?

✳ REFERENCE CHECK

You have now narrowed your choice to two or three people. So, why is it important to check references? Well, for starters, it is an important part of the selection process; they are also more likely to help ensure successful hires by screening for a good fit for the organization/department. A reference check may also help avoiding a probation failure and can help avoid charges of *negligent hiring*.[19]

The reference check is the final step before hiring. It is a way to weed out applicants who have falsified or stretched their credentials or who in other jobs have been unsatisfactory. Reference information can be thought of in two ways: substance and style. *Substance* concerns the factual information given to you by the applicant. *Style* concerns how the person did in previous jobs, how he or she got along with others, how well he or she worked under pressure.

When requesting a reference check, prepare specific job-related questions and do not ask questions that are not permitted during the interview.[20] First, verify the substance issues, such as dates of employment, job title, salary, and so on. You may wonder why applicants would falsify information on an application, but they do. One applicant writes that he graduated from a culinary school that he only attended briefly; another says that she was the front desk manager when in reality she filled in twice for the regular manager. If your job requires a particular educational degree or certification, ask applicants to supply a copy of the appropriate document. Otherwise, get the applicant's written permission to obtain a transcript.

Once you have confirmed that the person is who they say they are on paper, you can start checking previous work references. Often, former employers will only reveal neutral information such as job title, dates of employment, and salary, because of fear of being charged with libel, slander, or defamation of character by the former employee.

Although there is nothing wrong with providing objective documented information, such as an attendance problem, past employers are often reluctant to discuss this sort of concern or even answer the one question you really need an answer to: "Would you rehire?" To reduce any possible liability, you should ask applicants to sign a release on the application form (Figure 6.7) that gives you permission to contact references and holds all references blameless for anything they say.

Because it is fast, checking references by phone is very common. Be sure to document your calls on a form. Ask to speak to the employee's former supervisor. Always identify yourself and your company, and explain that you are doing a reference check. Start by asking for neutral information such as salary and job title and work your way up to more telling information.

Despite the importance of checking references, few people in the hospitality industry bother with a reference check. It may be habit or tradition, or it may be fear and desperation: fear of finding out there is a reason not to hire and desperation to fill the job. It may just be too time consuming or you may think that your gut feeling or intuition says it all. But it is really a serious mistake to neglect the reference check and thus run the risk of hiring a problem worker.

When calling for a reference check, talk to human resources, not the department supervisor—who might be a friend of the applicant or who might want to be rid of the applicant and therefore give him or her a good reference regardless. Do get background checks: these will include a credit check—you don't want someone with credit problems working in a cash-handling situation. Do also get a criminal background check—you don't want to give a sex offender access to guest rooms.

✳ MAKING THE CHOICE

Choosing a new employee is your decision and your responsibility. Making the choice may mean choosing between two or three possibilities or looking further for the right person for the job. When making the hiring choice, avoid making any of these common mistakes:

1. Don't jump to hire someone who simply reminds you of yourself. Also try not to fall prey to the halo effect. Look at the big picture!
2. Many problems in hiring come about when you hire too quickly. Use the time involved in the selection process to go through each step thoughtfully. Aim to hire the best candidate, not simply the first reasonably qualified applicant who comes forth.
3. Don't rush to hire the applicant who interviewed the best. Although the interview process can certainly tell you a lot about an applicant, the applicant with the best interviewing skills (which can be learned and practiced by anyone) is not necessarily the best person for the job. Also, keep in mind that during an interview, some applicants will use their charismatic personalities and ability to tell you what you want to hear to get top consideration for the job in question.

4. Don't hire someone just because your "gut feeling," or intuition, says that this applicant is the best. Intuition is fine to use, but always combine it with the other tools of the trade, such as reference checking and testing.

5. Don't hire someone just because the person comes highly recommended. Perhaps an applicant comes highly recommended as a breakfast cook, but you are looking for an experienced pizza maker. It's fine to listen to a recommendation for an applicant, but as usual, that's only part of the story.

Every time you hire someone, even when you feel confident about your choice, there is the chance that you have made a mistake. You will not know this, however, until your new people have been with you awhile and you can see how they do the work, whether they follow instructions and learn your ways easily and willingly, how they relate to the customers and the other workers, whether they come in on time, and all the other things that make good workers. To give yourself the chance to make this evaluation, it is wise to set a probationary period, making it clear that employment is not permanent until the end of the period.

If you see that some of your new people are not going to work out, let them go and start over. Do not let them continue beyond the end of the probation period. It is hard to face the hiring process all over again, but it is better than struggling with an incompetent employee. It can be as hard to fire as it is to hire—but that's another story.

✳ MAKING THE OFFER

Offers for all jobs should be made in writing. The offer letter typically is sent, or given, to the new hire after an offer has been made and accepted over the phone. When you are making an offer, be sure to include all the conditions that were discussed with the applicant. The following points should appear in the offer letter, as appropriate:

- Department
- Position title
- Supervisor
- Location
- Rate of pay
- Schedule of shift, days off
- When jobs start, where to report, whom to report to
- Clothing and equipment needed
- Meal arrangements
- Parking
- Arrangements for orientation/training
- Brief description of benefits
- Probationary period
- Appointment time or whom to call for an appointment concerning filling out additional personnel forms (such as the I-9 form)

Negligent Hiring

Fear of negligent hiring and retention litigation is a hiring manager's worst nightmare and the most compelling reason to conduct in-depth criminal records searches of job applicants. A multilevel jurisdictional criminal records search is the greatest protection an employer has against a negligent hiring lawsuit.[21]

Could your employer be sued if a guest were injured by a hostile employee who had a violent background that would have been uncovered if a proper reference check had been done? Yes, your employer could be sued for **_negligent hiring_**. In the past ten years, lawsuits for negligent hiring have been on the rise. If a violent or hostile employee injures a guest or employee, the injured party may sue the employer and will probably win if he or she can prove that the employer did not take reasonable and appropriate precautions to avoid hiring or retaining the employee.

As a leader, you have the responsibility of taking reasonable and appropriate safeguards when hiring employees to make sure that they are not the type to harm guests or other workers. Such safeguards include conducting a reasonable investigation into an applicant's background and, especially, inquiring further about suspicious factors such as short residency periods or gaps in employment.

You also have a responsibility to counsel or discipline your employees when they become abusive, violent, or show any other deviant behavior. Follow up on complaints your employees and customers may make about another employee's negative behaviors. Use your employer's policies to dismiss dangerous or unfit employees after appropriate warnings. For hospitality companies, a well-oiled human resource team trained to screen for such hidden characteristics (prejudice) and identify people who will fit into a corporate culture with zero tolerance for prejudice is of the utmost importance.[22]

negligent hiring
The failure of an employer to take reasonable and appropriate safeguards when hiring employees to make sure that they are not the type to harm guests or other workers.

Orientation

Orientation introduces each new employee to the job and workplace as soon as he or she reports for work. It is not uncommon in the hospitality industry for people to be put to work without any orientation at all: "Here is your workstation; do what Virginia tells you." You don't even know what door to come in and out of and where the restrooms are, and on payday everyone else gets paid and you don't, and you wonder if you have been fired and didn't even know it.

The primary purpose of orientation is to tell new staff members (1) what they want to know, and (2) what the company wants them to know. As with any training, it takes time—the new person's time and the supervisor's time—anywhere from 30 minutes to most of the day.

Nevertheless, it is worth the time needed to do it and to do it well. It can reduce employee anxiety and confusion, ease the adjustment, and tip the balance between leaving and staying during the first critical days. In addition, it provides an excellent opportunity to create positive employee attitudes toward the company and the job.

Therefore, you have two goals for an orientation:

1. Communicating information: getting the messages through
2. Creating a positive response to company and job

orientation
A new worker's introduction to a job.

Let us look at the second one first because it makes the first one easier and because it is more likely to be overlooked.

✳ CREATING A POSITIVE RESPONSE

If you do not have an orientation for each new employee, somebody else will—your other workers. Their orientation will be quite different from yours, and it may have a negative impact. They want to give a new person the inside story, the lowdown, and it will include everybody's pet gripes and negative feelings about the company and warnings to watch out for this and that, and your new worker will begin to have an uneasy feeling that this is not such a good place to work. People are always more ready to believe their coworkers, their peer group, than their boss, so it is important for you to make your impact first. Then, in the days that follow, you must live up to what you have told them in your orientation or their coworkers might undermine the impression you have made.

You want to create an image of the company as a good place to work. You also want to foster certain feelings in your new people: that they are needed and wanted, that they and their jobs are important to the company. You want to create the beginnings of a sense of belonging, of fitting in. You want to reduce their anxieties and promote a feeling of confidence and security about the company and the job and their ability to do it.

You do all this not only through what you say but how you say it and even more through your own attitude. You speak as one human being to another; you do not talk down from a power position. You assume that each is a person worthy of your concern and attention who can and will work well for you. You do not lay down the law; you inform. You treat orientation as a way of filling their need to know rather than *your* need to have them follow the rules (although it is that, too). You accentuate the positive.

If you can make a favorable impact, reduce anxieties, and create positive attitudes and feelings, new employees will probably stay through the critical first seven days. It will be much easier for you to train them, and they will become productive much more quickly.

✳ COMMUNICATING THE NECESSARY INFORMATION

Employees want to know about their pay rate, overtime, days and hours of work, where the restrooms are, where to park, where to go in and out, where the phone is and whether they can make or receive calls, where their workstation is, to whom they report, break times, meals, and whether their brother can come to the Christmas party. The company wants them to know all this plus all the rules and regulations they must follow; company policy on holidays, sick days, benefits, and so on; uniform and grooming codes; how to use the time clock; emergency procedures; key control; withholding of taxes; explanation of paycheck and deductions. They must also fill out the necessary forms and get their name tags, and they should have a tour of the facility and be introduced to the people they will work with.

employee handbook
A written document given to employees that tells them what they need to know about company policies and procedures.

It is a lot to give all at once. It is best to give it one-on-one rather than waiting until you have several new people and giving a group lecture. A lecture is too formal, and waiting several days may be too late.

You can have it all printed in a booklet, commonly called an *employee handbook*. But you cannot hand people a book of rules and expect them to read and absorb it. It will really turn them off if you ask them first thing to read a little booklet about things they cannot do. *Tell them.* Give them the booklet to take home.

An orientation checklist, shown in Figure 6.9, is an excellent tool for telling your employees what they need to know. It lists sample topics covered during an orientation program, such as how to request a day off. These topics are grouped into three

INTRODUCTION TO THE COMPANY

_____   Welcome.

_____   Describe company briefly, including history, operation (type of menu, service, hours of operation, etc.) and goals (be sure to mention the importance of quality service).

_____   Show how company is structured or organized.

POLICIES AND PROCEDURES

_____   Explain dress code and who furnishes uniforms.

_____   Describe where to park.

_____   How to sign in and out and when.

_____   Assign locker and explain its use.

_____   Review amount of sick time, holiday time, personal time, and vacation time as applicable.

_____   Review benefits.

_____   Explain how to call in if unable to come to work.

_____   Explain procedure to request time off.

_____   Review salary and when and where to pick up check, as well as who can pick up the employee's paycheck. If applicable, explain policy on overtime and reporting of tips.

_____   Discuss rules on personal telephone use.

_____   Explain smoking policy.

_____   Explain meal policy, including when and where food can be eaten.

_____   Review disciplinary guidelines.

_____   Explain guest relations policy.

_____   Review teamwork policy.

_____   Explain property removal policy.

_____   Explain responsible service of alcohol, if applicable.

_____   Explain Equal Employment Opportunity policy.

_____   Discuss promotional and transfer opportunities.

_____   Explain professional conduct policy.

_____   Explain guidelines for safe food handling, safety in the kitchen, and what to do in case of a fire.

_____   Explain notice requirement if leaving your job.

THE NEW JOB

_____   Review job description and standards of performance.

_____   Review daily work schedule including break times.

_____   Review hours of work and days off. Show where schedule is posted.

_____   Explain how and when employee will be evaluated.

_____   Explain probationary period.

_____   Explain training program, including its length.

_____   Describe growth opportunities.

_____   Give tour of operation and introduce to other managers and coworkers.

FIGURE 6.9: Sample orientation checklist.

categories: "Introduction to the Company," "Policies and Procedures," and "The New Job." One benefit of using such a checklist is that it ensures consistency among managers and supervisors who are conducting orientation and makes it unlikely that any topic will be forgotten.

Similarly, you cannot expect new employees to soak up everything you say. As you are aware, communication is a two-way process, and you can send message after message but you cannot control the receiving end. They will listen selectively, picking out what interests them. Try to give each item an importance for them. (For example: "You can get any entrée under $5 free." "The employee parking lot is the only place that isn't crowded." "The cook will poison your lunch if you come in through the kitchen.") Give reasons. ("The money withheld goes to the government.") Phrase things positively. ("You may smoke on breaks in designated areas outside the building" rather than "Smoking is forbidden on the job.")

Watch your workers carefully to make sure that you are understood, and repeat as necessary. Encourage questions. ("Can I clarify anything?") Be sure you cover everything (use a checklist). Even so, you will need to repeat some things during the next few days.

Taking the trouble to start new employees off on the right foot will make things easier as you begin their training for the job. They will feel more positive, less anxious, and more receptive to the new work environment.

 # KEY POINTS

1. *Labor market* refers to the supply of employees looking for jobs and the jobs available in a given area.
2. Many hospitality jobs require hard physical labor. The days and hours of work vary, but many employees work part-time hours, including weekends and evenings.
3. Possible sources of employees include those already working in your operation, people looking for their first job, women, immigrants, retired people, moonlighters, the unemployed, the disabled, and people who just want to get away from what they have been doing.
4. You will find it helpful to know something about the labor market in your own area, such things as prevailing wages for various jobs, unemployment rates for various types of workers, demographics, and the kinds of companies you are competing with for workers.
5. To determine labor needs, you must define the qualifications for each job in a document called a job specification. Job qualifications include knowledge, skills and abilities, work experience, and education and training.
6. When forecasting staff needs, look at your schedules and consider the amount of time it takes to replace an employee and get the new employee trained. Anticipate openings using a staff forecast form, shown in Figure 6.3.
7. Figure 6.2 shows recommended ways to ask questions of job applicants to avoid charges of discrimination.

8. Recruiting should be appropriate, competitive, constant, and use a multifaceted approach.

9. Recruiting is either internal or external. Examples include employee referral programs, direct recruiting, advertising, employment agencies, community organizations, personal contacts, and word of mouth.

10. The selection process includes the application form, the interview and evaluation, testing, the reference check, and making the choice.

11. Tips for interviewing are given in Figure 6.8.

12. To be usable, a test must be valid, reliable, and relevant to the job.

13. When hiring, you must make good-faith efforts to safeguard employees and guests from harmful people. If the proper checks are not made, your employer could be charged with negligent hiring.

14. Orientation tells new staff members what they want to know and what the company wants them to know.

KEY TERMS

can-do factors	job specification
demographics	labor market
direct recruiting	negligent hiring
employee handbook	orientation
Employee Polygraph Protection Act of 1988	patterned interview
	private employment agencies
employee referral programs	projection
employment requisition form	promoting from within
external recruiting	recruiting
halo effect (overgeneralization)	scheduling
internal recruiting	temporary agencies
job posting	truth in hiring
job service centers	will-do factors

REVIEW QUESTIONS

Answer each question in complete sentences. Read each question carefully and make sure that you answer all parts of the question. Organize your answer using more than one paragraph when appropriate.

1. Describe the labor market in the area in which you live. What jobs are available? Are there many jobs advertised in the classified section of the newspapers? Is it hard to get a job because of a large number of applicants?

2. Describe five sources of potential employees.

3. List the job qualifications detailed in a job specification.

4. Which of the following questions are okay to ask applicants?

- Do you own a car?
- Do you own a home?
- In this job, you will be lifting boxes up to 50 pounds. Can you lift 50 pounds?
- Are you healthy?
- Can you supply a photograph?
- If you came from Greece, are you a Greek citizen?
- Are you married?
- What professional organizations do you belong to?
- What ages are your children?
- What clubs do you belong to?
- Are you 40-something?
- Do you have any disabilities?
- Are you able to perform the job I have just described?
- Do you have any outside activities that would keep you from observing the required days and hours of work?

5. What is negligent hiring? How can you avoid it?
6. Describe two methods of internal recruiting and three methods of external recruiting.
7. Discuss three methods you might use to evaluate your recruiting efforts.
8. List seven dos and seven don'ts for interviewing.
9. Why is checking references so important? Why is it so difficult to check references?

ACTIVITIES AND APPLICATIONS

1. Discussion Questions

- What recruiting methods would be most appropriate to the situation in your area?
- Which is better in your opinion: to hire experienced workers or to train people? Defend your opinion. Are there other alternatives?
- How can you guard against your own subjectivity in an interview?
- How could performance standards be used in recruiting and selection?
- Do you think you have ever been discriminated against while trying to get a job? If so, describe.
- Describe various experiences you have had when taking a job interview. Which interviewers struck you as being good? What did poor interviewers do or forget to do?

2. Role-Play: Interviewing

Using the job description for a server that was presented in Chapter 5, work in groups of four to develop a series of interview questions for a part-time server position (Thursday through Saturday evenings) in an Italian restaurant serving pizza, pasta, and other Italian meals. When completed, have two students role-play an interview, with the two extra students acting as observers. When the first role-play is done, the observers will act as interviewer and interviewee. The role of the observers is to look for questions that are illegal and also to judge the ability of the interviewer to do a good job.

3. Group Activity: Job Specifications

Working in groups of four, each group decides on a job classification, such as cook or housekeeper, for which they will write a job specification. Use the format in Figure 6.1.

4. Case Study: The One That Got Away

Dennis is dining-room manager in the coffee shop of a large hotel. He is about to interview Donna, a drop-in applicant who is filling out an application form. A natural server type, smiling, good voice, well groomed. He'd like to hire her to replace Rosa—these married women with kids don't show up half the time. Dennis is on duty as host for the lunch-serving period. He is seating a party of guests when Donna brings him her application. "Enjoy your lunch!" he says to the guests as he hands them the menus. Then he hurries over to ask Eleanor, a server who sometimes acts as hostess, to sub for him for a few minutes, and seats Donna at a table near the entrance. He can keep an eye on things while he interviews her. He glances at the application. A year as waitress at Alfred's Restaurant—good! A high school graduate taking a couple of courses at the community college—good! The application is filled out neatly and carefully—good! He looks up to compliment her but sees Eleanor waving at him. "Excuse me, I'll be right back," he says to Donna. He deals quickly with a customer who wants to get a recipe. Donna is fiddling with a spoon and looks up soberly when he comes back. "I'm sorry," he says. "Now, where were we? Oh yes, I was going to tell you——" Another waitress presents herself at the table. "Listen, Dennis," she says, "tell Eleanor to get off my back. I'm not taking orders from her, she's not my boss." "Look, Dolores, I'll talk to you in a minute. The guest at Table 9 is signaling you. Go tend to her." Donna has a fixed smile on her face. "I really think you'd like it here," says Dennis, "there's never a dull moment. Now tell me about your job at Alfred's." After getting a chance to discuss Donna's work experience, he sees that Eleanor is gesturing that he is wanted on the phone, so he excuses himself. "Yes, of course, I'll take care of it," he says to his boss, and rushes back to Donna, who is sitting with hands folded, looking straight ahead. "Now tell me about yourself." "Well . . . what would you like to know?" She smiles politely. "Are you married?" Dennis asks abruptly. "Yes." Not so good. "Any kids?" "A baby boy." Worse! She looks at him levelly and says, "My mother takes care of him." "Would you—oh damn!" Eleanor is gesturing madly and a customer looking like very bad news is heading his way. He rises hastily. Donna rises, too. "I have to go," she says. "I'll call you," Dennis says over his shoulder before facing a furious man with a long string of complaints. The day goes on like this, one thing after another. The next morning he thinks about Donna again. Never mind about the baby: He decides to hire her on a probationary basis. When he finally finds time to call her, she tells him she has taken a job at the hotel across the street.

Case Study Questions

1. Dennis has made a number of mistakes in this interview. Identify as many as you can and discuss their adverse effects.
2. What did he find out about Donna during the interview?
3. What did he tell her about the job? What did she learn about the job in other ways?
4. On what basis did Dennis decide to hire her? Is it a good basis for making a hiring decision?
5. Do you think Donna would have decided to work for Dennis if he had gone about the interview differently?

WEB ACTIVITY

- Go to the following website: www.eeoc.gov.
- Click on federal EEO laws to answer the following:
  1. Which laws does the U.S. Equal Employment Opportunity Commission (EEOC) enforce?
  2. What is the Civil Service Reform Act of 1978 (CSRA)?
  3. Who enforces the CSRA?
  4. Which law prohibits discrimination against qualified individuals with disabilities who work in the federal government?
  5. What does the EEOC also provide?

RELATED WEBSITES

Federal Wage and Labor Law Institute	www.fwlli.com
Hospitality Careers	www.hcareers.com
Hospitality Employment	www.chefsatwork.com
	www.entreejobbank.com
	www.escoffier.com
	www.foodservice.com
	www.gotajob.com
	www.restaurantsjobs.com
	www.restaurantmanagers.com
STAT-USA	www.statusa.gov

ENDNOTES

1. Diana Berta, "Maintaining Labor Levels Easier During Recession," *Nation's Restaurant News*, vol. 43, no. 8 (March 2, 2009), p. 16.
2. "United States Unemployment Rate," *Trading Economy*, April 1, 2011. Available at www.tradingeconomics.com/united-states/unemployment-rate. Also see Robin Lee Allen, "Restaurants Hungry for Workers as U.S. Unemployment Rate Continues to Drop," *Nation's Restaurant News*, vol. 40, no. 36 (September 4, 2006), p. 29.
3. Jim Sullivan, "Word to the Wise: Stop Hiring or Retaining People who Make Your Job as a Restaurant Operator Harder," *Nation's Restaurant News*, vol. 41, no. 10 (May 7, 2007), p. 22.
4. Personal conversation with David Watkins, director of human resources for the Suso Beach Resort, July 12, 2007.
5. Christine La Fave, "The Ten-Minute Manager's Guide to Attracting Top Talent," *Restaurants and Institutions*, vol. 118, no. 10 (July 1, 2008), p. 24.
6. Ibid.

7. Dina Berta, "Study: Online Should Diversify Not Replace, Traditional Hiring," *Nation's Restaurant News*, vol. 42, no. 45 (November 17, 2008), p. 8.

8. Mary Bolz Chapman. "Do Green Efforts Aid?" *Chain Leader* (February 1, 2009).

9. Anonymous, "Keeping Current: Recruitment and Hiring," *Partner's Report*, vol. 04, no. 3 (March 2004), p. 5.

10. Phillip Perry, "A Carrot a Day," *Restaurants USA* (January–February 2001).

11. Leslie A. Weatherly, Selection Tests, SHRM Research. Retrieved from www.shrm.org/research/briefly_published/Employee%20Testing%20Series%20Part. February 14, 2008.

12. Diana Berta, "Recruiter's Explore Using Podcasts to Attract Workers," *Nation's Restaurant News*, vol. 41, no. 25 (January 18, 2007), p. 14.

13. Personal conversation with Charlotte Jordan, October 25, 2004.

14. Personal correspondence with Chris Chapman, September 14, 2004.

15. Liz Hall, "Looks Good on Paper?" *Personnel Today* (March 2004), p. 17.

16. Sullivan, p. 22.

17. Getting Hired Practice Questions. Hospitality Jobs Online. Obtained at: www.hospitalityonline.com. July 16, 2007.

18. Katerina Ameral, presentation to USF HR class, November 4, 2004.

19. Obtained online from www.admin.mtu.edu/hro/forms/checkingreferences.pdf. Retrieved July 16, 2007.

20. Ibid.

21. Robert Capwell, "Due Diligence in Screening: No Room for Shortcuts," Society for Human Resource Management, Staffing Management Library—Reference Checking. January 2008.

22. Ellen Koteff, "Lethal Weapon: Use Zero Tolerance Policies to Eradicate Prejudice in the Workplace," *Nation's Restaurant News*, vol. 40, no. 50 (December 11, 2006), p. 25.

Chapter 8

Motivation

Overview

Employee Expectations and Needs

Motivation

Theories of Motivation

Applying Theory to Reality: Limiting Factors

Building a Positive Work Climate

Focus: The Individual

Motivational Methods

Focus: The Job—Providing an Attractive Job Environment

Focus: The Leader

Susan just started working a month ago at the front desk of an airport hotel. So far, she is not very happy with the job. To begin with, she has trouble finding a parking spot every afternoon when she comes to work, although she was promised that there were plenty. When she reports to work, she is lucky if she can find her boss, who is often away from the work area, to question him about her training program, which is going very slowly. Most of her peers manage to say hello, but that is usually all. She wonders if anyone would notice if she just took off out the front door and did not come back.

Randy, a cook in a downtown restaurant, loves where he works. Although his pay and benefits are good, there are many other reasons why he loves his job. He feels like part of a quality team at work, management always keeps him informed of what's going on, hourly employees frequently get promoted when there are open positions, the kitchen is comfortable to work in and he has just the equipment he needs, everyone is on a first-name basis, he gets bonuses based on the number of guests served, and the restaurant owners give him time off to go to college and pay his tuition.

Employees want to be treated as individuals first and as employees second. They want a lot more out of work than just a paycheck. They want, for example, respect, trust, rewards, and interesting work.

In the first section of this chapter, we discuss employee expectations and needs. The concept of motivation is then discussed, followed by a section on how to build a positive work climate.

Today's employees tend to have higher expectations from their jobs, and they have less tolerance for mismanagement, frustrating coworkers, or poor working conditions. They expect companies to invest in them—in coaching and job development—so they can grow professionally and personally. They want to be contributing members of a

259

team. If they do not feel valued personally, they will leave. If the economy is good, they will leave quickly. To retain good workers—and even to transform mediocre workers into good workers—supervisors must know how to motivate employees.

After completion of this chapter you should be able to:

- **Explain common employee expectations of their leaders.**
- **Define the term** *motivation* **and explain the leader's responsibility to motivate his or her employees.**
- **Discuss the essential points of current theories and practices for motivating employees on the job.**
- **Explain the challenge of applying common motivational theories in the hospitality work environment.**
- **Identify nine ways to build a positive work climate by focusing on employees as individuals.**
- **Describe two ways a leader can build a positive work climate by focusing on him- or herself.**

Employee Expectations and Needs

When you become a leader, you will have certain expectations of your employees. You will expect them to do the work they have been hired to do—to produce the products and services to the quality standards set by the enterprise that is paying you both. You sometimes wonder whether their performance will meet your expectations, and you have some plans for improving productivity.

But you might not realize that what these people expect from you and how *you* meet *their* expectations has as much to do with their performance as your expectations of them. If you handle their expectations well, if they recognize your authority willingly, you will have a positive relationship going for you—one on which you can build a successful operation. Let us look at some categories of things workers typically expect and need from the boss.

✳ YOUR EXPERIENCE AND TECHNICAL SKILLS

Employees expect you to be qualified to lead. First, they want you to have worked in the area in which you are leading: a hotel, a hospital kitchen, a restaurant, whatever it is. Coming into a restaurant from a hospital kitchen might discount your experience, and you will have to prove yourself. Coming into a big hotel from a job in a budget motel, you will also have to prove yourself. Your associates want to feel that you understand the operation well and appreciate the work they are doing. They want to feel that they and their jobs are in good hands—that you are truly capable of leading them and their work.

In some circumstances, being a college graduate will make you distrusted. Your associates might assume that you think you know it all and that you will look down on them. They might think that *they* know it all and that you have not paid your dues by coming up the hard way.

In other places, if you are *not* a college graduate and other leaders have college degrees—in a hospital setting, perhaps—you will have to work harder to establish yourself with your associates. If they are satisfied with what you have done on other jobs and how you are doing on this one, they will each decide at some point, okay, you are qualified to lead here. But it will take time and tact and determination on your part.

Second, they want you to be not only experienced but also technically competent. Every employee who works with you expects you to be able to do his or her particular job. This can become a sort of game. Employees will question you, they will check you, they will make you prove you know what you are doing: "Why doesn't the bread rise?" "Why doesn't the sauce thicken?" There will be instances when they will have sabotaged that recipe just to see if you know what is wrong. They may unplug the slicer and tell you it is broken, and you will start checking the machine and the fuses before you catch on. You are going to have to prove your right to supervise. You don't have to know how to do every job *as well as* each person doing that job—but you do have to know how to do it.

✳ THE WAY YOU BEHAVE AS A LEADER

Nearly everyone wants a leader who will take stands and make decisions, who will stay in charge no matter how difficult the situation is, who is out there handling whatever emergency comes up. Hardly anyone respects a boss who evades issues and responsibilities, shifts blame, hides behind the mistakes of others, or avoids making decisions that will be unpopular even though they are necessary.

Many people expect authority and direction from the boss. These people want you to tell them what to do; they do not know how to handle too much independence. Some of them will want you to supervise every single thing they do—"Is that okay?" "Is this the way you want it?" Others just want you to define the job, tell them what you want done, and let them go at it—"Hey, get off my back and leave me alone."

Sometimes you will have an employee who is totally opposed to authority, who will reject everything you say simply because you are the boss; this one will give you a hard time. When you get to know each person's special needs and expectations, you can adjust your style of directing them accordingly—your style, but not what you require of them. You must do what is correct, not what pleases them.

Your people expect you to act like a leader toward them, not like one of the gang. They want you to be friendly, but they expect you to maintain an objective, work-oriented relationship with each person. They do not want you to be everyone's pal, nor will they like it if you have special friends among the workers.

If you do socialize off the job with some of the people you supervise, you are running certain risks. Can you go out and party with them, form close friendships, and then come back and supervise them on the job without playing favorites or making other workers jealous? Maybe you can. But can your worker friends handle this closeness, this double relationship? Will they think they are special and that they can get away with things? These are friendships to approach with caution or to avoid altogether.

Your people expect you to treat them fairly and equally, without favoritism. The fairness that people expect is fairness as *they* see it, not necessarily as you see it.

If there is someone on your staff that you don't like, it is going to be difficult, if not impossible, for you to treat this person without bias. If there is someone else who you like a lot, you will tend to favor that person. Will employees think you are being fair when there is a difference in the way you instruct, discipline, and deal with these two people? They might think that you are playing favorites or are really putting somebody down. You must always think of how these things look to the other associates and how it will affect their acceptance of you. Sometimes they might be right and you are not aware of it.

Fairness includes honesty with your associates and with the company. Your people expect you to evaluate their work honestly, to follow company rules, to put in your time, to fulfill your promises, and to carry out your threats. One of the worst mistakes you can make is to promise something you cannot deliver, whether it is a threat or a reward. People will not respect the authority of a leader who does this. If you do not come through for your workers, they will not come through for you.

Consider Joe Clark, operator of a Chick-Fil-A restaurant. "The people who work for me are my guests," says Clark. He greets them when they arrive, and says goodbye when they leave, and talks with them in between. "The most fun I have is right before we open, when everyone is doing food prep," he says. "It's an opportunity for us to catch up with each other." Some of Clark's employees have been with him for eight, nine, and even ten years. "They've found job satisfaction right here."[1]

✳ COMMUNICATION BETWEEN LEADER AND EMPLOYEES

Your workers expect several things from you in the way of communication. First, *they expect information.* They expect you to define their jobs and to give them directions in a way they can comprehend. Probably 90 percent of the people who work for you want to do a good job, but it is up to you to make it clear to them what the job is and how it should be done. It often takes a little extra time to make sure that each associate has grasped the full meaning of what you have said. But if you expect them to do a good job, they expect you to take the time necessary to tell them exactly what a good job is.

Telling them what to do and how to do it should include the necessary skills training. In the foodservice industry, it is typical to skip this training or to ask another associate to train the new person while the two of them are on the job. It is not uncommon to hire people to bus tables, put them to work without training, yell at them for doing everything wrong, and then fire them for breaking so many dishes. Unless they quit first. Lack of clear direction is a major reason for the high rate of employee turnover in this industry. The leader does not meet the associate's expectations.

The second type of communication that people want from the boss is *feedback on their performance.* The most important thing a worker wants to know is, "How am I doing? Am I getting along all right?" Yet this expectation, this need, is usually met only when the worker is *not* doing all right. We tear into them when they are doing things wrong, but we seldom take the time to tell them when they are doing a good job. A few seconds to fill that basic human need for approval can make a world of difference in your associates' attitude toward you, and the work they do for you.

Clear communication between supervisors and associates is critical in a creative and positive work climate.
Photo courtesy of the author.

A third form of communication that employees expect from you is to have you *listen* when they tell you something. They can give you useful information about their jobs and your customers, and they can often make very valuable suggestions if you will take the time to listen—really listen—to what they have to say. But they do expect you to take that time and to take them seriously, because they are offering you something of their own.

Two cardinal rules on suggestions from employees are:

1. Never steal one of their suggestions and use it as your own.
2. If you cannot use a suggestion, explain why you can't, and express your appreciation.

If you violate either of these rules, suddenly your associates will stop telling you anything. They will not even respond when you ask for their input. You have closed the door they expected to be open, and they are not going to open it again.

✳ UNWRITTEN RULES AND CUSTOMS

In most enterprises certain work customs become established over the years, and employees expect a new supervisor to observe them. They are not written down anywhere, they have just become entwined in the culture, and they are treasured by workers as inviolable rights, never to be tampered with, especially by newcomers. In many kitchens, for example, a new worker is always given the grungy jobs, such as vegetable prep or cleaning shrimp.

In a hotel, a new night cleaner will have to clean the lobby and the public restrooms. If the leader brings in somebody new and he or she isn't started off with the grungy jobs, that's just not right. If a new waiter is brought in and given the best station in the restaurant—the one with the best tips or the one closest to the kitchen—there's going to be a mutiny; that's just not done.

People will lay claim to the same chair day after day to eat their lunch, they will park their cars in the same place, and if you disrupt one of these things established by usage and custom, they will take it as a personal affront. If you want to make changes to the established customs, you will be wise to approach them cautiously and introduce changes gradually.

Another type of rule or custom, sometimes written down but more often unwritten, is the content of a job as seen by the person performing it. When people begin a new job, they quickly settle in their own minds what constitutes a day's work in that job and the obligations and expectations that go with it. If you as a leader go beyond your workers' expectations, if you ask them to do something extra or out of the ordinary, you have violated their concept of what they were hired to do, and they feel you are imposing on them, taking advantage. They will resent you, and they will resent the whole idea.

Suppose that you are a dishwasher and you finish early, and the leader is so pleased that she asks you to clean the walk-in. The next day you finish early again and the boss says, "This is terrific, today we are going to clean the garbage cans." "Hey, no," you say, "I was hired to wash dishes, not to clean walk-ins and garbage cans." And you are about ready to tell her off but you think better of it; you need the job. On the third day you have only 30 people for lunch instead of your usual 300, but how long does it take you to finish the dishes? All afternoon and 30 minutes of overtime, at least.

In sum, people expect the leader to observe what associates believe their jobs to be, whether they have been defined on paper by management or defined only in the associates' own minds. Rightly or wrongly, they resent being given more to do than they were hired to do, and they may refuse to do the extra work, or won't do it well, or will take overtime to do it.

One way to avoid this kind of resistance is to make clear when you hire people that you may ask them to vary their duties now and then when the work is slow or you are shorthanded or there is an emergency. An all-purpose phrase included in each job description—"other duties as assigned"—will establish the principle.

However, as a new supervisor you need to be aware of the way people perceive what you ask them to do. In our example, the worker who finishes early is rewarded with two unpleasant jobs totally unrelated to running the dish machine. There is no immediate and urgent need and no warning that the worker might be expected to fill idle time with other tasks. We will have more to say about defining job content in later chapters. A clear understanding is essential to a successful relationship between associate and leader.

✳ PERSON-TO-PERSON RELATIONSHIPS

Today's associates expect to be treated as human beings rather than as part of the machinery of production. They want the leader to know who they are and what they do on the job and how well they are doing it. They want to be treated as individuals, and they want to feel comfortable talking to the leader, whether it is about problems on the job or about hunting and/or fishing and/or the weather and the new baby at home. They want the leader's acceptance and approval, including tolerance for an occasional mistake or a bad day. They want recognition for a job well done. Whether they are aware of it or not, they want a sense of belonging on the job.

To your people, you personify the company. They don't know the owners, the stockholders, the general manager, and the top brass. To most hourly workers, you are the company—you are it. If they have a good working relationship with you, they will feel good about the company. If they feel good about the company, they can develop that sense of belonging there. And if they feel that they belong there, they are likely to stay.

Successful leaders develop a sensitivity to each person, to the person's individual needs and desires and fears and anxieties as well as talent and skills. They handle each person as much as possible in the way that best fills the associates' personal needs. If you can establish good relationships on this one-to-one level with all your workers, you can build the positive kind of work climate that is necessary for success.

Check Your Knowledge

1. Name expectations that employees often have of their leaders.
2. Why is communication between leader and employees important?

Motivation

motivation

The why of behavior; the energizer that makes people behave as they do.

The term *motivation* refers to what makes people tick: the needs and desires and fears and aspirations within people that make them behave as they do. Motivation is the energizer that makes people take action; it is the *why* of human behavior. In the workplace, motivation goes hand in hand with productivity. Highly motivated people usually work hard and do superior work. Poorly motivated people do what is necessary to get by without any hassles from the leader, even though they may be capable of doing more and better work. Unmotivated people usually do marginal or substandard work and often take up a good deal of the leader's time.

Sometimes, people are motivated by resentment and anger to make trouble for the supervisor, to beat the system, or to gain power for themselves. Such motivations are at cross-purposes with the goals of the operation and have a negative effect on productivity. Motivation, as we have noted many times, is a major concern of the leader.

Leadership success is measured by the performance of the department as a whole, which is made up of the performance of individuals. Each person's performance can raise or lower overall productivity and leadership success. The big question is how to motivate poor performers to realize their potential and raise their productivity, and how to keep good performers from going stale in their jobs or leaving for a better opportunity.

Actually, you cannot motivate people to do good work. Motivation comes from within. The one thing you as a leader can do is to turn it on, to activate people's own motivations. To do this you must get to know your associates and find out what they respond to. It may be the work itself. It may be the way you lead. It may be the work environment. It may be their individual goals: money, recognition, achievement, or

FIGURE 8.1: **Needs, desires, fears, and aspirations lead to motivation.**

whatever. Figure 8.1 shows the relationship of key motivators: needs, desires, fears, and aspirations.

How do you find out what will turn people on? It isn't easy. There are many theories and few answers. What motivates one person might turn someone else off completely. Everybody is different. People do the same things for different reasons and different things for the same reasons. People's needs and desires and behaviors change from day to day and sometimes from minute to minute. You can never know directly why they behave as they do, and they might not know why either, or would not tell you if they could.

In sum, motivation is a complicated business, and motivating people to do their jobs well has no one simple answer. It takes something of an experimental approach; you try to find out what each person responds to, and if one thing doesn't work, maybe the next thing will. But it need not be just a trial-and-error process. You can get quite a bit of insight into human behavior from people who have spent their lives studying the subject, and you will find much in their theories that will help you to figure out how to motivate individual associates to do their best for you.

The one thing that you can seldom do is to develop a set of rules applying this or that theory to a certain person or particular situation on the job. For this reason, we give you the various theories first. Then we spend the balance of the chapter investigating ways of motivating people by using your broadened understanding of human nature along with a mixture of theory, sensitivity, and ingenuity.

✳ WHAT MAKES YOU WORK?

In *Why Work?* MacCoby suggests that there are five different character types of work. Each responds to different values. Recognizing the kind of person you are will help determine why intrinsically motivates you:[2]

1. *Expert*: Motivated by mastery, control, autonomy. Example: Craftsman—Excellence in making things.
2. *Helper*: Motivated by relatedness, caring for people. Example: Institutional helper—Skill in resolving conflict.
3. *Defender*: Motivated by protection, dignity. Example: Supporting the oppressed—Power, self-esteem, survival.
4. *Innovator*: Motivated by creating, experimenting. Example: Gamesman—Glory, competition.
5. *Self-developer*: Motivated by balancing competence, play, knowledge, and personal growth. Example: Seeking harmony.

In the workplace, motivation goes hand in hand with productivity.
Courtesy of ImageState.

Today's best supervisors and managers, says MacCoby, are self-developers—a well-rounded person who seek to balance personal growth, knowledge, and competence.[3]

Theories of Motivation

Whether they realize it or not, everyone has a theory of how to get people to perform on the job. Several are familiar to you, although you might not think of them as theories. Chapter 2 introduced some of them in terms of leadership; now we look at those theories and others in terms of motivation.

✳ MOTIVATION THROUGH FEAR

One of the oldest ways of motivating people to perform on the job is to use fear as the trigger for getting action. This method makes systematic use of coercion, threats, and punishment: "If you don't do your job and do it right, you won't get your raise." "I'll put you back on the night shift." "I'll fire you."

This approach to motivation is sometimes referred to as a "kick in the pants." It is still used surprisingly often, with little success. Yet people who use it believe that it is the only way to get results. They are typically autocratic, high-control, authoritarian bosses with Theory X beliefs about people, and they think other theories of motivation are baloney—you must be tough with people.

Motivation through fear seldom works for long. People who work in order to avoid punishment usually produce mediocre results at best, and fear actually reduces the ability to perform. At the same time, it arouses hostility, resentment, and the desire to get even. Absenteeism, tardiness, poor performance, and high turnover are typical under this type of supervision.

Fear will sometimes motivate people who have always been treated this way, and it can function as a last resort when all other methods have failed. But it will work only if the supervisor is perceived as being powerful enough to carry out the punishment. If the boss continually threatens punishment and never punishes, the threats have no power to motivate. In fact, not even fear works in this situation.

No one recommends motivation through fear except the people who practice it. On average, workers in the United States simply will not put up with that kind of leader unless they are desperate for a job.

✳ CARROT-AND-STICK METHOD

A second philosophy of motivation is to combine fear with incentive reward for good performance, punishment for bad. You may recognize this as carrot-and-stick motivation: the carrot dangled in front as a promised reward, the stick hitting the worker from behind as goad and punishment. It is another high-control method, one that requires constant application. Once the reward is achieved or the punishment administered, it no longer motivates performance, and another reward must be devised or punishment threatened or applied.

In effect, the leader is pushing and pulling workers through their jobs; they themselves feel no motivation to perform well. At the same time, employees come to feel that they have a continuing right to the rewards (such as higher wages, fringe benefits), and these get built into the system without further motivating effect. Meanwhile, the punishments and threats of punishment breed resentment and resistance.

✳ ECONOMIC PERSON THEORY

economic person theory
The belief that people work solely for money.

A third motivation theory maintains that money is the only thing that people work for. This classical view of job motivation was known as the *economic person theory*. Frederick Taylor was perhaps its most influential advocate. Taylor developed his scientific management theories on the cornerstone of incentive pay based on amount of work done. He firmly believed that he was offering workers what they wanted most, and that the way to motivate workers to increase their productivity was to relate wages directly to the amount of work produced. What he did not know was that the employees in his plant were far more strongly motivated by their loyalty to one another. In fact, for three years they united to block every effort he made to increase output despite the extra wages that they could have earned.

There is no doubt that money has always been and still is one of the most important reasons that people work. For some people it may be the most important reason. That paycheck feeds and clothes and houses them; it can give them security, status, a feeling of personal worth. For people who have been at the poverty level, it can be the difference between being hungry and being well fed or between welfare and self-support with self-respect. For teenagers, it can mean the difference between owning a car and being without transportation. For most people on their first job, whether it is an hourly job or an entry-level management job, money is often the primary motivator.

But the amount of money in the paycheck does not guarantee performance on the job. The paycheck buys people's time and enough effort to get by, but it does not buy quality, quantity, and commitment to doing one's work well. If people work for money, does it follow that they will work better for more—the more the pay, the better the performance?

There are certainly instances in which it works: the expectation of wage increases, bonuses, tips, and rewards is likely to have this outcome. But money does not motivate performance once it is paid; the incentive comes from the expectation of more to come.

Furthermore, people do not work for money alone. A number of research studies have shown that, for most people, money as a motivator on the job has less importance than achievement, recognition, responsibility, and interesting work. In sum, money is only one of the resources you have for motivating people, and it does not necessarily have a direct relationship to productivity.

✳ HUMAN RELATIONS THEORY

social person theory
The idea that fulfillment of social needs is more important than money in motivating people.

After the Hawthorne experiments uncovered the human factors affecting productivity, the *social person theory* succeeded the economic person in motivation theory. The human relations enthusiasts pushed their convictions that if people are treated as people, they will be more productive on the job. Make people feel secure, they said, treat them as individuals, make them feel they belong and have worth, develop person-to-person relationships with each one, let them participate in plans and decisions that affect them, and they will respond by giving their best to the organization.

Putting this theory to work brought about higher wages, better working conditions, pension plans, paid vacations, insurance plans, and other fringe benefits, making workers happier but not necessarily more productive. The question remained: What motivates people to work?

✳ MASLOW'S HIERARCHY OF NEEDS

hierarchy of needs
A theory proposed by Maslow that places human needs in a hierarchy or pyramid. As one's needs at the bottom of the pyramid are met, higher-level needs become more important.

An influential answer to this question was the motivation theory of psychologist Abraham Maslow. Human beings, he pointed out, are *wanting animals,* and they behave in ways that will satisfy their needs and wants. Their needs and desires are inexhaustible; as soon as one need is satisfied, another appears to take its place.

In *Motivation and Personality,* Maslow proposed a hierarchy of universal human needs representing the order in which these needs become motivators of human behavior.[4] This *hierarchy of needs* is represented by the pyramid in Figure. 8.2.

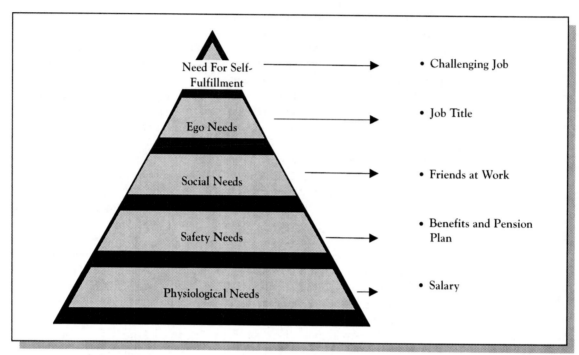

FIGURE 8.2: Relating Maslow's hierarchy of needs to a work setting.

At the bottom of the pyramid are people's most basic needs—the *physiological needs* related to *survival,* such as food and water. When these needs are not being met, every effort is directed toward meeting them. People who are truly hungry cannot think of anything but food. For many hospitality employees, this equates to salary or wages.

But when survival needs are being met, they no longer motivate behavior, and the next level of needs comes into play. These relate to *safety;* they include protection, security, stability, structure, order, and freedom from fear, anxiety, and chaos. For hospitality employees, this equates to benefits and pension plans.

As these needs, in turn, are more or less satisfied, *social needs* become the predominant motivators. These include the need to be with others, to belong, to have friends, to love, and be loved. For hospitality employees, this means socializing at work—and we do plenty of that, don't we?

Above these three groups of needs (sometimes called *primary needs*) is a higher level of needs centered on esteem. These are sometimes referred to as ego needs. One of them is the desire for *self-esteem* or *self-respect* and for the strength, achievement, mastery, competence, confidence, independence, and freedom that provide such self-esteem.

Another is the desire for the *esteem of others*: for status, fame and glory, dominance, recognition, attention, importance, dignity, appreciation. The need for esteem gives rise in some people to the need for power as a way of commanding the esteem of others. Satisfaction of the need for self-esteem leads to feelings of self-confidence, strength, and worth. When these needs go unsatisfied, they produce feelings of inferiority, weakness, and helplessness. For hospitality employees, this equated to job title and perks.

self-actualization
According to the motivational theorist Maslow, the desire to fulfill one's own potential.

At the top of the hierarchy is the need for *self-fulfillment,* or what Maslow called *self-actualization*. This includes the need to be doing what one is best fitted for, the desire to fulfill one's own potential. For the hospitality employee this equates to a challenging job where people can always learn more.

One or another of all these personal needs or various combinations of needs is what motivates people to do what they do. If a lower need goes unsatisfied, people will spend all their time and energy trying to fill it, and they will not experience the next level of needs until the lower needs are met. When a need is satisfied it is no longer a motivator, and the next level of needs becomes the predominant motivation.

Thus, motivation is an unending cycle of need and satisfaction, need and satisfaction. You have a need, you look for a solution, you take action to satisfy the need, and another need appears, because human beings are wanting animals whose needs and desires are never completely satisfied. This continuing cycle explains why workers' needs evolve and change as their own situation changes.

Maslow's theory of motivation does not give you a tool you can use directly; you cannot sit down and analyze each person's needs and then know how to motivate that person. What it can do is to make you aware of how people differ in their needs and why they respond to certain things and not to others. It can help you understand why some of your associates behave as they do on the job.

✳ THEORY Y AND MOTIVATION

Maslow's theories were the springboard for McGregor's Theory X and Theory Y, two opposing views of the way that supervisors and managers look at their workers. Theory X and Theory Y applied Maslow's theories directly to the problem of motivating workers on the job. McGregor made two particularly significant contributions with Theory Y. One was to revise the typical view of the way that people look at work: It is "as natural as play or rest" when it is satisfying a need. This is a flat reversal of the Theory X view of the worker, and it suggests a clear reason why people work willingly.

McGregor's second contribution to motivational theory was the idea that people's needs, especially their ego and self-actualization needs, can be made to operate on the job in harmony with the needs and goals of the organization. If, for example, people are given assignments in which they see the opportunity for achievement, for responsibility, for growth, for self-fulfillment, they will become committed to carrying them out. They will be self-directed and self-controlled, and external controls and the threat of punishment will be unnecessary. In other words, if you can give people work that will fill some basic need, their own motivation will take care of its performance. People will work harder and longer and better for the company if they are satisfying their own needs in the process.

✳ HERZBERG'S MOTIVATION-HYGIENE THEORY

The work of another psychologist, Frederick Herzberg, explained why human relations methods failed to motivate performance and identified factors that truly motivate (see Figure. 8.3).[5] Herzberg found that factors associated with the job environment

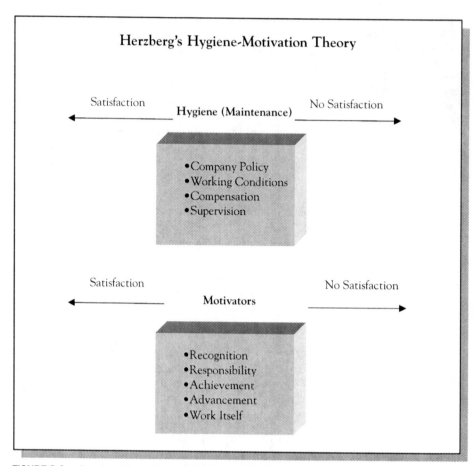

FIGURE 8.3: An adaptation of Herzberg's Hygiene-Motivation Theory, which was originally proposed by Dr. Frederick Herzberg, B. Mausner, and B. Snyderman in *The Motivation to Work* (New York: John Wiley, 1958).

dissatisfiers
A factor in a job environment that produces dissatisfaction, usually reducing motivation.

hygiene factors (maintenance factors)
Factors in the job environment that produce job satisfaction or dissatisfaction but do not motivate performance.

(compensation, supervision, working conditions, company policy, and so on) create dissatisfaction and unhappiness on the job when they are inadequate; they become *dissatisfiers*.

But removing the causes of dissatisfaction (the human relations approach) does not create satisfaction, and it therefore does not motivate performance. Herzberg called these environmental factors *hygiene factors*. They are also commonly called *maintenance factors*. For example, if you think you are underpaid, if you don't get along with your boss, if the kitchen isn't air-conditioned—these things can reduce motivation and cause absenteeism, poor work, and less of it.

They are related to motivation only in the sense that they reduce it. Such factors must be maintained at satisfying levels to avoid negative motivation. But air-conditioning the kitchen or raising wages will not make the cooks work harder once the novelty wears off. In contrast, a second group of factors provides both motivation and job satisfaction.

These, Herzberg found, consist of opportunities in the job itself for achievement and growth—such factors as recognition, responsibility, achievement, advancement, the work itself. He called these factors *motivators*. If you give a cook who loves to invent new dishes a chance to develop a special menu item, you will see a motivator at work.

The answer to motivating employees, then, lies in the job itself. If it can be enriched to provide opportunity for achievement and growth, it will not only motivate the worker to perform well but will also tap unused potential and use personnel more effectively. We look at job enrichment in more detail later in the chapter.

✳ BEHAVIOR MODIFICATION

Behavior modification, a newer method for improving performance, simply bypasses inner motivation and deals instead with behavior change. It takes off from the behaviorist's theory that *all behavior is a function of its consequences;* people behave as they do because of positive or negative consequences to them. If the consequences are positive, they will tend to repeat the behavior. If they are negative, they will tend not to.

If you want to improve performance, then, you will give *positive reinforcement* (attention, praise) whenever people do things right. You look actively for such behavior, and when you catch people doing something right, you praise them for it.

If you were going to carry out the theory literally, you would provide some form of negative consequence for undesired behavior, but in practice negative consequences (blaming, punishment) tend to have side effects such as hostility and aggressive behavior. However, you cannot ignore the undesired behavior. You can deal with it positively without threatening the person by suggesting the correct behavior in coaching fashion: "Let me show you how." But the really important side of behavior modification is positive reinforcement. It reverses the usual story of nothing but negative feedback ("The boss never notices me except when I do something wrong"), and it satisfies the need for attention with the kind of attention that builds self-worth.

The use of behavior modification has burgeoned in recent years, and it can sometimes be very effective. There have been instances where positive reinforcement has not only corrected undesired behavior but has actually increased productivity. Whatever its theoretical base, positive reinforcement can be another resource for you to try out with your people.

✳ REINFORCEMENT AND EXPECTANCY THEORY

The reinforcement theory praises and rewards employees' good behavior. Undesired behavior is not reinforced. Supervisors can modify behavior by giving appropriate praise and rewards. Positive reinforcement should be given right after the behavior occurs. Good performance is rewarded by praise, preferably in front of other associates, and other incentives like bonuses, gifts, promotions, pay increases, and other perks can be given. *Negative reinforcement* is the withholding of praise and rewards for inferior performance.

motivators
Whatever triggers a person's inner motivation to perform. In Herzberg's theory, motivators are factors within a job that provide satisfaction and that motivate a person to superior effort and performance.

behavior modification
Effecting behavioral change by providing positive reinforcement (reward, praise) for the behavior desired.

positive reinforcement
Providing positive consequences (praise, rewards) for desired behavior.

negative reinforcement
Withholding praise and rewards for inferior performance in order to encourage better results.

The expectancy theory explains that employees are concerned about three important questions:[6]

1. How much effort, diligence, and care should I devote to my work?
2. If I perform well as a result of my effort, diligence, and care, will I obtain desired outcomes to satisfy my needs?
3. Does my employer provide work outcomes that satisfy my needs?

Check Your Knowledge

1. Explain what is meant by person-to-person relationships.
2. Define motivation.
3. Briefly discuss the motivation theories.
4. Define behavior modification and positive reinforcement.

With the work expectancy theory it is vital that supervisors provide the training and coaching necessary so that the associates will have the expectancy of achieving superior performance. If, however, the superior performance goes unrewarded or even if the reward does not match up to the associates' expectations, then dissatisfaction will result. It is important to realize that not all employees want the same reward. The best approach is to find out what will motivate them and offer a selection of rewards.

Applying Theory to Reality: Limiting Factors

Now, what can you do with all this theory? There is a great deal in it that you can put to work if you can adapt it to your particular situation and to your individual workers. There are also circumstances that limit how far you can go. One limiting factor that immediately comes to mind is the *nature of many jobs* in the hospitality industry.

They are dull, unchallenging, repetitive, and boring. On the surface, at least, there does not seem to be much you can do to motivate the pot washer, the security guard, the cleanup crew, the makers of the beds, and the changers of the light bulbs to keep them working up to standard and to keep them from leaving for another job.

Even among the less routine jobs there is little you can change to make the work itself more interesting and challenging. The great majority of jobs are made up of things that must be done in the same way day after day. At the same time, many jobs depend to some extent on factors beyond your control: What people do each day and how much they do varies according to customer demand. Unless your workers happen to find this interesting and challenging (and some people do), it is difficult to structure such jobs to motivate people. But the situation is not hopeless. Later in the chapter we will see what creative management can do for even the dullest jobs.

A second limiting factor is *company policy, administration, and management philosophy.* Everything you do must be in harmony with company goals (customer-oriented and cost-effective) and must meet company rules and regulations. Furthermore, you do not control wage rates, fringe benefits, promotion policies, controls, and other companywide systems and practices. If jobs are totally standardized by scientific management methods, you cannot tamper with job content and method at all unless you go through proper channels and procedures established by the company.

Positive reinforcements can encourage associates to improve their performance.
Photo courtesy of the author.

The style of leadership characteristic of the organization will greatly influence what you can and cannot do. If the philosophy of management is authoritarian and high-control, you will have a hard time practicing another approach. In particular, your relationship with your own boss and your boss's management style will influence the nature and scope of what you can do to motivate your people.

A third factor, closely related to the second, is the *extent of your responsibility, authority, and resources*. You cannot exceed the limits of your own job. You may be limited in your authority to spend money, to make changes in job duties, and so on. Remember, too, that your boss is responsible and accountable for your results, and this goes all the way up the chain of command. If you are going to innovate extensively, you will need the blessing of your superiors. But maybe you can get it!

Another limiting factor is the *kinds of people who work for you*. If they are only working there *until,* the job does not really motivate them; they are just putting in time. They do not put forth their energy and enthusiasm because work is not the central interest in their lives. They have something going on outside—family, studies—that takes care of most of their personal needs and interests, and they don't want to work any harder than they have to.

The large numbers of workers who are dependent personalities often pose a motivation problem—they want you to tell them what to do at every turn, until they sometimes seem like millstones around your neck. How do you shake them loose and put them on their own?

The *constant pressures* of the typical day in the life of the hospitality manager tend to fix attention on the immediate problems and the work itself. It is all too easy to become work-oriented rather than people-oriented, especially if you have been an hourly worker and are more at home managing work than managing people. This is a

PROFILE Bob Haber

Former director of human resources, Grand Hyatt Tampa Bay

Courtesy of
Bob Haber.

Early in my management career, I quickly realized how important it was to be able to motivate people and how this motivation would lead to the success of my department or the operation I was responsible for. I found this to be true no matter what type of profession or business I was in.

As a human resource professional, I believe that one of my most important responsibilities is to maintain and develop a motivated workforce. Associates who are motivated to perform are key to the successful operation of any business or company. This is especially true in the hospitality business. After all, true hospitality requires associates to perform in a genuine, caring manner that is perceived by the guest as such.

This genuine approach is largely derived from an associate's desire to want to be hospitable or enjoy what they do. So, how do you get associates to enjoy their work? One important part is the way you motivate or lead them in the workplace. Although everyone has different wants and needs to be motivated, there are several things you can do as a leader to motivate your associates to perform to their fullest.

Associates should be "bought in" to what you want the end result to be. They have to see what's in it for the company and them. Understanding the "why" of what is expected of them is important. People rarely perform well for no reason. Being part of the process requires their understanding of the desired end result and why it is important. Because of this, leaders must engage their associates. They have to communicate openly and directly. They have to give information freely and accept it from their associates. This is especially true with today's younger workforce who will

limitation that managers can deliberately strive to overcome once they see how motivating people can help to accomplish the work better.

Another limitation is *time*. You probably think your day is already too full, and it may well be. It takes time to get to know your people. It takes time to figure out ways of changing things that will make people more motivated.

It takes a lot of time to get changes through channels, if that is necessary. It takes time to get people used to changes in their jobs, and it usually takes time before you begin to see results. But the effective manager will make the time and will gain time in the end by making more effective use of people.

There are limitations in the theories themselves when it comes to applying them. The primary one is that there is no law of motivation or set of laws that you can apply as you can apply scientific or mathematical formulas. This, of course, is true of everything having to do with human beings. Everyone is different, and their needs and desires and behavior respond in a kaleidoscope of change triggered by anything and everything—other people, the environment, the task, their memories, their expectations, *your* expectations, and what they ate for breakfast.

The theories themselves change. New experiments shed new light. The enthusiasms of the past give way to the fads of the future.

Who has the answers? What works? You have to translate the findings of others in terms of your individual workers and the jobs you supervise. These are judgments you make; there are no sure-fire answers. But there is plenty of guidance along the way.

not perform with the "because I said so" approach. In order to motivate associates, leaders must both communicate needed information regularly and listen to feedback on an ongoing basis.

The environment you provide as a leader is also a key part of an associate's motivation. Having someone who enjoys what they do and the surroundings they do it in will help maximize their contributions. I don't mean the physical surroundings, rather the environment they are provided through dignity and respect.

Treating associates with respect greatly adds to their emotional or mental well-being, and as a result will help them be more productive for you and the company. You must also ensure that this mutual respect is shown from coworker to coworker. Get to know your associates and provide them with a comfortable workplace that makes them feel good and want to come to work each day.

Making it rewarding to work hard and perform will also add a lot of value to your motivation techniques. Both formal and informal praise, on an ongoing basis, are crucial. Associates want to know they are doing well, and what it takes to be good. There are many long-term or formal types of recognition that will help motivate your associates. Although this is important, positive reinforcement and praise that is timelier will motivate continued performance and behavior like no other.

This on-the-spot reward will best relate the performance with your desired outcome and motivate for continued good performance. Praise often and be genuine! Say thank you when a job is well done. Provide ongoing coaching when associates don't quite perform as expected. Give them the tools and opportunity to succeed through their own efforts. As I said, associates want to know what it takes to be good.

I like to measure our motivation efforts by seeing how much associates will rally around you and the company when the "going gets tough." How difficult it is to get someone to perform out of a normal routine, or to take on an unusually difficult task. This can be an excellent indicator of how well motivated they really are. In any case, proper motivation will only lead to good things and help maximize your associate's contributions.

Building a Positive Work Climate

A positive work climate is one in which employees can and will work productively, in which they can do their best work and achieve their highest potential in their jobs. Meeting employee expectations and needs is one way to create a positive work climate. Before we take a look at others, let's discuss a similar concept: morale.

Morale is a group spirit with respect to getting the job done. It can run the gamut from enthusiasm, confidence, cheerfulness, and dedication to discouragement, pessimism, indifference, and gloom. It is made up of individual attitudes toward the work that pass quickly from one person to another until you have a group mood that everyone shares. It may change from moment to moment. You see it when it is very high, and you notice it when it is very low; and if it is average, nobody says anything about it.

When people are unhappy in their jobs, they just plain don't feel good at work. They feel exhausted, they get sick easily and miss a lot of days, and eventually they give up because the job is not worth the stress and unhappiness. In an industry where many people are working "until" and do not have a sense of belonging, these kinds of feelings and behavior are contagious, and morale becomes a big problem. Absenteeism, low-quality work, and high employee turnover multiply production problems and cost money. It probably costs at least $1,000 every time you have to replace a busperson.

morale
Group spirit with respect to getting a job done.

Do You Know?

What seven things can a leader do to create a positive work climate?

> 1. Write effective vision, mission, and goals statements, and ensure everyone knows them.
> 2. Actively listen to your employees.
> 3. Give a hand to your employees when appropriate.
> 4. Treat employees fairly and consistently.
> 5. Keep your employees informed.
> 6. Involve and empower your employees.
> 7. Use up-to-date and accurate job descriptions.
> 8. Orient, train, and coach your employees.
> 9. Formally evaluate employee performance at least twice yearly.
> 10. Praise and reward your employees.
> 11. Pay for performance.
> 12. Institute a profit-sharing or other gain-sharing program for employees.
> 13. Let your employees make as many of their own decisions as possible.
> 14. Cross-train employees, rotate their positions, and have a career ladder and promote from within.
> 15. Be able to perform the job you supervise.
> 16. Manage your time.
> 17. Be a good role model.
> 18. Establish competitive and equitable pay rates.
> 19. Offer a competitive benefit package suited to your employees.
> 20. Provide a pleasant, safe, and clean work environment.

FIGURE 8.4:   Twenty ways to build a positive work climate.
Source: Jay R. Schrock.

High morale has just the opposite effects and is the best thing that can happen in an enterprise. To build a positive work climate, you need to focus on these three areas: the individual, the job, and the supervisor. Figure 8.4 lists 20 ways to build a positive work climate. Let's look at some of the most important ways that you can make work enjoyable.

✳ PURPOSE = MOTIVATION

You've got to have a purpose in life![7] Before you can motivate, you need a purpose. People yearn for purpose—for doing something that's important, that engages their full potential in a way that's meaningful beyond their bank accounts. And that makes your job as their supervisor a little harder. You may not have as much control over their compensation and benefits as you would like to have. But you do have control over how inspired they are and how connected they feel to the mission their jobs serve.[8]

Most people want to feel that, thanks to their efforts, the world is a little better off by nightfall than it was when the day started. You just have to figure out how what they do makes it happen that way. The first thing is for you to understand how your company improves the world—and how your job serves that mission.[9] After connecting your job to the mission, you can help your employees make the connection. For example, hospital custodians are not just sweeping floors—they are helping to save lives. The "connection" can come from the product itself, the guests, the community co-employees, even the employees' families and the dream future that the employees' jobs with your company are helping them realize.[10]

Focus: The Individual

The starting point is your individual workers—one by one. The idea that everybody works for some one thing, like money, is no longer credible. Employees are glad to have the paycheck, but whether they are willing to work hard for that money or for something else or for anything at all is what you want to determine. Because everybody is different, you are going to need an individual strategy of motivation for each person—not a formal program, just a special way of dealing with each one that brings out their best efforts and offers them the greatest personal satisfaction.

Getting to know your people takes an indirect approach. People are not going to open up to the boss if you sit down with them at the coffee break and ask them questions about what they want from their jobs. They will tell you what they think you want to hear, and they will probably feel uncomfortable about being quizzed.

You may have hired them for one reason, but they probably come to work for altogether different reasons, which they may think is none of your business. They have taken the job as a vehicle for getting where or what they want, but that is a hidden agenda. For some people it is money, for some it is pride, for some it is status, for some it is something to do *until*. If you can find out what kind of satisfactions they are looking for, it will help you to motivate them.

High morale helps keep employee turnover low. At this hotel, the employee turnover rate is 23 percent per year.
Photo courtesy of the author.

You can learn about them best by observing them. How do they go about their work? How do they react to you, to other workers, to customers? What questions do they ask, or do they ask any? How do they move—quickly, slowly, freely, stiffly? How do they look as they speak or listen? Notice their gestures and facial expressions. What makes them light up? What makes them clam up? Pay special attention to what they tell you about themselves in casual conversation. This may be an entirely new approach for you, but people-watching is really quite interesting, and you can quickly become good at spotting clues.

Clues to what? Needs and desires, discontents and aspirations. Frustrations, drive, and achievement. Ability and performance, too, and whether performance is up to par for that job and whether this person has abilities the job does not call on. But primarily needs, desires, and responses, because these are the motivators you want to channel into high performance that will satisfy both you and them.

Observing your people has a purely practical purpose. You are not going to try to psychoanalyze them, probe for hidden motives, delve into what really makes them tick. You can't. That takes years of training you don't have, and a great deal of time you don't have, either. Furthermore, you shouldn't.

If you are wrong in your amateur analysis, your employees will consider you unjust, and if you are right, they will feel vulnerable—you know them too well. Either way, it is going to interfere with motivation rather than improve it. Your approach, in contrast, should be practical, pragmatic, and experimental; you could even call it superficial.

You observe your people and get ideas of what you might do to motivate this or that person to perform better for you, as well as get more personal satisfaction from the work. You try out an idea, and if this person does not respond, you try something else. What they respond to is what is important and what you have to work with. The personal whys—the inner needs—are simply clues that you sometimes use to reach the what-to-do.

John Kotter, former Matsushita Professor of Leadership at Harvard Business School, has observed that only companies whose employees are "intellectually and emotionally convinced that their business creates something that adds value to the world" will survive in the new economy.[11] But in an economic climate characterized by rapid change and job anxiety, can companies legitimately expect their employees to bring their hearts and minds to the workplace? And if so, what do employers need to do to or be willing to do to make this happen?[12] We should realize that fear and coercion don't work and that compensation alone is not the answer.

But giving employees information about how compensation decisions are made, and giving them the freedom to question it, is important. There's no quicker way to demonstrate your commitment to loyalty and trust than to let employees know what you know. For example, say your company faces a huge task of reducing costs. If you share the real situation with employees, you are more likely to receive several good ideas for cost cutting that will add up to substantial savings.

Employees want their work to connect to a greater purpose—yes, people want to work in order to bring more good to the world. Hence, the importance of sustainability. Efforts to increase sustainable operations are likely to be embraced by employees, as they can identify with the cause. By focusing on values beyond profitability, companies can actually increase profitability.

Motivational Methods

Consider being a first-time supervisor and the youngest in the department. With ten senior guys around me, how do I secure and maintain their trust as their boss?

Answer: Put not your trust in people, but put your people in trust, if that's what you mean. Really, if your subordinates don't trust you, then you won't be able to get their full cooperation.[13] Mr. Elbo adds that the problem is that you just don't earn the trust of people overnight. It requires a long process on your part, along with a considerable amount of time and energy. There are seven best approaches:

1. *Empower the workers.* Give them the chance to participate in problem-solving and decision-making processes, whenever possible.
2. *Share vital information.* If they know that you trust them with sensitive information, they could easily reciprocate by performing better in their jobs.
3. *Work objectively with everyone.* Don't play favorites. People have different personalities, but just the same, they should be given equal treatment, as this promotes teamwork.
4. *Be a decisive boss.* Avoid being wishy-washy. If you don't have a ready answer, then be honest, and promise to immediately return to the concerned worker with the right answer or decision.
5. *Show appreciation to people's good deeds as soon as it becomes apparent.* Don't drag your feet. But be specific by citing what you appreciate.
6. *Maintain a two-way, personal, and eyeball-to-eyeball communication with everyone on a regular basis.* Even with technology around us, there is still no substitute to having an active dialogue with people.
7. *Be polite.* No matter the amount of pressures that you are carrying, you need to be nice.[14]

✳ LEADING ENERGY

The major challenge facing leaders and human resource professionals over the next 20 years will be leading human energy. The challenge of energy management, though, is not just an individual endeavor; it extends to organizations—big time. Many people, if not most people, seldom bring their best efforts to work; they seem to save them for evenings and weekends.

If you ask managers, "Of all the people you have met in your career, what percentage of them are fully engaged at work?" most say, "Less than 10 percent."[15] The authors James G. Clawson and Douglas S. Newburg comment, "One does not need nationwide polls or leadership seminar participants' opinions to observe this phenomenon; virtually every working establishment is full of people going through the motions." The authors add: "How many times in your career has your manager/supervisor asked you how you want to feel today?"[16] Most HR professionals and leaders *assume* that professionals will do what they have to do and not let their feelings get in the way. And that is the problem—feelings affect our performance—plain and simple! Sadly, this is true and presents a challenge to human resource professionals and supervisors.

The dilemma in motivating associates is knowing when the effect of goals becomes demotivating. For example, a company was having a motivational retreat when a senior vice-president came to give a pep talk. He said, "Our stock value is currently $95, and if it's not up to $125 by December 31, the CEO and I will not be getting our bonuses, so you need to get your rears in gear!"[17] Imagine how the associates felt. But we also need to realize that similar examples happen all the time: If a company gets a 10 percent increase in sales one year—yes, you guessed—it wants 12 percent the next. You've just worked your butt off and now they want more! So, what's the answer?

✳ DEALING WITH SECURITY NEEDS

It is relatively easy to spot people with high security needs. They look and act anxious, uncertain, and tentative. They may be among those who ask you how to do everything, or they might be too scared even to ask. Fear and anxiety are demotivators; they reduce motivation. When security needs are not satisfied, people cannot function well at all; in fact, these people are among those who leave during the first few days on the job.

Here is where Maslow's theories come in handy. If you see that someone has a need for security and you can help that person satisfy that need, you ease that person along to a higher motivational level. To satisfy these needs, you do all the things that we have been recommending in earlier chapters. You tell them what to do and how to do it; you tell them exactly what you expect. You train them. All these things provide a reassuring structure to the work that protects them from the uncertainties of working. It reduces their mistakes and builds their motivation and confidence.

You let them know where they stand at all times. You support them with coaching and feedback and encouragement. You give them positive reinforcement for things they do right, and you retrain them to help them correct their mistakes. You do not solve their problems, you do not cuddle and coddle; you help *them* to do their jobs *themselves*.

You keep on making positive comments about their work even when they are fully trained and you are satisfied with their performance. It is natural for a supervisor to stop paying attention to a worker once things are going well, but even a short absence of approving comments can trigger doubt and uncertainty again in workers who are insecure. Recognition, even if it is only a big smile and a passing, "Hey, keep up the good work!" is an affirmation that life on the job is, after all, not uncertain and threatening. Above all, you must avoid any use of fear as a motivator. This is the last thing that these people need.

Evaluate their work frequently, and give praise for things done right, especially for improvement of any sort. Use improvement to build confidence: Accentuate the achievement and the potential—"See how far you have come; see where you can go from here." Show them that you expect them to do well. Your confidence will give them confidence. And if you can build confidence, you may eventually activate self-motivation and aspiration. Satisfaction of primary needs allows these higher level needs to emerge.

✳ DEALING WITH SOCIAL NEEDS

Everybody has social needs (Maslow again). You might not think of work as being a place to satisfy them, but it often is. For many people, a job fills the need to be with others, the need to be accepted, the need to belong. These are powerful needs. Often, they will fall into Herzberg's category of hygiene factors: They cause dissatisfaction when they are unsatisfied, but they do not motivate when satisfied. But for some people they can be motivators, too.

For example, consider the homemaker who gets a job because she wants to talk to people who are more than three feet tall. If you hire her as a cashier or a switchboard operator, she probably won't be very good at it because this is not what she came to work for. But if you make her a desk clerk or a server or a sales rep where she can talk to people all day long, she could easily become a higher achiever.

Whether or not social needs can be turned into motivators, it is useful when people find such needs being satisfied on the job, both in terms of their individual development and in terms of the general work climate. People whose social needs are unmet may just not work very well, or they may even provoke trouble and conflict.

What can you do to help meet people's social needs? There are two specific needs you can work on, and it takes hardly any of your time. One is the *need for acceptance*. We have talked about this before: You build a person-to-person relationship and you treat each person as a unique individual who has dignity and worth. You respect their idiosyncrasies (unless they interfere with the work): You speak softly to Peter because that is what Peter responds to. You scream and yell at Paul because that is your unique way of relating to Paul and you both know it, and Paul will think he doesn't matter to you anymore if you treat him any other way.

You deal with each person differently, but you treat each according to the same standards, whether she is good-looking or plain, whether his mother is on welfare or owns the biggest bank in town. Each one is a person who has value, has worth, and you treat them all that way.

You also make it clear that you value each person's work and that it is important to the organization no matter how menial it is. The well-made bed, the properly washed salad greens, and the sparkling-clean restroom all please customers; the crooked bedspread, the gritty salad, and the empty tissue holder send customers away.

This attention to detail can be as important to the success of the hotel or restaurant as the expertise of the sommelier or the masterpieces of the chef. You can make people feel that they are an essential part of the entire organization, that you need them, that they belong there. A sense of belonging may be your most powerful ally in the long run—and it helps the long run to happen.

This *need to belong* is the other social need that you can do a lot to satisfy. Things you should be doing anyway help to satisfy this need, such as making people feel comfortable in their jobs by training them, coaching them, telling them where they stand, evaluating their work frequently. Open communications also encourage belonging; people feel free to come to you with suggestions or problems.

Keeping people informed about changes that affect them is a way of including them in what is going on—and if you leave anybody out, you reduce that person to a nobody. You can also include people in discussions about the work, inviting their ideas, feelings, and reactions. If you can build a spirit of teamwork, that, too, will foster a sense of belonging.

One's peer group also nurtures belonging. You need to be aware of social relationships among your workers and to realize that these relationships are just as important as their relationship with you, and sometimes more so. Often, peer pressure is more influential than the boss is. You need to have the group on your side—if it ever comes to taking sides—and that is best done through good relationships with each person.

These people work under you, and they look at you as their boss. They expect you to be friendly and to sit down with them if they invite you, but they do not expect you to be one of the gang. In fact, your uninvited presence for more than a moment or two may act as a constraint to their socializing.

Groups and group socialization are a normal part of the job scene. Often, groups break into cliques, with different interests and sometimes rivalries. You should not try to prevent the formation of groups and cliques. But if competition between cliques begins to disrupt the work, you will have to intervene. You cannot let employee competition interfere with the work climate.

✳ REWARDING YOUR EMPLOYEES

Incentive pay, bonuses, and various kinds of nonmonetary rewards can be very effective motivators if they activate people's needs and desires or are related to their reason for working. One of the problems, of course, is that what motivates one person leaves another indifferent, yet to treat people fairly you have to have rewards of equal value for equal performance.

These methods of triggering motivation begin with the carrot principle of dangling a reward for good performance. When people need or want the reward, they will work hard in expectation of getting it. If they do not want the carrot, it has no effect.

Rewarding associates contributes to a positive work climate.
Courtesy of Wyndham Hotels Group.

Once the reward is achieved, the cycle must start again: The desire must be activated by the *expectation of reward,* as Herzberg points out. No expectation, no achievement, and performance slumps back to a nonreward level unless people begin to derive satisfaction from the achievement itself. However, there is no doubt that rewards are useful motivators. In many jobs, the boring repetition of meaningless tasks precludes a sense of achievement that is fulfilling, and rewards may be the only resource you have for motivating.

The entire system of rewards, both monetary and otherwise, must be worked out with care, not only for getting the maximum motivation but also for fairness in the eyes of the employees. The performance required to achieve the reward must be spelled out carefully, and the goal must be within reach of everyone. People must know ahead of time what the rewards are and must perceive them as fair or they will cause more dissatisfaction than motivation.

How do you make rewards into effective motivators if people's needs and desires are so different? Somebody with eight children to feed might work very hard for a money reward or the chance to work more overtime. Another person might outdo himself for an extra day of paid vacation. Still another would do almost anything for a reserved space in the parking lot right near the door with her name on it in great big letters. Such rewards might be suitable prizes in an employee contest, with the winner being allowed to choose from among them.

You might get people involved by letting them suggest rewards (keeping the final decision to yourself or letting the team decide—within limits). Any involvement increases the likelihood of sparking real motivation. Actually, any reward can be more than a carrot.

It can be a recognition of achievement, of value, of worth to the company. It can build pride; it can generate self-esteem. It can also be a goal. Once employees earn a reward, if it gives them satisfaction, they will probably go for it again. Then you have activated motivation from within, with commitment to a person's own goal. And that, in miniature, is what successful on-the-job motivation is all about—fulfilling individual goals and company goals in the same process. The more both the employee's and the company's goals overlap, the greater motivation will be.

✳ DEVELOPING YOUR EMPLOYEES

Another way of maintaining a positive work climate is to help your people to become better at their jobs and to develop their potential. This may be one of the most critical things you do. A large percentage of the people in foodservice and hospitality enterprises are underemployed, and as managers we really do not utilize the skills and abilities of the people who work for us as fully as we could. Your goal should be to make all your people as competent as you can, because it makes your job easier, it makes you look better to your superiors, and it is good for your people.

You can develop your beginning workers through training, feedback, encouragement, and support, as well as by providing the right equipment and generally facilitating their work. By the way you deal with them, you can also give them a feeling of importance to the operation, a sense of their own worth, and a feeling of achievement and growth. Concrete recognition of improvement, whether it is an award, a reward, or merely a word of praise, can add to the pride of achievement.

If you have people with high potential, you should do all these things and more. You should try to develop their skills, utilize any talents you see, challenge them by asking for their input on the work, give them responsibilities, and open doors to advancement to the extent that you can. One thing is certain: If you have trained someone to take your place, it will be a lot easier for your company to promote you. But if none of your subordinates can fill your job, the company is less likely to move you up because it needs you where you are.

Developing your people also helps morale. It gives people that sense of moving forward that keeps them from going stale, marking time, moving on a treadmill. It is also important to your acceptance as a leader to have people feel that you are helping them to help themselves.

You develop employees by involving them. Employees who are asked to influence what happens at work tend to develop a sense of ownership; this feeling of ownership breeds commitment. Employees can become effectively involved in many managerial activities, such as evaluating work methods, identifying problems, proposing suggestions, and deciding on a course of action. Employees can tell you better than anyone else how their own jobs should be done.

For instance, McGuffey's Restaurants, a dinner-house chain based in North Carolina, asks for employee input on ways to improve service and also asks employees to elect representatives to an associate board at which employees' concerns will be addressed. In some cases, when you involve employees, you are actually empowering them. Empowering employees means giving them additional responsibility and authority to do their jobs. Instead of employees feeling responsible for merely doing what they are told, they are given greater control over decisions about work. For example, in some restaurants, servers are empowered, or given the authority, to resolve guest complaints without management intervention. A server may decide, in response to a guest complaint, not to charge the customer for a menu item that was not satisfactory.

At McGuffey's Restaurants, the company gives employees their own business cards, which they can use to invite potential customers in for free food or beverages. The company even lets employees run the restaurants two days a year, during which they can change the menu and make other changes.

Following are some guidelines for *empowering* your employees:

- Give employees your trust and respect, two essential ingredients for empowerment of employees.
- Determine exactly what you want employees to be empowered to do.
- Train employees in those new areas. Be clear as to what you want them to do.
- Create an environment in which exceptions to rules, particularly when they involve customer satisfaction, are permissible.
- Allow employees to make mistakes without being criticized or punished. Instead, view these times as opportunities to educate your employees.
- Reward empowered employees who take risks, make good decisions, and take ownership.

Finally, you should also continue to develop yourself. Chances are that you won't have much time for reading and studying, but you should keep pace with what is going on in other parts of your company and in the industry as a whole—read trade publications and attend trade association meetings. You can also watch yourself as you practice your profession, evaluating your own progress and learning from your mistakes. Make a habit of thinking back on the decisions you have made. What would have happened if you had done something differently? Can you do it better next time?

Focus: The Job–Providing an Attractive Job Environment

The employee's job environment includes not only the physical environment and working conditions but the other employees, the hours, rate of pay, benefits, and company policies and administration. You may recognize these as *hygiene* or *maintenance factors*.

As Herzberg pointed out, such job factors do not motivate. But any of them can cause dissatisfaction and demotivation, which can interfere with productivity and increase turnover. So it behooves the leader to remove as many dissatisfiers as possible. To the extent that you have control, you can provide good physical working conditions: satisfactory equipment in good working order; adequate heating, cooling, and lighting; comfortable employee lounges; plenty of parking; and so on.

You can see that working hours and schedules meet employees' needs as closely as possible. If you have anything to say about it, you can see that wages and benefits are as good as those of your competitors or better, so that your people will not be lured away by a better deal than you can give.

There is not much that you can do about company policy and administration if it is rigid and high-control, except to work within its limits, stick up for your people, and do things your own way within your sphere of authority. We will assume that the management philosophy is not based on fear and punishment or you would not be there yourself.

✳ PUTTING THE RIGHT PERSON IN THE RIGHT JOB

If you get to know your associates, you are in a good position to figure out what jobs are right for what people. People with high security needs may do very well in routine jobs: Once they have mastered the routine they will have the satisfaction and security of doing it well. Putting them in a server's job would be a disaster. Putting people-oriented associates in routine, behind-the-scenes jobs might be a disaster, too.

Many cooks enjoy preparing good things for people to eat. Even when they must follow other people's standardized recipes, there is the satisfaction of being able to tell exactly when a steak is medium rare, of making a perfect omelet, of arranging a beautiful buffet platter. Bartenders often enjoy putting on a show of their pouring prowess. These people are in the right jobs.

Pride in one's work can be a powerful motivator. Some people get a great sense of achievement from tearing into a room left in chaos by guests and putting it in order again, leaving it clean and inviting for the next guest. They, too, are in the right jobs. The professional dishwasher we have mentioned several times obviously took great pride in his work and wore his occupation as a badge of honor. He belonged in his job, and it belonged to him, and in a curious way it probably satisfied all levels of needs for him.

✳ MAKING THE JOB INTERESTING AND CHALLENGING

People do their best work when something about the work involves their interest and stimulates their desire to do it well. People who like what they are doing work hard at it of their own accord. People who don't like their jobs drag their heels, watch the clock, do as little as they can get by with, and are called lazy by the boss.

Different things about the work turn different people on. Some are stimulated by working with guests: They get a kick out of making them welcome, serving them well, pleasing them, amusing them, turning an irate guest into a fan by helping to solve a problem. Some people are miserable dealing with guests and enjoy a nice, routine job with no people hassles, where they can put their accuracy and skill to work straightening out messy records and putting things in order. Some people like jobs where there is always some new problem to solve; others hate problems and like to exercise their special skills and turn out products they are proud of.

What these people all have in common is that something about the content of their job both stimulates and satisfies them. Stated in theoretical terms, it satisfies their higher needs, those related to self-esteem and self-fulfillment. Specifically, people work

Making the job interesting and challenging is a key part of a supervisor's job.
Photo courtesy of the author.

hard at jobs that give them opportunity for achievement, for responsibility, for growth and advancement, for doing work they enjoy doing for its own sake.

There are two ideas here that you as a leader can use in motivating your people. One is to put people in jobs that are right for them, as just discussed. The other is to enrich people's jobs to include more of the motivating elements. Of course, there are limits to what you can do, but the more you can move in this direction, the more likely you are to create a positive work climate and motivate associates.

Workers who are bored are underemployed: The job does not make use of their talents, their education, and their abilities. They are only there until they find a more interesting and challenging job. Not only will you have to train their replacements sooner or later, but you are not making use of abilities right now that could contribute a great deal to your department and to the entire organization. Furthermore, as we said in Chapter 1, supervisors have an obligation to develop their people.

job loading
Adding more work to a job without increasing interest, challenge, or reward.

You cannot move associates into better jobs unless jobs are available, but you can look for ways to enrich their current jobs by building some motivators into them. This does not mean asking them to take on additional, but similar, tasks—that is called *job loading Job enrichment* means shifting the way things are done so as to provide more responsibility for one's own work and more opportunity for achievement, for recognition, for learning, and for growth.

You might start by giving people more responsibility for their own work. Relax your control; stop watching every move they make. Let them try out their own methods of achieving results as long as they do not run counter to the standards and procedures that are an essential part of the job. In other words, decrease controls and increase accountability. This must all be discussed between you, and there must be a clear understanding, as in any delegation agreement.

From there you can experiment with other forms of job enrichment. You can delegate some of your own tasks. You can rearrange the work in the jobs you are enriching to add more authority and responsibility for the workers. You can give new and challenging assignments. You can assign special tasks that require imagination and develop skills.

If, for example, you find that you have creative people in routine kitchen jobs, let them try planning new plate layouts or garnishes. If someone who majored in English is working as a payroll clerk, let her try her hand at writing menu fliers or notices for the employee bulletin board or stories for the company magazine. Look for people's hidden talents and secret ambitions and use them, and keep in mind reporting them when more suitable jobs are available.

Another idea that is being tried out in a number of industries is replacing the assembly-line method of dividing the work into minute, repetitious parts by giving a worker or group of workers responsibility for an entire unit of work or complete product, including quality control. Is there a way of avoiding assembly-line sandwich making that would give each worker or a group of workers complete responsibility for one kind of sandwich, letting them work out the most efficient method? Could you give a cleaning team responsibility for making up an entire corridor of rooms, dividing the tasks as they see fit?

There are many jobs in which the work is going to be dull no matter what you do. But even in these a shift in responsibility and point of view can work near miracles. A concerted program of job enrichment for cleaning and janitorial services carried out at Texas Instruments is an example of what can be done with routine low-skill tasks. These services were revamped to give everyone a role in the planning and control of their work, although the work itself remained the same. Extensive training embodying Theory Y principles was given to supervisors and working foremen, while worker training included orientation in company goals and philosophy and their part in the overall operation. A team-oriented, goal-oriented, problem-solving approach encouraged worker participation in reorganizing, simplifying, and expediting the work.

Increased responsibility, participation, and pride of achievement generated high commitment as well as better ways of doing the work. In the first year's trial the cleanliness level improved from 65 percent to 85 percent, the number of people required dropped from 120 to 71, and the quarterly turnover rate dropped from 100 percent to 9.8 percent. The annual savings to the company was a six-figure total.

The average educational level of these workers was fourth or fifth grade, proving that Theory Y management is applicable all up and down the scale. A major program such as this takes a long time to develop and implement and is out of the reach of the first-time supervisor working alone. But it shows what can be done when dedicated leadership and enlightened company policies activate employee motivation.

Any job enrichment effort is likely to produce a drop in productivity at first as workers get used to changes and new responsibilities. It takes a coaching approach to begin with and a lot of support from the boss. It is also essential to initiate changes slowly and to plan them with care. Too much responsibility and freedom too soon may be more than some associates can handle, either out of inexperience or because of the insecurities involved. Again, it is a situation in which your own sensitivity to your workers is a key ingredient.

Focus: The Leader

Ultimately, it is the leader who holds the keys to a positive work climate. It is not only the steps she or he takes, the things she/he does to spark motivation; it is also the way that leaders themselves approach their own tasks and responsibilities—their own performance of their own jobs.

If they themselves are highly motivated and enthusiastic about their work, their people are likely to be motivated, too. If they have high expectations of themselves and their people, and if they believe in themselves and their people, the people will generally come through for them. It is motivation by contagion, by expectation, by example.

In some operations the manager conveys a sense of excitement, a feeling that *anything is possible, so let's go for it!* You find it sometimes in the individual entrepreneur or the manager of a new unit in a larger company. If the manager is up, the people are up, too, and it is an exciting place to work. It is not unusual for people who have worked for such managers to end up as entrepreneurs themselves, putting their own excitement to work in an enterprise of their own.

Tony's Restaurant in St. Louis is a case in point. Owner Vincent Bommarito's enthusiasm, high standards, and involvement with employee development and performance, coupled with an anything-is-possible approach, have spawned at least 20 restaurants owned and operated by former employees. Of course, there are the added incentives of ownership in such cases, but it really begins with the excitement and enthusiasm of the original restaurant experience.

At the opposite extreme, leaders who are not happy in their jobs, who are not themselves motivated, will have unmotivated associates who are faithful reflections of themselves—management by example again. You cannot motivate others successfully if you are not motivated yourself. And if you are not, you need a change of attitude or a change of job.

If you give 75 percent of your effort to your job, your people will give 25 to 50 percent. If you put forth a 100 percent effort, your people will give you 110 percent. If you expect the best of people, they will give you their best. If you expect poor performance, poor performance is what you will get. If you tell people they can do a certain thing and they believe in you, they can do it—and they will. If you tell them it is beyond their ability, they won't even try.

This contagious kind of motivation can run back and forth between supervisor and workers; they can motivate you if you will let them. If you have good relationships with your people, they can spark your interest with new ideas about the work. They can help you solve problems. Their enthusiasm for the work will sustain your own motivation in the face of setbacks and disappointments. When a "we" attitude prevails, it builds belonging, involvement, and commitment.

✳ SETTING A GOOD EXAMPLE

role model

A person who serves as an example for the behavior of others.

management by example

Managing people at work by setting a good example—by giving 100 percent of your time, effort, and enthusiasm to your own job.

Whether you are aware of it or not, you set an example for your workers; they are going to copy what you do. The psychologist's term for this is *role model*. If you expect the best work from your people, you've got to give your best work to your job. If you give 100 percent of your time and effort and enthusiasm, chances are that your workers will give you 110 percent. But if they see you giving about 75 percent and hear you groaning about your problems, they will give you only 25 to 50 percent of their effort. So if you want a fair day's work from your people, give a fair day's work to them: *management by example*, it is sometimes called.

Giving your best means keeping your best side out all the time. Everybody has a good side and a bad side, and most of us are vulnerable to a certain few things that can turn that bad side out and cause us to lose our cool. This is disastrous when you are a role model, particularly if you are supervising people who deal with customers.

If you lose your temper with a group of workers and shout at them, they are going to carry the echo of your voice and the feelings it arouses in them right into the hotel lobby or the dining room or the hospital floor. They are going to be impatient and hostile and heedless of the guests' needs. And there goes the training you have given them in guest relations.

Your good side is as influential as your bad side. If you want your people to treat guests courteously and serve them well, treat your associates courteously and well. If bad moods are contagious, so are good moods. Enthusiasm is contagious. If you would like your associates to enjoy their work, be enthusiastic yourself. Is that a big order? Sometimes. But if you can do it, it works. Set your sights high; expect the best of your associates.

On the one hand, if you expect their best, they will usually give you their best if you approach the subject positively. If you show them you believe in them and have confidence in their ability to do the job, if you cheer them on, so to speak, they will attach the same value to their performance that you do. They will take pride in their work and in their own achievements. On the other hand, if you suddenly tell them to improve their work, without warning and in a critical way, implying that they are slackers and don't measure up, they are likely to resent the criticism and resist the demand.

✳ ESTABLISHING A CLIMATE OF HONESTY

A positive work climate requires a climate of honesty. We have talked about honesty as one of the things that workers expect of the leader. It means that you are honest with them when you talk to them about their performance and their potential and their achievements and mistakes. It means that you keep your promises and give credit where credit is due.

It means that you do not cheat, lie, or steal from the company: You do not take food home from the kitchen or booze from the bar, you do not take money from guests in return for a better room or a better table. You are a role model and you do not do these things, not only because they are unethical, but also because you want your associates to be honest; they are going to imitate you. This is another example of leadership by example.

You do not say one thing and do another. Nothing confuses an associate more than a supervisor who gives good advice but sets a bad example. You are consistent and fair. You do not manipulate; you are open and aboveboard; you can be trusted. A climate of honesty encourages the growth of loyalty. If you are loyal to the company that employs you and are honest and fair and open with your associates, they will develop loyalty to both you and the company.

If you put down the company, you destroy your entire work climate because your workers will begin to believe that the company is a lousy place. If you feel like running down the company now and then, keep it to yourself. If you feel like that all the time, get out. You cannot do a good job as supervisor with those feelings bottled up inside.

 # KEY POINTS

1. Employees want their leader to be qualified to supervise, be experienced, take charge, treat people fairly and equally, communicate, and treat people as human beings.
2. Motivation is the "why" of human behavior.
3. There are various theories of motivation: Use fear (McGregor's Theory X); combine fear with incentives (carrot-and-stick motivation); give money (economic person theory); give them consideration (human relations or social person theory, Maslow's hierarchy of needs); satisfy employee work needs, such as a need for growth or achievement (McGregor's Theory Y); and give positive reinforcement when a worker does something right (behavior modification).
4. Factors that limit your use of motivational techniques include the boring nature of many jobs, company management policies, the extent of your authority and resources, the employees themselves, and the constant time pressures.

5. A positive work climate is one in which employees can and will work productively.
6. Morale is a group spirit surrounding getting a job done.
7. Motivational methods include vision, goals that individuals have contributed toward, expectations, empowerment, sharing information, frequent one-on-one communication, resources, appreciation and recognition, fun, advancement opportunities.
8. In order to build a positive work climate, you need to focus on the individual, the job, and yourself (the leader) by getting to know your people, dealing with security and social needs, rewarding and developing your people, providing an attractive job environment, providing a safe and secure work environment, making the job interesting and challenging, setting a good example, and establishing a climate of honesty.
9. Besides causing pain and suffering to the injured employee and the cost of lost work time, there are other direct and indirect costs to consider when an accident occurs, such as lost business and possibly a lawsuit.

KEY TERMS

behavior modification
dissatisfiers
economic person theory
hierarchy of needs
hygiene factors
job loading
maintenance factors
management by example

morale
motivation
motivators
negative reinforcement
positive reinforcement
role model
self-actualization
social person theory

REVIEW QUESTIONS

Answer each question in complete sentences. Read each question carefully and make sure that you answer all parts of the question. Organize your answer using more than one paragraph when appropriate.

1. Name five expectations that employees often have of their leader.
2. Briefly discuss five motivational theories that make the most sense to you.
3. Which motivational theorist thinks that most people will "become all they are capable of becoming"?
4. What limits the leader from using motivational theories to their fullest?
5. Compare the terms *positive work climate* and *morale*. In what ways are their meanings similar, and in what ways different?
6. To what do the terms *demotivator* and *dissatisfier* refer? How do demotivators and dissatisfiers affect productivity? How can the leader avoid them?
7. What is meant by *develop your people*?
8. Describe leadership by example.

ACTIVITIES AND APPLICATIONS

1. Discussion Questions

- When you go to work, what are some of your expectations and needs? What is positive about the work climate? What is negative?
- Why can't motivation theory be reduced to a set of rules that a supervisor can apply to maintain or increase productivity?
- What motivates you when you are working? Does your supervisor make any effort to determine what motivates your actions and use this knowledge to increase your productivity or try a new task?
- Do you think that one motivational theory is especially better than others in motivating workers to perform well? Defend your answer.
- Several factors are mentioned in this chapter to help build a positive work climate. Which three are most important to you? Can you think of any other factors? Refer to Figure. 8.4 for more factors.

2. "Dear Boss" Letter

Write a letter to a future leader about how you want to be treated. For example, you could ask to be listened to, to be thanked, to be challenged, and so on. List at least ten things describing how you want your future boss to work with you.

3. Group Activity: Rewards

Working in a group, number in priority order what you think employees want from their jobs. Then number in priority order what supervisors believe that employees want from their jobs. A real survey like this was done with supervisors and employees. The top three concerns for employees, and how supervisors ranked their concerns, are listed at the end of this chapter.

Employees Want:		Leaders Think Employees Want:
_____	1. Promotion and growth	_____
_____	2. Interesting work	_____
_____	3. Job security	_____
_____	4. Feeling of being in on things	_____
_____	5. Full appreciation of work done	_____
_____	6. Good wages	_____

WEB ACTIVITY

- Go to one of the following websites: Monster.com, Careerbuilder.com, Jobs.com, or Careers.org. See if you are motivated by any career opportunities at one of these sites.

RELATED WEBSITES

HR tools	www.hrtools.com
Employee of the month system	www.eaward.com
Team member motivation	www.billmain.com
Team member motivation	www.employer-employee.com
Team member motivation	www.generationsatwork.com
U.S. Office of Personnel Management	www.opm.gov

ANSWER TO GROUP ACTIVITY: REWARDS

Employees: 2, 5, 4
Supervisors: 6, 3, 1

ENDNOTES

1. Charles Wardell, *Building Front Line Morale in Motivating People for Improved Performance* (Boston: Harvard Business School Press, 2005), pp. 22–23.
2. Adam Tobler, *Making Work Meaningful in Motivating People for Improved Performance* (Boston: Harvard Business School Press, 2005), pp. 37–38; and Michael MacCoby, *Why Work?: Motivating the New Workforce,* 2nd ed. (Alexandria, VA: Miles River Press, 1995).
3. Ibid.
4. Abraham Maslow, *Motivation and Personality* (New York: Harper & Row, 1954).
5. Frederick Herzberg, B. Mausner, and B. Snyderman, *The Motivation to Work* (New York: John Wiley, 1958).
6. Joseph W. Weiss, *Organizational Behavior and Change: Managing Diversity, Cross Cultural Dynamics, and Ethics* (Minneapolis: West, 1996). As cited in Charles R. Greer and Richard W. Plunket, *Supervision: Diversity and Teams in the Workplace* (Upper Saddle River, NJ: Prentice Hall, 2003), p. 234.
7. Personal conversation with Betty Schoenbaum, June 1, 2010.
8. Martha I. Finney, *The Truth about Getting the Best from People* (Upper Saddle River, NJ: Pearson Education Financial Times Press, 2008), p. 10.
9. Ibid.
10. Ibid., pp. 11–12.
11. Loren Gray, *Enlisting Hearts and Minds in Motivating People for Improved Performance* (Boston: Harvard Business School Press, 2005), pp. 27–28.
12. Ibid.
13. Reylito Elbo, "In The Workplace," *Business World Manila* (August 11, 2006), p. 1.
14. Ibid.
15. James G. Clawson and Douglas S. Newburg, The Motivator's Dilemma, *in The Future of Human Resources Management.* Edited by Mike Losey, Sue Meisinger, and Dave Ulrich. (Hoboken, NJ: John Wiley & Sons, 2005), p. 15.
16. Ibid., p. 18.
17. Ibid., p. 16.

Chapter 9

Supervising Teams, Teambuilding, and Coaching

Overview

One vital factor is necessary in order to be successful in the hospitality industry: having an effective team. But, what is an effective team, and how do we turn groups into teams and make them winning teams? Many hospitality corporations realize that their main competitive advantage is their employees.

One hospitality product is much the same as another until we add personal service. We have all likely experienced a hospitality service that was less than what was expected and, hopefully, many more of the opposite.

Why is it that in one place the employees are standing around talking amongst themselves and not attending to their guests' needs? Yet, in another, there is a group **synergy**, with employees helping and encouraging each other to excel? Figure 9.1 illustrates the synergy created by a team. In this chapter, we will examine teams and teamwork and how to establish winning teams, a vital part to achieving success in the hospitality industry. Successful concepts such as total quality management (TQM) and empowerment are presented with industry examples to reinforce the learning. After completing this chapter you should be able to:

synergy
The actions of two or more people to achieve an outcome that each is individually incapable of achieving.

- Explain the difference between *groups* and *teams*.
- Describe *team norms, cohesive teams*, and three ways to influence a team.

297

- **Discuss the building of teams, turning groups into teams, creating successful teams, and the characteristics of successful teams.**
- **List and describe the steps in installing a TQM process.**
- **Discuss empowerment and coaching.**

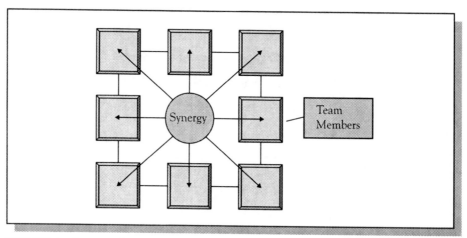

FIGURE 9.1: Team members can create a synergy (when the output is greater than the sum of the individual input). This is accomplished by group members encouraging each other to accomplish goals.

group

A number of people working together, or considered together because of common characteristics.

team

A group of individuals who share a common goal and the responsibility for achieving it.

What Is a Team?

Teams are very different from groups. A *group* is defined as a number of people working together, or considered together because of similarities. If working together, they interact to achieve a certain objective. The group usually shares information but remains neutral.

A *team* is a special kind of group. A team is a group of individuals who share a common goal and the responsibility for achieving it.[1] Teams are task-oriented work groups; they can evolve or be appointed, either formally or informally (which will be discussed further in the following section).

The team attempts to achieve a positive collaboration among its members. A successful team will work well with each other, achieve set goals, and each member will have a feeling of self-worth. The successful team will also be adaptive, flexible, and able to deal with conflicts as they arise.

formally appointed team
A team that has a formally appointed leader who may have more influence and decision-making authority than other team members.

delegation
The act of giving a portion of one's responsibility and authority to a subordinate.

informally appointed team
A team that evolves on its own.

interdependency
Reliance on others to accomplish a task such as work responsibilities.

team morale
Confidence and enthusiasm that come from a team working in harmony.

teamwork
The cooperative actions that a team performs.

team players
Individuals who participate in the collective effort to get a job done efficiently.

A *formally appointed team* has an appointed team leader. The team leader possesses the power to influence others and may have more decision-making authority than others. The power to influence others is not the only difference between team members and leaders.

A head server is a good example of a formally appointed team member within a restaurant. Power may be *delegated* to this server from management. **Delegation** is when one gives a portion of his or her responsibility and authority to a subordinate. The leader may delegate the head server to do nightly checkouts or voids throughout the evening.

An *informally appointed team* will evolve on its own. It has a rotation of leadership. The group leader does not have formal power over the group. The informally appointed team has some advantages over the formally appointed one. For instance, one person probably does not possess every quality needed to be the perfect leader.

With the rotation of leadership, everyone has a chance to show the qualities that they possess. Formally appointed team leaders may also lose popularity among the group because of their connection with management. With an informally appointed team, this is not likely to happen due to the fact that when their turn comes, everyone is linked with management.

People join teams for many different reasons. One main reason for joining a team in the hospitality industry is to accomplish tasks as efficiently and swiftly as possible. It would be a lot harder to survive a night as a server if you tried to do everything on your own. In actuality, it would be virtually impossible to expedite, deliver, and serve food, while clearing, resetting tables, and waiting on people!

Being part of the team assures you that you have others to fall back on if the going gets rough. People may also simply join a team to feel like they are a part of a whole. They want to feel that they contribute something to the overall success of the team. This may help to develop, enhance, and/or confirm some underlying identity needs.

A team that will be highly successful consists of members who care for and trust each other. They know how to listen to each other as well as express their own ideas. This will form *interdependency* within the team. The interdependence leads to a team collaboration. They find that working together is more effective than working apart.

Efficiency will increase, as well as *team morale*. Team morale is another factor in having a successful team. A team with high morale has harmony among its members. They work well together, know how to communicate openly, and trust each other. In order to have high team morale within the team you must have teamwork, as well as team players.

Teamwork is the actual action that a team performs. It is defined as the cooperative effort by a group of persons acting together as a team. In order to have teamwork in the hospitality industry, you must have *team players*. Team players are individuals who participate in a collective effort and cooperate to get the job done efficiently.

This may range from clearing tables for coworkers on a busy night to taking orders for them because they seem overburdened. One common form of teamwork in the restaurant industry is the rule of having "full hands" going in and out of the kitchen whenever possible.

It is interesting to note that with self-managed teams, the dynamics change if a member leaves or transfers to another "store" (as in restaurant) or hotel. Is this true only for self-managed teams? The new member takes time to adjust to the dynamics and culture of the group. Because we frequently work in groups in the hospitality industry, the ability to work with a team is a major requirement for selection of the associate. Being a team player is more important than being an independent-minded superstar. Ask any team coach.

Working Together

team norms
Implicit as well as explicit rules of behavior that result from team interaction.

Now that we have learned the differences between a team and a group, let's consider how team norms affect work behavior. In the hospitality industry, teams as well as *team norms* are constantly evolving. Team norms are defined as implicit, in addition to explicit rules of behavior. Norms occur inevitably within every type of group—or, should we say, *team*—interaction. They are how team members communicate and conduct themselves in the workplace. Norms work best when the team is allowed to create them. Teams will resent it if preexisting norms are imposed on them or are appointed to them.

This makes it sound like norms should be stopped because they are inherently negative. However, norms can be led in a positive direction. Positive team norms are behaviors that are agreed on and accepted within the group. They range from communication to performance.

The team should have a positive norm for open communication, as well as wanting to strive for peak performance. For example, a team might agree that if a team member is running late, the other team members will cover for him or her. This can help service overall by ensuring that one person's delayed bus won't delay service for customers. However, a supervisor must keep an eye out for the employee who decides to come in late frequently. Negative norms can develop by abusing team norms.

One way a leader may increase positive team norms in the hospitality industry is by giving rewards for high sales. This could be a weekly or monthly contest where all the servers get a reward when sales reach a goal. The rewards could range from a dinner on the house to a gift certificate. This creates a positive norm among the team members and allows them to have fun, while all of them are striving for the same goal.

Negative team norms are behaviors that are against the interest of and are not accepted by the overall group. An example of a negative team norm is an employee who feels that he does not need a preshift meeting; therefore, he always comes to work late.

This employee should not just be made an example of in this book; he should also be made an example of at work. As a supervisor, it is your duty to evaluate anything or anyone that negatively affects your team. You will never be able to stop negative norms from arising, but you can assess them so that the team may move forward.

project teams
Teams that are brought together for the completion of a project.

In hospitality companies, there are work-area teams such as a dining room team in a hotel restaurant. There may also be *project teams* where a member of the dining room team joins a project team for a period of usually about two months to work on a special project. The project could be creating a new menu or making suggestions for reconception of the theme of the outlet.

Working together becomes all the more important when we consider that in a recent Zagat survey, service ratings ranked behind food by an average of nearly two points. Some 72 percent of complaints by diners responding to the survey were service related.[2]

It's called cooperation—sharing the load to ensure that your guests leave smiling. And if you've never worked in the hospitality industry, you don't know just how important cooperation is on the job. As members of the team, everyone pitches in with one goal in mind—to keep the guests happy.[3]

✳ COHESIVE TEAMS

Why are some teams more efficient than others? Think of it as putting pieces of a puzzle together. Each member of the team is interconnected and represents a piece of this puzzle. In order for the puzzle to be put together correctly, you must have cohesion. Building a *cohesive team* is a major factor in the success of any hospitality company. A cohesive team communicates well with each other and has well-defined norms, unity, respect, and trust among its members.

As in all teams, the members of cohesive teams have strengths and weaknesses; hopefully, what one member lacks another will make up for. This cohesion will result in a team that works well and fits together well. When members of the team fit well together, there is more of a chance that the team will reach its peak performance. If a team lacks cohesion, performance will be hindered because the group will not have any sense of unity.

To build a cohesive team, goals and objectives need to be set. How would a team be able to strive for cohesion if members do not know what their goals are? Through close interaction with one another, the team will learn each other's strengths and weaknesses and how each member works. Interaction and communication among the members of the team will eventually lead to group norms, respect, trust, and unity.

In the restaurant industry, everyone should have the same objective and goals in mind: let's make this shift as smooth and efficient as possible, and have fun while we are doing it. It is also easier to give negative feedback when there are agreed-on goals.

Just as there is incredible power in a strong team, there is a disaster waiting to happen in a weak team environment. A strong team overachieves and accomplishes results that it could never reach working independently. Unfortunately, a strong team does not happen by accident. It takes management awareness, focus, and effort.[4]

The best team-building experiences in the world are the ones that allow passionate, dedicated, and talented people to get the chance to give their best toward a common goal.[5]

Let your people take the lead and you'll be amazed at how far they'll take you on the strength of their vision:[6]

- Let them know you want to intentionally pass on some of the power. Get their buy-in.
- Brainstorm with the entire group on what shared leadership will look like in your team.
- Find out what their personal hidden beliefs are about leadership and management.
- Work with your team members to discover what additional training they need to exercise their new leadership responsibilities well.
- Learn to consider your team members as an advisory board.

cohesive team
A team that communicates well and has well-defined norms, respect, unity, and trust among its members.

The author and philosopher Johann Wolfgang von Goethe wrote, "Treat people as if they were what they ought to be, and you will help them to become what they're capable of being." So if we treat our team members as if they are already leaders, they will rise to the occasion.[7]

When acting as a consultant to hospitality industry clients, the author begins with the purpose or main aim of the company or restaurant. The president might say the main purpose is X but, when the different levels of the organization are asked, the answer is frequently Y, especially from the lower levels of the organization. That is, management and employees are not on the same page. Other factors that are considered are the degree of overlapping values and goals. Figure 9.1 shows the degree to which an employee's personal values and goals overlap with those of the company. The more overlap there is, the more motivated the employees will likely be.

✳ LEADING A KITCHEN TEAM

Chef Gary Colpits at Manatee Technical Institute says that kitchen leadership and teamwork begin with respecting everyone and making sure that everyone is and feels a part of the team. Everyone has to have a say and can help make decisions. Chefs need to let their team members know that team members' opinions and feelings do matter. As leaders, we must be sensitive to their needs and concerns.

Before a shift, the kitchen team comes together for a "battle plan" briefing so that everyone is on the same page. These briefings underline the importance of communications—imagine what chaos and misunderstanding there would be without communication. Every station discusses its action plan for what needs to be accomplished, from *mise en place* to making their own prep list—because it might be necessary to start with the dessert if it needs to gel.

participative leadership
A system that includes workers in making decisions that concern them.

Each station needs to *prep to par* using standardized recipes. Then the chef/kitchen leader must demonstrate ***participative leadership***, leading by example, working with the team—not only to show team members that the leader can do it but also to encourage and coach them in a "we can have fun but it is work" approach.

✳ LEADING A RESTAURANT SHIFT

Every shift is unique and presents different obstacles to overcome. Nevertheless, leaders must be ready to lead their staff through a successful shift. There are many things to do before and after the doors open and close! This is where checklists come in handy. The following is an example of an opening checklist for a restaurant:

____ Arrive in facility, take care of alarms.
____ Check outside for trash, litter, etc.
____ Check A/C or heat, ice machines, walk-in coolers.
____ Survey the interior for general cleanliness.
____ Check all registers/computers.
____ Proceed to office, check notes in log.
____ Complete safe audit, sign in daily log, and confirm banks from previous shift.
____ Confirm deposit amount and prepare change order.

___ Review previous day's daily sales report, record sales, set the budget, and make forecasts (expected number of sales and guests based on the previous year) for the day.

___ Review private party function sheets.

___ Review staff schedule and determine preshift meeting topics (discussed in the next section).

___ Recheck manager's log for items that need attention.

___ Meet with chef to review preparation lists and specials.

___ Prepare seating chart for lunch.

___ Enter lunch specials into computer.

___ Issue bar bank to bartender.

___ Check bus stands, bar, and restrooms for cleanliness and proper setup.

___ Complete line check with chef.

___ Conduct a preshift meeting with the front of the house staff.

___ Do final walk-through of dining area.

___ Set music volume, lighting level, and thermostat.

___ Unlock the front door.

___ GO TIME![8]

❋ CONDUCTING PRESHIFT MEETINGS

preshift meetings
Interactive meetings that offer the leader managing a shift the opportunity to address problem issues and lay out the strategy for a successful shift.

Preshift meetings offer the leader managing a shift the time and opportunity to motivate employees. Preshift meetings should be interactive, allowing for questions to be answered, but straightforward and to the point. A typical preshift meeting should last 10 to 15 minutes. It should cover the following:

- Any problem issues should be addressed (avoiding names).
- Service practices should be emphasized.
- New products ought to be covered.
- Promotional items and specials should be highlighted.
- Provide the shift's forecast (number of expected guests).
- Note items to up-sell for the shift (such as a certain wine).
- Employees should know the status of any incentive programs in place (such as the employee who sells the most food for the week gets a dinner on the house).

The leader of the preshift meeting should note these guidelines:

- Outline the topics to be covered beforehand.
- Make sure that all staff members (to be in attendance at the meeting) are ready and in place 15 minutes prior to the shift.
- Hold the meeting somewhere that will decrease the number of distractions.
- Have someone designated to answer the phones.
- Show enthusiasm to help motivate the staff!

Throughout the shift, managers must be present and available for their staff. Managers should never go hide in the office to complete paperwork, which can be done at another time. They need to be involved with their staff and in the guest experience. There is nothing worse for a server than being in the weeds while having unhappy guests and not a manager in sight.

Leaders are present when needed and are in touch with what is going on in the entire restaurant, from the front-of-the-house to the back-of-the-house. Priorities when leading a shift include the following: safety and sanitation; driving revenue and repeat business, or service and selling; delivering on the brand promise; conflict resolution and prevention, among both guests and team; and connecting with, not merely interacting with, every customer.[9]

✳ USING CLOSING CHECKLISTS

As the evening shift begins to come to a close, the manager refers to a *closing checklist* that may include the following:

_____ Close stations/cut appropriate staff.
_____ Collect server checkouts, check side work and closing duties.
_____ Check with chef to ensure orders for next day's deliveries are set up.
_____ Close kitchen and bar.
_____ Lock the door.
_____ Collect remaining server and bar checkouts.
_____ Check bar for cleanliness and restock.
_____ Check out dining room cleanliness.
 _____ Tables and chairs.
 _____ Trash.
 _____ Restrooms.
 _____ Bus station.
_____ Check out kitchen with chef to see that the following items were completed:
 _____ Walk-ins cleaned, stocked, and organized.
 _____ Floors cleaned.
 _____ Equipment turned off and cleaned properly.
 _____ Dish area cleaned, stocked, and organized.
 _____ Sales abstract recorded properly.
_____ Run all register/computer reports and Z (clear) machines.
_____ Batch all credit card processing machines.
_____ Complete manager's daily sales report.
_____ Complete deposit and drop in safe.
_____ Make up banks for the next day.
_____ Leave all necessary notes in manager's daily logbook.
_____ Do final walk-through; check to see that everything is locked.
_____ Recheck to secure all exterior doors.
_____ Set unit alarm.
_____ GO HOME.[10]

One thing great managers/leaders share is continuous and *purposed motion*. They are continually moving, helping, spreading energy, confidence, direction, and coaching. They move between kitchen, storeroom, back door, expo line, dining room, greeter

Getting team members' input is crucial to obtaining their full commitment to achieving goals.
Photo courtesy of Manatee Technical Institute.

area and front door, assessing and directing flow, focus, food, and fun.[11] One restaurant manager attached a pedometer to his belt and logged nearly seven miles during a single shift—that is a lot of walking! Interaction with your staff and guests is the key to leading a successful and enjoyable shift.

✳ THREE WAYS TO INFLUENCE AN INFORMAL TEAM

feedback

Giving information about the performance of an individual or group back to them during or after performing a task or job.

There are some ways that you can influence an informal team. One question that you might ask yourself is, have you been giving the team enough and appropriate *feedback*? What type of feedback are you giving them? You should not give only negative feedback (or only positive feedback).

The amount of feedback given to employees generally should meet somewhere in the middle. Unfortunately, it is more common in the restaurant industry to hear when something is done wrong than when something is done right. Positive reinforcement is often neglected, but employees need it just as much as criticism. It takes only two words from you to change an employee's whole perspective—those two words are, "Great job!" Therefore, employees need to be told when their actions are unacceptable as well as when they've done a job well.

In addition to feedback, you should be able to *identify the key players within the group*. Although, as already noted, there are no formally appointed leaders in the informal team, there are always some members who have more of a control over the team.

The leader should identify the "unappointed" leaders and assess whether they are positive or negative impacts. If they are negatively impacting the group, then appropriate steps should be taken to address the issue. (The manager talks with the individual to find out why they are doing negative things, and to formulate a plan to get them to change their ways.)

Finally, another way to influence the informal team is *communication*. *Open* communication not only builds a trusting, open relationship with the staff but also helps to confirm that you are addressing the right issues. If you are consistent at openly communicating with staff, they are more likely to come to you with problems that are occurring within the establishment. If you had a manager who never or rarely spoke to you, the chances of your going to him or her with an issue are slim to none.

communication
Productive expression of ideas; the key to building trust and resolving conflicts.

Do You Know?

How are successful teams built?

Building Teams

One of the biggest challenges a leader will face is building a successful team. Before actually implementing the plan of building a team, managers should consider what they want out of the team they are about to build. What needs to be the focus of the team? What is the major goal that you want the team to accomplish? In the restaurant/hotel industry, the goal might be increased sales or simply more customer appreciation and/or feedback. After you have a clear answer to these questions, you may then start on building the team.

The first step to take is clarifying these goals to preexisting members (if there are any). Next, you should be very selective about whom you hire, and always conduct a reference check! It happens often in this industry, but you should never hire employees simply to fill a position.

You should always hire based on the idea that the applicant will provide something for the team (skills, personality, good attitude, etc.). There is rarely a shortage of applicants in this industry; more often, managers make rash decisions on hires due to a lack of time.

In the long run, these rash decisions will take more time to fix than the time it would have taken to screen out possibilities before the rash hire. Management should also seriously take recommendations about whom to hire from team members. It is not likely that a team would intentionally recommend a "bad apple" as a new team member.

Keep in mind that one team member's problem affects the whole group. Essentially, if a team member has a problem that is not addressed, it will create a downward spiral. One team member's problem will end up being the entire staff's problem. Although you are working on a team, you should consider each person as an individual, and even work with him or her on issues that do not concern the group. Once team members see that you are concerned with them individually, in addition to the team as a whole, you start to build a sense of trust and confidence.

Build a positive work environment. If you are delegating tasks to team members, or simply asking the team to kick performance up a notch, provide incentives. Incentives range from actual rewards to extra positive feedback to the chance promotion. You want the team to know that you are actively looking for rising stars. Once the team knows that you have appreciation for those who work hard and that you recognize those who are slackers, chances are, you will find more team members rising in performance.

✳ TURNING GROUPS INTO TEAMS

Many leaders mistakenly assume that they have a team when, in actuality, what they have is a group. A group is two or more interacting and interdependent individuals who come together to achieve particular objectives. Groups may be formal or informal. *Formal groups* are work groups established by the company.

formal groups
Work groups established by the company.

Formal groups include committees, group meetings, work teams, and task forces. Formal groups are either permanent or temporary. For instance, the executive committee of a resort hotel is permanent and meets regularly to run the resort. A temporary committee is established to work on a particular project such as a staff appreciation banquet. After the banquet, the temporary committee, having achieved its goals, is disbanded.

As a leader, you will want your group to become an effective team. To accomplish this, you will need to understand how groups can become true teams, and why groups sometimes fail to become teams. Groups become teams via basic group activities, the passage of time, and team development activities.[12] According to a theory advanced by Bruce Tuckman, teams building goes through four stages:[13]

1. *Forming.* Group members attempt to lay the ground rules for what types of behavior are acceptable.
2. *Storming.* Hostilities and conflict arise, and people jockey for positions of power and status.
3. *Norming.* Group members agree on their shared goals, and norms and closer relations develop.
4. *Performing.* The group channels its energies into performing its tasks.

(Tuckman added a fifth stage, *adjourning*, or breaking up the team.)

informal groups
Groups that form naturally in the workplace due to friendships and common interests.

By contrast, *informal groups* are more social by nature. These groups form naturally in the workplace due to friendships and common interests. Examples are people sharing lunchtime together or forming a club. Remember, a group is based on independence; a team is based on interdependence. In order to have a team you must have trust, communication, and collaboration. There are many ways that a supervisor can attempt to change a group into a team. Here we will discuss a few of the most critical.

First, as a supervisor you want to get the team's input toward establishing team goals. Working with the group to define goals involves the individual as a part of the whole, and a group with common goals is more likely to work as a team to achieve them.

Second, allow some team decision making. When a decision needs to be made about something concerning the team members, consult them and hear them out. This does not necessarily mean that the outcome decision has to be that of the team, but give them a say. They will appreciate having a voice in the workplace, but understand that the final decision comes from management.

If you have a cohesive team, then team members should all want to participate in the decision-making process. If you have a group, conformity tends to appear, and not everyone has an interest in the decision-making process or the outcome. Some ways to

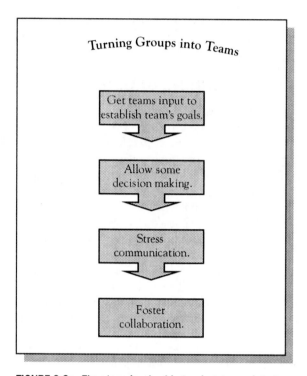

FIGURE 9.2: The steps involved in turning groups into teams.

involve the team in decision making are to have a regular meeting at which changes in policy are discussed. Make it clear that the supervisors take employees' suggestions seriously. Figure 9.2 shows the steps involved in turning groups into teams.

Third, stress *communication.* In a team, members know each other's motives and what makes each other tick. In the typical group the members do not really know each other and might even distrust other members of the group because communication is not key. In a team, communication is the key that builds trust and resolves conflict.

Supervisors must stress the importance of communication. When team members feel comfortable enough to communicate their point of view to each other, they, in turn, are more apt to give other members of the team support and trust. If it seems that there are problems, address them. Make sure the team feels comfortable enough with each other and with management to point out problems. Letting employees know about changes, even those that don't affect them directly, can make them feel like they are working as a part of a whole.

Finally, you must have collaboration among team members. In a group the members might all have individual goals, but a successful team strives together to reach the same goal. Team members must be committed to reaching the goal. If members are not striving for the same goal then you have a group, and you may want to do some reassessing of the group members to establish a team.

As we stated in the Working Together section, keep in mind that even if the team is striving for the same goal, team members have strengths and weaknesses;

hopefully, what one member lacks another will make up for. If the team collaborates and works through each other's strengths and weaknesses, they will have a sense of unity. When members of the team have unity, there is more of a chance that the team will reach its peak performance.

Fostering teamwork is creating a work culture that values collaboration. In a teamwork environment, people understand and believe that thinking, planning, decisions, and actions are better when done cooperatively. People recognize, and even assimilate, the belief that "none of us are as good as all of us."[14]

❊ CREATING SUCCESSFUL TEAMS

Creating successful teams depends on creating the climate for success. We know that teams must have a passion for the company's vision, mission, and goals, but supervisors need to give clear guidelines as to exactly *what* is to be done *by whom, when, where*, and *what resources* are required.

The supervisor also ensures that the resources are available when needed. The word TEAM can be used as an acronym for Together Everyone Achieves More. Team members should be selected for their attitudes and skills and trained by a "coach," not a boss. Training for group decision making and interpersonal communications as well as cross-training makes for success.

Select people who like teamwork—not everyone does—and reinforce behaviors that make for good teamwork by having formal recognition awards for those who "walk the talk." Some companies make a DVD and give copies along with framed photos taken with senior management to team members.

Other companies profile members in newsletters. Give teams an opportunity to show their work to senior management. Team selection, especially team leader selection, is important. It's best not to select the most senior member, who may be a member of the executive committee or guidance team (to use the Ritz-Carlton term) because other team members will simply agree with whatever the senior manager says. It's better to select another team member.

A good example of creating a successful team was at a major resort hotel where the servers at the Beach Club reported to two different departments. Guest comments alerted management to a *challenge* (which sounds better than *problem*) of poor timeliness in the delivery of food and beverage orders, yet the service received an outstanding score. The pool and beach attendants reported to one department and the bartenders and cooks to another. When both groups were united to form one team, there was some initial resentment, but as the teamwork improved, so did the tips. Figure 9.3 illustrates the elements of a successful team.

Team effectiveness is defined by three criteria:[15]

1. The *productive output* of the team meets or exceeds the standards of quantity and quality.
2. Team members realize *satisfaction* of their personal needs.
3. Team members remain *committed* to working together.

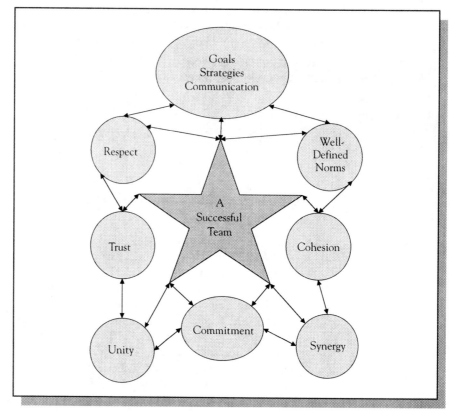

FIGURE 9.3:   Elements of a successful team.

If you think of the interaction of participants on television shows such as *Survivor* or *The Apprentice*, you can appreciate the nuances of teams.

✳ CHARACTERISTICS OF SUCCESSFUL TEAMS

Having described the creation of successful teams, we can now take a look at how a successful team looks and behaves. There are ten main characteristics of successful teams:

1. The team understands and is committed to the vision, mission, and goals of the company and the department.
2. The team is mature—not necessarily in age—in realizing that members sometimes need to place the team before their personal interests.
3. The team works to continually improve how it operates.
4. Team members treat each other with respect: they listen and feel free to express their thoughts.
5. Differences are handled in a professional manner.
6. Members have respect for their supervisor.
7. Members are consulted and their input is requested in decision making.

Courtesy of
Macarena Nieto.

When supervising a team, I establish positive norms of behavior by having a discussion on what we want for our team norms. By encouraging all team members to participate and contribute I am more likely to get their buy-in. I also stress the importance of mutual respect and cooperation. The same technique applies to setting team goals.

I stimulate discussion on the goals and am amazed to find that many of the goals set by the team exceed those set by management—so we all get bonuses!

We come together as a team for each shift and go over topics of importance—past, present, and future. I spend time on each shift ensuring that everything is going according to plan. I make a checklist with the times that the various tasks should be done by. At the end of the shift we have a quick wrap-up to discuss what went well and what could be improved.

8. Members encourage and assist other team members to succeed.
9. The team meets or exceeds its goals.
10. There is a synergy where the output of the team is greater than the input of each team member.

In order to become successful, teams need to have the skills required for the job. They also need to be empowered to do the job and to be held accountable for their performance. Teams should be rewarded for meeting or exceeding goals. In the fast-paced hospitality industry, people with insufficient skills are quickly discovered. They need to be trained or replaced for the benefit of the other team members; otherwise, the team morale will suffer.

Installing Total Quality Management

total quality management (TQM)
A process of total organizational involvement in improving all aspects of the quality of a product or service.

Given an increasingly competitive market and fluctuations in guest service levels in many hospitality organizations, it is no wonder that so many companies have adopted a ***total quality management (TQM)*** continuous improvement process. TQM is a concept that works well in the hospitality industry because its goal is to ensure continuous quality improvement of services and products for guests.

With TQM, the word *guest* is preferred over *customer*, the inference being that if we treat customers like guests, we will exceed their expectations. Successful and progressive companies realize that quality and service go hand in hand. A good meal poorly served results in guest dissatisfaction and a consequent loss of revenue. TQM works best when top management, middle management, supervisors, and hourly employees all believe in the philosophy and concept of TQM. It is a never-ending journey of continuous improvement, not a destination.

TQM is applied in all areas of the business at every level. It works like this: A detailed introduction of the TQM concept and philosophy is given by a senior member of management to underline the importance of the TQM process. The best example of a TQM philosophy is The Ritz-Carlton Hotel Company, which has built a reputation for exceptional guest service. Horst Schulze, former president and CEO, nurtured the tradition of excellence established by the celebrated hotelier, Cesar Ritz, beginning with the motto, "We are ladies and gentlemen serving ladies and gentlemen."[16]

"We practice teamwork and lateral service to create a positive environment." The mission, "To provide the finest personal service and facilities, instill well-being, and even fulfill the unexpressed wishes of our guests," expresses the need for uncompromising service. It is no wonder that the Ritz-Carlton was the first hospitality company to win the coveted Malcolm Baldrige National Quality Award. The main reason for The Ritz-Carlton Company winning this award, not once but twice, is due to TQM (1992 and 1999).[17] Ritz-Carlton associates are empowered to "move heaven and earth" to fulfill a guest's request.

All associates are schooled in the Company's Gold Standards, which include a credo, motto, three steps of service, and 20 Ritz-Carlton basics. Each employee is expected to understand and adhere to these standards, which describe the process for solving guest problems.

Figure 9.4 shows the steps for a successful TQM continuous improvement process. Top and line management is responsible for the process. Once they commit to ownership of the process, the team participants will be energized to focus their energy

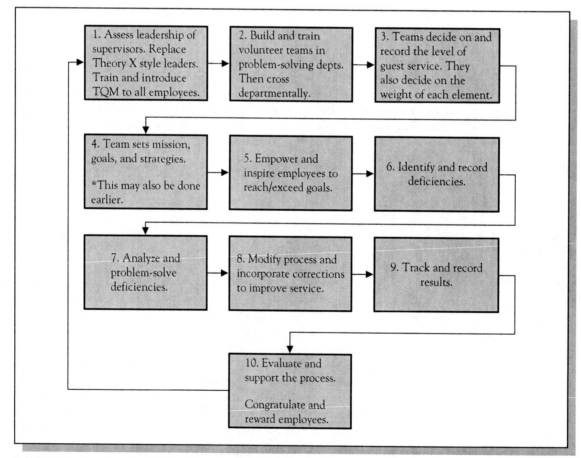

FIGURE 9.4:   Ten steps to a total quality management continuous improvement process.

TQM being introduced to a team.
Courtesy of Sodexo.

on the process. Notice how step one calls for leadership (existing, or in need of leadership training). It is critical to have good leader-managers in place to maximize the effectiveness of TQM.

- *Step one* in the process: Have excellent leaders as supervisors and managers. The more successful companies develop leader-managers who can inspire the TQM teams to exceed guest expectations.
- *Step two*: Build and train teams of volunteer associates within each department and later cross departmentally in problem solving.
- *Step three*: Have the teams decide on and write down the appropriate levels of guest service and relative weighting for "their guests" because front-line associates best know the service expectations of "their" guests.

Of course, management has input, but the whole point of TQM is that management has to give up some of its power and allow associates to share in the decision-making process for determining the criteria and performance levels for guest service.

For example, how many rings should the telephone give before it is answered? Or, how long should guests have to wait for a hostess to seat them at a restaurant? The answers are, answer the phone within three rings if possible, and, in the absence of the hostess, appoint someone to acknowledge the guests and let them know that the hostess will be there momentarily. The list of performance criteria for each department will vary according to the type of hospitality business and the guest expectations. In a restaurant situation, guests can be asked in a survey how much they liked their food. A Likert scale of 1 to 10 or 1 to 7 (using descriptors such as "Very much" on one end and "Not at all" on the other) can be used to score each criterion. Food quality is further broken down into taste, smell, appearance, and temperature.

Other restaurant meal quality criteria include service equals courtesy, friendly, efficient, prompt, professional, and so on. The total dining experience includes ease of access to the restaurant, parking, curbside appeal, cleanliness, condition of bathrooms, decor, noise levels, lighting, ambiance, music, and so on.

Once a score has been determined for each element of the guest experience, a base has been arrived at for future comparison. The team of associates comes up with ideas and how-tos for improving the guest experience for each of the elements that is below the level of quality expected by guests.

- *Step four*: Set mission, goals, and strategies based on guest expectations. Write the company, property/unit, or department mission and goals, and create strategies to meet or exceed those goals.
- *Step five*: Empower and inspire associates to reach goals.
- *Step six*: Identify deficiencies, which are areas where service falls below expectations.
- *Step seven*: Analyze and resolve identified deficiencies.
- *Step eight*: Modify processes to incorporate corrections and to improve service to expected levels.
- *Step nine*: Track results—improvements in service, guest satisfaction, employee satisfaction, cost reduction, and profit.
- *Step ten*: Evaluate and support the process. If the goals are not being met, begin again with step one. If the goals are met, congratulate team members for their success and reward them.

Installing TQM is exciting because once everyone becomes involved, the teams find creative ways of solving guest-related problems and improving service. Other benefits include increased guest and employee satisfaction, cost reductions, and, yes, increased profit. TQM is a top-down, bottom-up process that needs active commitment and involvement of all employees, from top managers to hourly paid employees. With TQM, if you are not serving the guest, you had better be serving someone who is serving the guest. To the guest, services are experiential; they are felt, lived through, and sensed.

Empowering Employees

empowerment
To give employees additional responsibility and authority to do their jobs.

More hospitality companies are empowering teams and employees to deliver outstanding guest service. *Empowerment* means ensuring that employees have the skills, knowledge, and authority to make decisions that would otherwise be made by management. The goal of empowerment is to have enthusiastic, committed employees who do an outstanding job because they believe in it and enjoy doing it. Empowerment encourages employees to be creative and to take risks, both of which can give a company a competitive edge.

There are two types of empowerment: *structured* and *flexible*. Structured empowerment allows employees to make decisions within specified limits, an example being *comping* (giving at no charge) an entree, not the whole meal. Flexible empowerment gives employees more scope in making decisions to give outstanding guest service.

As described in the TQM section, employees are empowered to problem-solve and do whatever it takes to delight the guest (so long as it's legal). With Ritz-Carlton, associates are empowered by *owning* the guest's request. Associates can spend up to $2,000 without consulting management to solve a guest's problem. An example was when the laundry was pressing a bridesmaid's dress and accidentally burned a hole in it. The concierge took the guest to the nearby Versace store and bought a new dress on her own credit card.

Empowerment enables companies to get quick decisions to satisfy guests. An associate no longer has to find a manager to approve a request; the associate is *empowered* to handle the situation. Empowerment also means fewer levels of management are required. For example, a hotel had several floor housekeepers whose job it was to inspect all rooms serviced by housekeepers. Finally, managers wised up and asked themselves the question, why aren't we doing it right to start with?

Now, certified housekeepers no longer need their rooms checked; the first person in the room after it is cleaned is the guest. This has saved thousands of dollars in salaries and benefits. Empowered employees can schedule, solve TQM problems, budget, do performance evaluations, and participate in employment selection. Today, the supervisor's role is to formulate a vision, show trust, provide resources, coach, train, offer encouragement, and help when needed.

The steps in establishing an empowerment program are similar to those for TQM—a meeting of all employees to announce (with the use of specific guest survey data) the need to increase guest satisfaction. This is followed by an introduction and explanation of empowerment. A training session goes over problem resolution, decision making, and guest service.

The program is monitored and recorded so guest and employee satisfaction—both of which hopefully increase—can be celebrated. The number of times a manager is called to deal with a request is also recorded, along with any costs involved with empowering employees to give away or *comp* a service. Hospitality companies find that the cost of reducing or comping a few charges is more than made up by the increased business they receive as a result of any "guarantee" program.

Another story that illustrates how empowerment can encourage an associate to go the extra mile is: Picture a fabulous resort hotel on a cool day in February. Two guests arrive and decide that they want to have their lunch out on the terrace, rather than in the restaurant.

A table was duly set for them, and, because it was cold, the server went to the laundry and had them put two blankets in the dryer to warm them up. When the guests were presented with the blankets, they were really impressed. It so happened that the guests were travel writers for a major newspaper, and they wrote up the story as an example of exemplary service.

Empowered employees tend to feel more in control of and have a greater commitment to their work and are also more productive than nonempowered employees. So it's no wonder that many hospitality companies such as Marriott and T.G.I Friday's gain their associates' feedback and ideas on a regular basis. They empower their employees and they, in turn, score highly in guest and employee satisfaction surveys. It's a win–win situation.

Check Your Knowledge

1. Describe TQM and how it works.
2. What does empowering employees really mean?

Guest feedback is an important part of TQM. Some hospitality businesses have outside companies conduct guest surveys, asking such questions as: Did you have a sense of well-being? Did you feel cared for as an individual? Did you feel wanted as a guest? These questions are measuring the emotional attachment that the guest has with the company and brand.

Overcoming Team Challenges

Every team must overcome some challenges to be successful. Regardless of how much supervisors strive to overcome them, some of these challenges must work out on their own. For instance, you can implement ways that the team may gain personal development, cohesion, positive norms, and so on, but the supervisor cannot simply make them happen. The people in the team must want to gain these qualities and must want a positive workplace.

One major team challenge that management must help to overcome is negativity—including "us versus them." No matter how selective supervisors are at hiring employees, they will always come across an unexpected negative hire. You must remember that when you are interviewing someone, they always have their best face on. The first impression is not necessarily what is behind the real person. If someone is applying for a position in the company, they are probably not going to come in being negative (if they do, then you should not hire them in the first place).

Therefore, it is important (once again) for the supervisor to be an active part of the team. If one person is bringing everyone down, either the active supervisor will recognize it or a team member will be comfortable enough with the supervisor to bring it to his or her attention. This issue should be immediately addressed; otherwise it may create a domino effect.

Another major challenge that management must overcome is learning how to delegate responsibilities. Supervisors must learn how to let go of certain responsibilities, and which responsibilities are to be let go of. Even if you think that it will be much quicker and easier to just do it yourself, this is another way to gain the respect of the team.

Some examples of things that may be delegated to the team in a restaurant are reservations, server cash-outs, nightly station checks, and time for evening "cuts" (when you cut the server staff down from a full staff to a smaller staff at the end of the night). When a job is delegated, make sure you explain what to do clearly and precisely. Also make sure that the person you are delegating the job to possesses a full understanding of what is to be done and that he or she is confident in doing it.

High turnover is one of the major obstacles in the hospitality industry. You cannot have a cohesive, successful team if the team members are always changing. Although there is no clear-cut way of how to overcome high turnover, there are some strategies to reduce it. One way is to be in tune with your staff. If it seems that members of the team are distraught, take the time to talk with them. Ask what the problem is and try to reach a solution. Maybe the only problem is that they are having scheduling conflicts, and it can be resolved simply by giving them more or fewer hours.

Finally, supervisors must overcome the challenge of gaining the respect of the team. This is a tricky one because you must learn how to be their friend to gain trust as well as their leader to gain respect. A supervisor who is too friendly will get walked all over. A supervisor who is not friendly enough will not gain trust. Where do you draw the line?

The answer to this is not so simple. You should always be professional when talking with the staff. Never use inappropriate language; you never really know whom it will offend. Also, limit activities that you attend together outside of the company. Take part in organized activities, but do not make a regular appearance at the local hangout after shifts.

Coaching

In today's workplace, the *leader as a commander* approach is no longer acceptable. This type of approach follows the rule that employees will do as told what to do, how to do it, and when to do it. Often employees find this type of leadership style to be unmotivating and even somewhat demeaning. Today, employees want their voices to be heard and to be more integrated as part of the operation, not simply a warm body.

Coaching is a process involving observation of employee performance and conversation focusing on job performance between the manager and the employee. Coaching can take place informally at the employee's workstation or formally by having coaching sessions in an office. It is different from *counseling*, a process used to help employees who are performing poorly because of personal problems such as substance abuse.

The first step in coaching is to observe employees doing their jobs. Be sure you are completely familiar with pertinent performance standards and job duties. Coaching focuses on enhancing skills of the employee, productivity of the employee, and elevating employee motivation. When employees feel that they are part of a team working together to achieve a goal, they are more likely to excel in performance.

As taught today in management and education circles, the notion of a *self-fulfilling prophecy* was conceptualized by Robert Merton, a professor of sociology at Columbia University. This is the notion that once an expectation is set, even if it is not accurate, we tend to act in ways that are consistent with that expectation.[18]

If managers try to control their workers, they will manage them in a restraining way that will condition employees to do nothing unless they are directly under supervision. If they act as coaches and lead their employees in the direction to assume responsibility, they manage their employees in such a way that the self-fulfilling prophecy will prepare them to take on those responsibilities.

Therefore, if high expectations for employees are set, they will be more likely to strive toward achieving those expectations. If low expectations are set, then the employee will not be motivated to go beyond the low expectations.

Based on an in-depth study, an eight-step coaching model has been developed:

1. *Be supportive.* Be flexible, assist when needed, show understanding, listen, provide positive feedback, encourage, and be open to new ideas.
2. *Define the problem and expectations.* Give the employee the chance to explain the situation. The coach should make sure the problem is understood and then clarify expectations.

coaching
Individual, corrective, on-the-job training that is focused on improving performance.

counseling
Counseling occurs when a counselor meets with a client in a private and confidential setting to explore a difficulty the client is having, distress he may be experiencing, or perhaps his dissatisfaction or loss of a sense of direction or purpose.

3. *Establish impact.* Make sure that the negative impact of the problem is understood.

4. *Initiate a plan.* The coach and employee should collaborate to develop a plan to correct the problem.

5. *Get a commitment.* Make sure the employee knows what is expected of him or her and is willing to commit to the plan that was collaboratively developed.

6. *Confront excuses/resistance.* Do not accept excuses or resistance. Make sure that the focus is on what can be done to be successful instead of what might not work.

7. *Clarify consequences.* Be clear about what will happen if the plan is not completed.

8. *Don't give up.* Coaching is hard; it takes time. There is never one right answer or solution. Working together, the coach and the employee can resolve problems successfully.[19]

What every good leader needs is continuous feedback about his or her performance as well as their employees. Anyone who has sat in the manager's chair knows how little feedback you get during the course of a day. In fact, being promoted often means the end of virtually all feedback.[20] This does not have to be so. If the leader takes the coach approach, he or she will still be part of the team, involved in employee performance. In turn, the leader will still know what is going on in the operation, how

Coaching a team can be fun and stimulate productive teamwork.
Photo courtesy of the author.

employees feel about it, and what changes need to be made. The coach views the leadership process as a collaborative venture in which every voice is heard.

The overall purpose of coaching is to evaluate work performance and then to encourage optimum work performance either by reinforcing good performance or confronting and redirecting poor performance. Coaching therefore provides your employees with regular feedback and support about their job performance and helps you to understand exactly what your employees need to know. It also prevents small problems from turning into big ones that may require much more attention later. If coaching employees is so beneficial, why do supervisors often avoid it?

Possible reasons are:

- Lack of time. (In most cases, coaching requires only a few minutes.)
- Fear of confronting an employee with a concern about his or her performance. (A mistake—the problem not faced may only get worse, not better.)
- Assuming that the employee already knows that he or she is doing a good job, so why bother saying anything? (Your employee would love to hear it anyway.)
- Little experience coaching. (You can start practicing now.)
- Assuming that the employee will ask questions when appropriate and does not need feedback. (Many employees are too proud or shy to ask questions.)

There are many skills needed to be an effective coach. Many of us already have them, but we do not understand how to implement them in a workplace setting. After complete understandings of these skills are reached, the rest should come naturally!

Most important is being present—not just physically being there on the job, really be there mentally. Avoid distractions and focus on building the performance of your team. The more you are focused on your employees' needs, the better rapport you will build with them.

This is the foundation of building a team that looks up to you as a coach, not a manager. Goals need to be set for you and your employees. Don't assume you or your employees already know what goals need to be reached; brainstorm and interact with them. Come to shared, clear agreements and make sure to follow up on them to be sure they are being kept. If the agreements are come to interactively, employees will be more apt to feel responsible for their upkeep.

A coach does not tell their employees what needs to be done and how to do it. A coach asks and teaches. Resist the temptation to "give them a fish"; instead, teach them *how to fish* for their own answers. If you feel compelled to offer advice, it can be packaged in a way that puts the person fully at choice and in charge. For example, try, "I have an idea that you might find useful."[21]

If an employee is doing the job well, do not hesitate to say so. Everyone likes to be told that they are doing a good job, so praise employees as often as you can. Work on catching your employees doing things right, and then use these steps:

1. Describe the specific action you are praising.
2. Explain the results or effects of the actions.
3. State your appreciation.

In some cases, you might want to write a letter of thanks and make sure that a copy goes into the employee's personnel file. You could instead use a standard form, which is quicker to complete.

When observing employees, sometimes you will see what appears to be a problem with performance. If Ted left a pallet of canned goods outside the storeroom, ask him, "Is there a reason why these canned goods are not put away yet?" If Sally is not using the new procedure for cleaning flatware, ask her, "Are you aware of the new procedure for washing flatware?" It could be that Ted stopped putting the canned goods away when a delivery of milk (which has to be put in the refrigerator immediately) came in, or perhaps Sally was on vacation when the cleaning procedure was changed. Consider the following questions before correcting an employee:

- Does the employee know what is supposed to be done, and why?
- Are there any reasons for poor performance that the employee cannot control, such as inadequate equipment?
- How serious are the consequences of this problem?
- Has the employee been spoken to about this concern before?

By asking questions before you point a finger at someone, you help maintain the self-respect of the employee. After asking questions, if it is obvious to you that a correction is needed, be careful not to correct one employee in front of another. No one likes being corrected in front of his or her peers. Arrange to talk privately with the employee to define the performance problem, agree on why it is happening, make your standards clear, and work with the employee to set goals for improvement.

Let's say that Kim's performance as a cocktail server has deteriorated noticeably in the last few weeks and there have been guest complaints of poor service, ill temper, and rudeness. If you tolerate her poor performance, it will reduce her respect for you, for the job, and for herself. So you arrange to talk to her privately and try to get her to do most of the talking. You get Kim to tell you what is wrong and let her know how you perceive the problem as well.

The goal is to resolve the problem, and you encourage her to make her own suggestions for doing this. This leads to her commitment to improve. You make sure that she understands the performance you expect, and you get her to set her own improvement goals: measurable performance goals such as a specific reduction in customer complaints within a certain period of time.

- If the problem is related to the job, you do what you can to solve it. For instance, one fast-food employee's poor performance turned out to be caused by a large puddle of water in which she had to stand while working. The supervisor had the plumbing fixed, and that solved the performance problem. Kim's problem might have an equally simple solution.
- If the problem involves other people on the job, the solution might be more complex, but you do everything you can to resolve it. In the meantime, you have a management obligation to help Kim meet performance standards.

- If the problem is personal, it might help Kim to talk about it, but you cannot solve it for her. You can only listen in order to help her overcome its interfering with her work.
- If the problem is burnout, you might be able to motivate her with some change of duties and responsibilities that would add variety and interest to her job. In any case, she will probably respond to your supportive approach, and when she has set her own goals, she will feel a commitment to achieving them.

When goals have been set that you both agree to, establish checkpoints at which you meet to discuss progress (get Kim to set the times—perhaps once a week or every two weeks). You express your confidence in her ability to meet her goals, make it clear that you are available when needed, and put her on her own.

During the improvement period, you observe discreetly from the sidelines, but you do not intervene. Kim is in charge of her own improvement; you are simply staying available. You compliment her when you see her handle a difficult customer; you give her all the positive feedback you can; you keep her aware of your support.

You wait for the checkpoints to discuss the negatives, and you let Kim bring them up. You use the checkpoints as informal problem-solving sessions in which you again encourage Kim to do most of the talking and generate most of the ideas. To summarize, make sure that a counseling session includes the following:

1. Speak in private with the employee. Be relaxed and friendly.
2. Express in a calm manner your concern about the specific aspect of job performance you feel needs to be improved. Describe the concern in behavioral terms and explain the effect it has. Do so in a positive manner.
3. Ask the employee for his or her thoughts and opinions, including possible solutions. Discuss together these solutions and agree mutually on a course of action and a time frame.
4. Ask the employee to restate what has been agreed on to check on understanding. State your confidence in the employee's ability to turn the situation around.
5. At a later time, you should follow up and make sure that the performance concern has been addressed.

In many operations, you will be asked to document (meaning you will need to write on paper) coaching sessions. Some leaders document coaching sessions in a logbook, which is much like a diary of day-to-day events in the operation. Depending on the policy, coaching sessions may be recorded on forms intended for that purpose.

Any documentation of coaching sessions should include the date and place of the coaching and a summary of the coaching session. Although this might seem time-consuming, documentation is essential if you ever need to terminate an employee or simply to do yearly performance evaluations, the next topic.

Making coaching behaviors part of what you do is essential to the process. Here is a recap of some behaviors that you, as a coach, should focus on:

1. Do not think about employees as people who need to be controlled.
2. Listen, listen, listen!

3. Develop the individual strengths of each employee.
4. Endorse effort and growth (instead of pointing out mistakes).
5. Stop providing solutions. Give your employees an opportunity to figure it out.
6. Stop making all the decisions. Delegate decisions where appropriate and engage your employees.
7. Be unconditionally constructive. Take responsibility for how you are heard, even if you meant something different but came across the wrong way.
8. Create an environment where people want to work with you and feel valued, respected, and part of a team.[22]

Check Your Knowledge

1. What is counseling used for?
2. Explain the self-fulfilling prophecy.
3. What is coaching?
4. Why do supervisors often avoid coaching?

 # KEY POINTS

1. A group is defined as a number of persons working together, or considered together because of similarities. They share information but remain neutral. A team is a special kind of group that attempts to achieve a positive collaboration among its members.
2. A formally appointed team has an appointed team leader. The team leader possesses the power to influence others; power may be delegated to this server from management. An informally appointed team will evolve on its own, it has a rotation of leadership, and the group leader does not have formal power over the group.
3. One main reason for joining in a team in the hospitality industry is to accomplish tasks as efficiently and swiftly as possible. People may also simply join a team to feel like they are a small part of a whole (this may help to develop, enhance, and/or confirm some underlying identity needs).
4. Teamwork is the actual action that a team performs. It is defined as the cooperative effort by a group of persons acting together as a team. In order to have teamwork in the hospitality industry you must have team players.
5. In the hospitality industry, teams as well as team norms are constantly evolving. Team norms are defined as implicit, in addition to explicit, rules of behavior. Positive team norms are behaviors that are agreed-upon and accepted within the group. Negative team norms are behaviors that are against the interest of and are not accepted by the overall group.
6. A cohesive team communicates well with each other, and has well-defined norms, unity, respect, and trust among its members. To build a cohesive team, goals and objectives must be set.
7. Three ways to influence an informal team are: feedback, identification of the key players, and communication.
8. Before actually implementing the plan of building a team, managers should consider what they want out of the team they are about to build. They should be very selective with whom they hire and should conduct reference checks. A supervisor should also keep in mind that one team member's problem affects the whole group.
9. Groups may be formal or informal. Formal groups are work groups established by the company; informal groups are more social by nature.

10. There are four steps to take in turning a group into a team: (1) Get the team's input into establishing team goals; (2) Allow some team decision making; (3) Stress communication; (4) Have collaboration among team members.

11. A team that will be highly successful understands and is committed to the vision, mission, and goals of the company and the department, is mature, works to continually improve how it operates, treats each other with respect, handles differences in a professional manner, has respect for the supervisor, is consulted for input in decision making, encourages and assists other team members to succeed, meets or exceeds its goals, and has synergy.

12. Total quality management's goal is to ensure continuous quality improvement of services and products for guests. TQM is applied in all areas of the business at every level. There are ten steps to total quality management.

13. There are two types of empowerment: structured and flexible. Structured empowerment allows employees to make decisions within specified limits; flexible empowerment gives employees more scope in making decisions to give outstanding guest service.

14. Major team challenges are negativity, learning how to delegate responsibilities, high turnover, and gaining the respect of the team.

15. The coach uses energy and positivity, not fear or status, as a form of motivation to get the job done.

 # KEY TERMS

coaching

cohesive team

counseling

communication

delegation

empowerment

feedback

formal groups

formally appointed team

group

informal groups

informally appointed team

interdependency

participative leadership

preshift meetings

project teams

synergy

team

team morale

team norms

team players

teamwork

total quality management (TQM)

 # REVIEW QUESTIONS

Answer each question in complete sentences. Read the question carefully and make sure that you answer all parts of the question. Organize your answer using more than one paragraph when appropriate.

1. Explain in detail the differences between a group and a team.
2. Compare and contrast a formally appointed team and an informally appointed team. What are some advantages and disadvantages of each?

3. What are norms? How do they evolve? When do they work best?

4. How do you build a cohesive team?

5. What are some ways to influence an informal team?

6. Explain total quality management.

7. What is empowerment? What are the two types of empowerment?

8. What are some of the major challenges a team must overcome in order to be successful?

9. Explain the differences between a coach and a supervisor.

 # ACTIVITIES AND APPLICATIONS

1. Discussion Questions

- Explain delegation. Other than the examples in the text, what are some appropriate duties in a restaurant that may be delegated? How about in a hotel?
- What are some of the main reasons that people join teams? This does not necessarily have to relate to the hospitality industry. Give examples inside as well as outside the industry.
- Give some examples of how a supervisor can contribute to heightening team morale.
- What are the steps in building a team?
- What does creating successful teams depend on?
- What does TEAM stand for?

2.1. Group Activity: Total Quality Management

You and three investors just bought a new restaurant. In groups of four, review the ten steps of TQM to implement a plan of action for your new establishment. Have one person keep a list of the plan as the other three brainstorm. Example: The first step is to have excellent leaders. As a new owner how will you find these leaders? Discuss it with the class.

2.2. Group Activity: Teambuilding Exercise

The class is assigned to teams of about six people each to participate in a scavenger hunt. Each team must create a team name and motto.

Scavenger Hunt:

Each team must collect and bring to class the following items:

- A photo of the group
- A meal pass for the cafeteria
- A copy of *USA Today*
- A CD-ROM
- A page of college letterhead paper
- A $50 bill
- A copy of this course outline/syllabus
- An athlete who represents the school
- A T-shirt with the school logo on it
- A hair clip

You have 30 minutes to bring the above items to class. After the winner is declared, reflect on how well your team did. What role did each member play? Did a leader emerge? Do you now feel more of a bonding with your team members?

3. **Case Study: "The Just Hired as a Supervisor Blues"**

Mike graduated from school a few months ago. He applied to various companies and has decided to take a position at a well-known local restaurant.

On his first day at work, Mike felt that everyone was out for himself. There was little teamwork going on and hardly any communication. Mike, in turn, was reconsidering his decision for taking this position. Before Mike decides if he is going to leave, he turns to you for some suggestions.

Case Study Questions

1. What do you think Mike should do to break the ice?
2. What are some ways Mike could try to turn the group into a team?
3. What are some reasons that this group could have such negative norms?
4. What would be some advantages for Mike if he implemented a TQM plan?

 # WEB ACTIVITY

- Go to the following website: humanresources.about.com/od/involvementteams/a/team_culture.htm#

  If you scroll down, you should find a heading: To make teamwork happen, these powerful actions must occur. Do you agree that these topics would make for a climate of teamwork at your place of work? Why or why not?

 # RELATED WEBSITES

Generations at work—a company site offering generational clips and articles.	www.generationsatwork.com
Team Member Motivation—a series of articles on motivation	www.employer-employee.com
American Society for Quality—a member organization devoted to Quality	www.asq.org

 # ENDNOTES

1. Jean M. Di Giovanna, "Five Components Needed for High Performing Teams," *Design Firm Management and Administration Report*, vol. 7, no. 4 (April 2007), p. 3.
2. Megan Rowe, "Secrets to Guest Service," *Restaurant Hospitality*, vol. 90, no. 3 (March 2006), p. 39.
3. "The Restaurant Team: 10 Ways to Build Cooperation," August 2006. hcareers.com.
4. "Your Business: Team Charter—Getting Buy-In to Get Results," April 2006. restaurantreport.com. Retrieved July 18, 2007.

5. Martha I. Finney, *The Truth about Getting the Best from People* (Upper Saddle River, NJ: Pearson Education, Financial Times Press, 2008), p. 46.

6. Ibid., p. 190.

7. Ibid., p. 191.

8. Adapted from: Chris Tripoli, "Operating Checklist," A'La Carte Consulting Group Online. www.alacartecon sultinggroup.com/article6.html. February 2008.

9. Jim Sullivan, "The Lost Art of Guest Finesse in the Dining Room," *Nation's Restaurant News*. findarticles .com/p/articles/mi_m3190/is_10_40/ai_n16101662. Retrieved February 2008.

10. Tripoli.

11. Sullivan.

12. Thomas S. Bateman and Scott A. Snell, *Management: Leading and Collaborating in a Competitive World*, 7th ed. (New York: McGraw-Hill Irwin, 2007), p. 464.

13. B. W. Tuckman, "Developmental Sequence in Small Groups," *Psychological Bulletin*, vol. 63 (1965), pp. 384–399. As cited in Thomas S. Bateman and Scott A. Snell, *Management: Leading and Collaborating in a Competitive World*, 7th ed. (New York: McGraw-Hill Irwin, 2007), p. 464.

14. Susan Heathfield, "How to Build a Teamwork Culture. Your Guide to Human Resources," November 2005. www.humanresources.about.com. Retrieved July 21, 2007.

15. Nadler, Hackman, and Lawler, *Managing Organizational Behavior*. As cited in Thomas S. Bateman and Scott A. Snell, *Management: Leading and Collaborating in a Competitive World*, 7th ed. (New York: McGraw-Hill Irwin, 2007), p. 67.

16. The Ritz-Carlton, "Working at The Ritz-Carlton," corporate.ritzcarlton.com/en/Careers/WorkingAt.htm. Retrieved April 28, 2011.

17. Vivian Deuschl, "The Malcolm Baldrige National Quality Award," corporate.ritzcarlton.com/en/Press/Kits/ Baldrige.htm. Retrieved April 28, 2011.

18. ACCEL, "Better Management by Perception." www.accel-team.com/pygmalion/index.html. Retrieved February 2008.

19. Steven J. Stowell and Matt M. Starcevich, Center for Management and Organization Effectiveness, "The Coach: Creating Partnerships for a Competitive Edge," U.S. Office of Personnel Management (August 1996), www.opm.gov/perform/articles/030.asp#Eight. Retrieved February 2008.

20. Ibid.

21. Daniel Robin & Associates, "Making Workplaces Work Better: The Eight Essential Skills of Coaching: How to Bring Out the Best in Others," www.abetterworkplace.com/075.html. Retrieved February 2008.

22. Megan Tough, "Coaching—The New Word in Management," www.siliconfareast.com/coaching.htm. Retrieved February 2008.

Chapter 11

Conflict Management, Resolution, and Prevention

Overview

Susan wants Friday night off. She requested it off, but she is on the schedule for Friday night anyway. Management had to put her on the shift because she is one of the restaurant's top servers and it is going to be a very busy night. Susan is not aware that management thinks of her as one of the top servers. Instead, she perceives management as trying to punish her because she had Jane cover her lunch shift last week. Here, a possible conflict with management may arise due to a misperception and a lack of communication. In this chapter, we will define conflict and discuss how it arises and how to manage it in the workplace.

After completion of this chapter you should be able to:

- **Define conflict.**
- **Identify the main ingredients of conflict.**
- **Understand how conflict arises in the workplace.**
- **Implement the steps in managing workplace conflict.**
- **Create a safe and secure workplace environment and know how to respond to incidents of workplace violence.**
- **Work on preventing conflict from happening.**

361

What Is Conflict?

Conflict. What do you think or feel when you hear that word? If you are like most people, you probably experience some sort of discomfort.[1] Why does conflict happen? To put it simply, because we are human and today we have many more choices in our lives and careers, which means more opportunity for conflict. We all have differing opinions. As a supervisor, the conflict at hand is not the real issue. How the conflict is dealt with is.

There are various ways to define conflict, but first, let's define **anger**. *Anger*, according to *Webster's Dictionary*, is defined as a feeling of great displeasure, hostility, indignation, or exasperation, wrath, trouble or affliction. **Conflict**, according to *Webster's Dictionary*, is defined as discord, a state of disharmony, open or prolonged fighting, strife, or friction.[2] We are likely to find anger where there is conflict but not always the reverse. One can certainly be angry without having any form of conflict with someone.

In this chapter, we define conflict as a disagreement resulting from individuals or groups that differ in opinions, attitudes, beliefs, needs, values, or perceptions. Conflict arises when two or more individuals, or groups, have opposing positions on the same subject.

Do You Know?

Describe the ingredients of conflict.

anger

Feeling of hostility, wrath, indignation, or great displeasure.

conflict

Discord, a state of disharmony, open or prolonged fighting, strife, or friction.

Most conflicts are fueled because one's interests or values are challenged.

Courtesy of Purestock.

❧ THE MAIN INGREDIENTS OF CONFLICT

desires
The things that we want.

Why do people get into conflicts in the first place? Most conflicts are fueled because one's interests or values are challenged, or because their needs are not met.[3] The main "ingredients" of conflict include desires, needs, perceptions, power, values, and feelings. *Desires* can also be thought of as "wants." These are things that we would like to have or have happen but do not *need* to have them or have them happen. *Needs* are those things that we feel are vital to our well being. Conflicts are bound to arise when needs are ignored—or we ignore the needs of others.

needs
The things that we feel are vital to our well being.

Perceptions are how people interpret things (situations, events, people, etc.). We all see things differently inside and outside of a situation. It is how people interpret, or perceive, a situation that determines whether a conflict will arise. Conflict may also arise when someone is rejecting, or seeking to gain, *power*. The way that managers utilize their power may have an effect on the number and type of conflicts that arise. Lack of leadership, as well as overuse of power, are both potential sources of conflict.

perceptions
How people interpret things—situations, events, people.

Feelings and emotions are a main cause of conflict. Many people are unable to separate themselves from their feelings and emotions, causing things to become "cloudy," so to speak. Conflicts can also occur when people ignore the feelings of others or if the feelings of two or more parties differ over an issue.

power
The capacity to influence the behavior of others.

Values are deeply held beliefs. When values are at the center of a conflict they are usually not up for negotiation, or any type of conflict management strategies. Here it might be best to just agree to disagree. These ingredients of conflict should not be viewed as negative. However, they can turn into elements that cause conflict if, and when, they are misunderstood. Figure 11.1 shows the main ingredients of conflict.

Check Your Knowledge

1. Explain the difference between a need and a desire.
2. Define the words *anger* and *conflict*.

❧ COMMON CAUSES OF CONFLICT IN THE WORKPLACE

feelings
Emotions or tendencies to respond in emotional ways.

There are many causes of conflict in the workplace. It would be virtually impossible to cover all of them in one chapter. Here are some of the most common causes:

values
Deeply held beliefs that are not open to negotiation.

- Lack of communication
- Feelings of being undervalued
- Undefined/not clearly defined roles
- Poor use of managerial criticism
- Preferential treatment
- Poor management/leadership
- Impractical expectations
- Overworked employees
- Stress
- Personality differences
- Internal conflict

Conflict can sometimes appear to be with another individual when at its center, it is not. Sometimes the person really has a conflict with him- or herself.

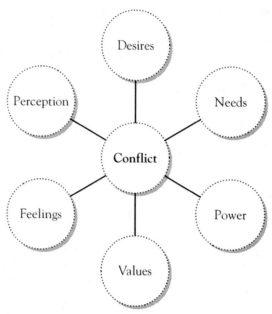

FIGURE 11.1: **The main ingredients of conflict.**

Workplace conflicts can be triggered by a variety of issues, such as the following factors suggested by Vicki Hess, principal of Catalyst Consulting:[4]

- *Different work methods.* Two employees have the same goal but approach the task two different ways.
- *Different goals.* Employees have goals that conflict with the goals for people in other areas of the company, such as front-of-the-house versus back-of-the-house.
- *Personalities.* People sometimes annoy each other just because of the way they look or act, or because of biases.
- *Stress.* On a good day, people can let issues roll off their back, but as stress increases, people often snap.
- *Different viewpoints or perspectives.* Someone might be so closely involved with an issue that he might have a different perspective from someone who sees the same issue more broadly. Hess also suggests that employees' viewpoints vary according to gender, age, upbringing, and cultural differences.

Okay, now go back and reread the common causes of conflict in the workplace. Try to find one answer to resolve them all. Did you come up with *communication* as your answer? It is the resolution to the majority of these conflicts. Poor communication is the number one topic raised by employees in questionnaires conducted in the workplace. Everyone wants to be valued. Showing a genuine interest in your employees fosters a positive workplace with open communication.

Not all conflict is bad—some is positive. But all conflict has a past, present, and a future, and resolving conflicts effectively requires that all three are dealt with.
Photo courtesy of the author.

Conflict Management

We might wrongly assume that all conflict is bad for individuals and the organization. This is simply not so—some conflict is not only natural but also productive, experts say. Learning how to manage it, however, does not come naturally.[5] Every relationship and every conflict has a past, present, and future, and resolving conflicts effectively requires that we deal with all three.[6]

conflict management
The application of strategies to settle opposing ideas/goals.

Conflict management is the application of strategies to settle opposing ideas, goals, and/or objectives in a positive manner. Managers are often put in the middle of conflicts. They must know how to manage themselves, as well as the situation, positively and delicately. Managers must be able to separate their own emotions and feelings from the situation at hand. They need to be able to act, not react! There are many ways to manage conflict. For the purpose of this chapter, we will use a five-step approach to conflict management, which is illustrated in Figure 11.2.

✳ ANALYZE THE CONFLICT

The first step is to *analyze* what is at the center of the conflict. To do this the supervisors need to ask themselves questions, as well as those involved in the conflict. Here are a few questions to ask:

- Who is involved?
- How did the conflict arise?

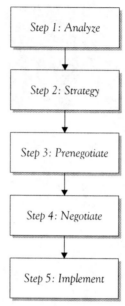

FIGURE 11.2: Five-step conflict management process.

- Can a positive spin be put on the situation?
- Are there any secondary issues?
- Have positions been taken?
- Is negotiation plausible?
- Is there a way to serve all interests at hand?
- Are there external constraints/influences?
- Is there a previous history of the conflict?

After the main source is identified and the source of the conflict is understood, it is helpful to brainstorm and write thoughts and ideas of resolution on paper.

❋ DETERMINE THE STRATEGY TO RESOLVE THE CONFLICT

The second step to managing conflict is to determine the type of *strategy* that will be used to resolve the conflict. Some examples of commonly used resolution strategies are collaboration, compromise, competition, accommodation, and avoidance.

Collaboration results most often when concerns for others are of high importance. This type of strategy results in a win/win outcome. Both parties cooperate with each other and try to understand the other parties' concerns, while also expressing their own. The parties both put forth a mutual effort and come to a solution that is completely satisfactory for both parties.

Compromise results from high concern for one's own interest or one's own group interest accompanied by moderate to high interest for the other parties involved. Both

collaboration
Strategy in which concern for others is of high importance and both parties try to cooperate with each other to come to a solution that is completely satisfying for both parties.

compromise
Concern for both one's own and the other parties' ideas or position—finding ways of agreeing (give and take) positions.

parties try to resolve the conflict by finding a resolution that partially satisfies both of them, but completely satisfies neither. This type of strategy either produces a win/win or lose/lose outcome, depending on if the solution chosen is the most effective. This varies, depending on the situation at hand.

Competition results when there is a high concern for one's own interest or one's own group. The outcome could vary from win/lose to lose/win, depending on who prevails. This strategy is not ideal, as it may cause increasing conflict. The losing party might try to even the score.

Accommodation is the result of low concern for your own interests or the interest of your group, which produces a lose/win outcome. The opposing party is allowed to satisfy their interest, while one's own interests are neglected.

Avoidance is exactly what it sounds like. The conflict is avoided by both parties and neither party takes action to resolve it. This produces a lose/lose outcome. In the hospitality industry, this strategy is generally useless because employees work in close quarters. This makes it virtually impossible to avoid each other.

✳ BEGIN PRENEGOTIATIONS

The third step to managing conflict is to start *prenegotiations*. This is a key part of the conflict management process. Being effective at negotiating is a fundamental skill for supervisors. During this step, there are several substeps. Initially, both of the parties involved in the conflict should be given the opportunity to come forth and offer a negotiation. If neither party is willing to come forth, then an outsider, in this case the leader, must step in.

Next, the situation should be *reassessed*. The key parties involved in the conflict must be willing to cooperate with each other in the resolution process. The issues should be laid out on the table. From here, what is negotiable, as well as what is not negotiable, must be determined. The parties involved should agree on what information is significantly related to the conflict, as well as how communication and decision making will take place. All of this should be completed before moving on to the fourth step.

✳ NEGOTIATE A SOLUTION TO THE CONFLICT

The fourth step to managing conflict is to begin the *negotiation* phase. All parties must be able to express their concerns and interests; they must also be willing to listen to each other. As a manager, you will be considered the neutral third party. This means that you should not judge or favor either of the parties' ideas or suggested options. You are there to facilitate a healthy discussion and keep the parties focused on the cause of conflict and how it is to be resolved (not to assign blame to a particular party).

The parties involved in conflict should make a list of options that might help resolve the conflict, as well as satisfy their interests. After the lists of possible solutions are completed, the options should be discussed and evaluated. Which option would best resolve the conflict and satisfy the most interests should be determined together. A commitment ought to be made to carry out the agreements, and both parties must feel assured that the other will carry out their part.

---

competition
When there is high concern for one's own interest—two different individuals/groups become rivals.

accommodation
Strategy in which concern for your own interests is of low importance, resulting in an outcome whereby the opposing party is allowed to satisfy its interests while one's own interests are neglected.

avoidance
Strategy in which conflict is avoided by both sides, resulting in a lose/lose outcome where problems continue to remain unresolved.

PROFILE Shirley Ruckl

Director of Human Resources, Longboat Key Club, Sarasota, Florida

Courtesy of Shirley Ruckl.

I have been with the Longboat Key Club & Resort (LBKCR) as director of human resources for three years, where I direct the human resource functions for the club and resort for 550 associates. Originally from Chicago, I attended Columbia College–Chicago for Business Management/minor in Advertising Art. I relocated to Orlando in 1995 and started my career in HR as a recruiter at the Walt Disney World Dolphin Resort and then joined Universal Studios Florida as a recruiting manager, where I helped open Citywalk—the entertainment complex for Universal. Prior to coming to the LBKCR, I worked for Wyndham International for five years. I was hired as a recruiting manager, but after six months I was promoted to assistant director of HR, and then director of human resources for an 1,100-room convention resort.

Conflict management is a very important topic because if it is handled in a professional manner, it can be a win–win for both parties to improve their working relationship. I'm sure you realize that some conflict is positive, but the conflict we mostly hear about is conflict that challenges both HR professionals and hospitality leaders alike. The objective of conflict management is to resolve workplace challenges by addressing the behavior, and by being solution-focused on changing the behavior.

I work with our team leaders and coach them to promptly sit down with the associate to discuss the situation in a quiet, neutral setting. A key to successfully coaching through conflict is remembering to always leave the associate's pride intact—regardless of the situation. Depending on the severity of the issue, the team leader and/or human resources director can talk with the individual(s) concerned. The goal is to communicate the challenge(s) effectively and candidly, and agree on a solution to correct the behavior moving forward.

When conflicts are dealt with immediately and professionally, there is a very good chance of the situation working out well for both the company and the individuals concerned. Remember to keep accurate documentation, and only discuss on a need-to-know basis.

✳ IMPLEMENT THE NEGOTIATED SOLUTION

The final step is for the parties to *implement* the negotiations made. As a supervisor, you need to support the resolution and continue to communicate. It is also beneficial to continue monitoring the situation in order to be certain that the agreement is in fact being carried out.

Conflict management is a very important human resources topic, because if it is handled in a professional manor it can be a win–win for both parties to improve their working relationship. I'm sure you realize that some conflict is positive, but the conflict we mostly hear about is conflict that challenges both HR professionals and hospitality leaders alike. I work with our team leaders and suggest that they immediately sit down to discuss the situation and hopefully clear the air. If it is a team issue, then the whole team needs to sit and address the situation. If it is an individual who is not carrying his or her weight, then escort the person to a neutral, quiet place where, depending on the severity of the issue, the team leader and/or human resource director can talk with the individual concerned—

at first alone, and then with supervisors or others with whom the person has a conflict. The goal is to state the differences, agree on what the differences are, and then find ways to resolve them.

When conflicts are dealt with immediately and professionally, there is a very good chance of the situation working out well for both the company and the individuals concerned. Remember to keep records and only discuss on a need-to-know basis.

Check Your Knowledge

1. Briefly list the five steps of conflict management.
2. What do resolution strategies *collaboration, compromise, competition, accommodation,* and *avoidance* each result from?

Conflict Resolution

Handling conflict in the workplace can be a challenging task. As a manager, you should always first keep the best interest of your company in mind, as detailed in Herb Kindler's book *Conflict Management Resolving Disagreements in the Workplace,* and Robert Friedman's article: "Knock Out On-the-Job Conflicts, Complaints with Six Simple Steps," published in *Nation's Restaurant News.* They discuss the following guiding principles for handling conflict.

✳ PRINCIPLES FOR HANDLING CONFLICT[7]

First of the guiding principles is to *preserve dignity and respect.* This means preserving the dignity and respect of all parties involved in the conflict, including yourself. The focus should stay on resolving the conflict, not on the individual characteristics of the parties involved. As a manager, you should never talk down to an employee, especially during a conflict; this could result in them feeling like they are being attacked. If you make everyone feel respected, this will lower defenses and help the process of resolution.

Second, listen with empathy and be fully present and identify the issues.[8] As you listen, try to determine what issues created the conflict. In some cases, the real issues may be beneath the surface. The flashpoint of a festering disagreement might ignite and result in serious consequences. For example, some employees in a restaurant might be hoarding cutlery; when it is discovered that there is a shortage of spoons and another employee finds out where they are being hidden, a fight breaks out.

Don't daydream while an employee is trying to voice an opinion. Listen carefully to everyone involved and withhold any judgments until everyone has had a chance to speak. Try to see from each differing perspective, put yourself in each of the individual's shoes. Give everyone a chance to speak with you on a one-on-one basis. Give your full attention and make direct eye contact. Most important, make sure that your employees feel heard. There is nothing worse than being left with the feeling that your opinion (or words) do not matter.

Third is to *find common ground without forcing change.* Agree on what the problem issues are. Recite for the participants what you perceive to be the issues and ask them to agree with you or correct you. Appealing as it might seem, as a manager it is important to not try to force others into changing. People don't change for others, they change for themselves. They change only when they believe that they will benefit from the change. Therefore, throwing weight around as a superior will result in getting nowhere. It is also important for your employees to trust and respect you. If they believe that you are always looking out for their best interest, they are more likely to believe in you, and look up to you as their mentor.

Fourth is to *discuss solutions*: The parties involved have some idea of how they want the situation to be solved—ask them for suggestions.

Fifth is to *honor diversity, including your own perspective*. According to *Webster's Dictionary*, **diversity** is defined as a difference, variety, or unlikeness.[9] To **diversify** is to give variety to something; to engage in varied operations; to distribute over a wide range of types or classes. During this step, it is important to honor diversity, as well as to foster diversification.

Sixth is to *agree on the solutions and follow up*. Discuss solutions with each participant until there is agreement on the issues. Keep detailed notes or have a recorder. Then, once agreement has been reached, document it and have the participants sign it. Then follow up to see if the agreement holds or needs further discussion. Figure 11.3 shows commonly used resolution strategies.

Okay, so let's say everyone has differing viewpoints on a certain issue. This can lead to a creative way of searching for the right resolution, or it can result in feelings of isolation. All too often, the search for a resolution during a conflict is a hasty one. When we rush, we rush others into an agreement.

We don't let them have time to understand what really matters to them, or come to an independent viewpoint from that of the group, a phenomenon known as *groupthink*. Let's say a group has to make a decision and you are the only person who holds a different viewpoint. If others are quickly (and perhaps enthusiastically) getting behind the prevailing idea, you will probably end up conforming to the group and not speaking your opinion in order to avoid conflict. What you should do, of course, is to speak out and let your voice be heard.

diversity
Differences, variety, characteristics that are not alike.

diversify
Provide variety; distribute assets, jobs, or other things over a wide range of types or classes.

groupthink
Phenomenon in which groups minimize conflict, resulting in a decision that excludes contrary opinions. Group members cheerlead what seems to be the prevailing idea, excluding critical evaluation.

Strategy	Results from	Results in
Collaboration	High concern for others.	Win/win
Competition	High concern for one's own interest.	Win/lose or lose/win
Compromise	High concern for one's own interests and moderate to high interest for the other parties.	Win/win or lose/lose
Accommodation	Low concern for one's own interests	Lose/win
Avoidance	Conflict is avoided by both parties.	Lose/lose

FIGURE 11.3: Commonly used conflict resolution strategies

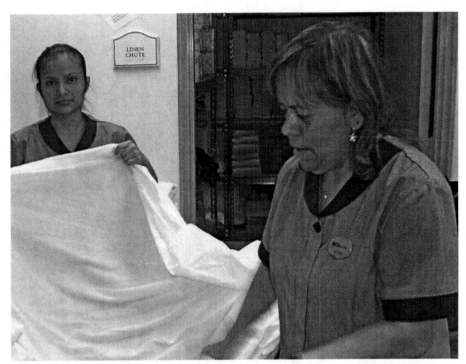

Having an in-house alternative dispute resolution process can save lots of problems and money.
Photo courtesy of the author.

We all know the cost of a lawsuit is very high, but in the case of employment litigation, many companies find that the cost of defending themselves against the charges of unfair employment practice is extremely high, often exceeding the amount of the employee's claim of damages. Cases for unfair employment practices may drag on for years, with increased legal expenses. So it makes sense to have an in-house dispute resolution process.[10]

✳ ALTERNATIVE DISPUTE RESOLUTION

Sometimes conflicts cannot be resolved within an organization, and the dispute might escalate to the point that it seems inevitable that the organization or an individual will be sued. There is an intermediary step that can be taken before that happens. *Alternative dispute resolution (ADR)* is a term for problem-solving and grievance-resolution approaches to address employee relations and disputes outside the courtroom. The purpose of ADR is to provide employers and employees with a fair and private forum to settle workplace disputes.[11] With ADR, a process is in place to offer the following options:[12]

Open-Door Policy
Employees have the opportunity to meet with managers to discuss issues.

alternative dispute resolution (ADR)
Problem solving and grievance resolution approaches to address disputes.

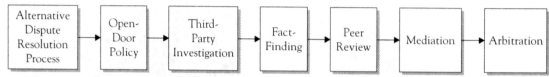

FIGURE 11.4:   **Alternative dispute resolution process.**

Third-Party Investigations

A neutral third-party, from inside or outside the organization, confidently investigates complaints and proposes resolutions.

Fact-Finding

A neutral third-party person or team from outside the organization examines the facts of the complaint and presents them in a report.

Peer Review

A panel of employees, or employees and managers, works together to resolve the employee complaints.

Mediation

Through a voluntary and confidential process, a neutral third-party facilitator trained in mediation techniques negotiates a mutually acceptable settlement. The steps in the process are gathering information, framing the issues, developing options, negotiating, and formalizing agreements. Participants in the mediation process create their own solutions, and settlements are not binding.

Arbitration

Disputes are settled by an arbitrator and may be either binding or nonbinding, according to the wishes of the participants. An arbitrator or panel of arbitrators hears both sides of an issue and then makes a determination.

As Nancy Lockwood, a human resource content specialist with the Society of Human Resources Management, suggests, the advantages of ADR are that the total cost is less than traditional means of resolving workplace disputes, legal costs are contained, the time spent on investigations is reduced and workplace productivity is not compromised. Figure 11.4 shows the steps in an ADR process.

Workplace Violence

Workplace violence is any act of physical violence, harassment, intimidation, or other threatening behavior happening at the workplace. The causes of workplace violence can be the result of a disciplinary measure or an employee bringing a domestic problem to work or a confrontation between two or more employees for any reason.

Workplace violence has become more problematic in recent years. The implications for HR professionals and managers are that they need to be more vigilant in

workplace violence
Any act of physical violence, harassment, intimidation, or other threatening behavior that occurs at the workplace.

creating a positive, safe, and secure workplace environment. We can see how several elements of HR come together: avoiding negligent hiring, creating a positive work environment, improving employee relations, leading, providing an open and inclusive culture. Management must be trained to spot potentially troubled employees, and the company should have a good employee assistance program.

The possibility of workplace violence can be significantly reduced by taking a few preventive measures: increased security by using employee name badges; reducing the number of entrances and exits to one or two; video surveillance cameras; entrances to have metal detectors and guest and employee security checks as hotels in Asia do; a complete background check on all employees; noting and reporting any use of threats, physical actions, frustrations, or intimidation.

A company might have a problem if it decides not to employ someone because the person has a criminal record. Several state and federal laws (Title VII of the Civil rights Act) restrict employers from making employment decisions based on arrest records, since doing so might unfairly discriminate against minority groups. Obviously, however, if an applicant stole money and was arrested and found guilty, you would not employ that person in a position that has access to money.

Spotting a potentially violent person is not easy, so prevention by careful background checks prior to employment is essential. Failure to do proper background checks can open up employers to lawsuits related to negligent hiring if an incident of workplace violence takes place (see Chapter 6). Supervisors are on the front line and can share with their employees information on employee assistance programs or refer all employees to the human resource office for further assistance. Sometimes an employee with a potential for violence displays some tendencies such as being irritable or irrational, constantly complaining, or having numerous conflicts with guests or other employees. Other tendencies include substance abuse, strong interest in violence, over-aggressiveness, problems with authority, and other inappropriate behavior.

Steps to be taken before and if violence happens are:

1. Make sure all employees know how to contact their supervisor, manager, security, and police.
2. Take all threats seriously and ensure all employees have received training on how to handle a violent situation.
3. Depending on the severity of the situation, employees need to remove themselves from harm's way and contact their supervisor/manager and call security or the police.
4. Do a threat assessment to determine the severity of the situation and have any suspect removed from the premises.
5. Ensure all employees know the emergency lanes and procedures to evacuate the building.

Following a violent incident, employees experience three stages of "crisis reactions" to varying degrees:

Stage one. In this stage, the employee experiences emotional reactions characterized by shock, disbelief, denial, or numbness. Physically, the employee experiences shock or a fight-or-flight survival reaction in which the heart rate increases, perceptual senses become heightened or distorted, and adrenaline levels increase to meet a real or perceived threat.

Stage two. This is the "impact" stage where the employee feels a variety of intense emotion, including anger, rage, fear, terror, grief, sorrow, confusion, helplessness, guilt, depression, or withdrawal. This stage may last a few days, a few weeks, or a few months.

Stage three. This is the "reconciliation stage" in which the employee tries to make sense out of the event, understand its impact, and through trial and error, reach closure of the event so it does not interfere with his or her ability to function and grow. This stage is sometimes a long-term process.

Although it is difficult to predict how an incident will affect a given individual, several factors influence the intensity of trauma. These factors include the duration of the event, the amount of terror or horror the victim experienced, the sense of personal control (or lack thereof) the employee had during the incident, and the amount of injury or loss the victim experienced (i.e., loss of property, self-esteem, physical well-being, etc.). Other variables include the person's previous victimization experiences, recent losses such as the death of a family member, and other intense stresses.[13]

Conflict Prevention

Just think of some of the recent outcomes of lawsuits. Millions of dollars would have been saved by companies if they had proper conflict prevention in place. In 2007, a jury awarded $11.6 million in punitive damages against the New York Knicks for sexual harassment and retaliatory discharge.[14] In March 2010, a McDonald's franchise owner paid $90,000 to settle a federal discrimination lawsuit on behalf of a worker with an intellectual disability. The worker was repeatedly harassed by supervisors, managers, and coworkers because of his disability, and at one point was threatened by a coworker with a box cutter.[15]

Conflict is bound to arise in any atmosphere that requires *interdependency* between people and work. Preventing it is substantially more effective than having to undo it! What can be done to prevent such conflict from arising? Well, the conflict itself is not really the root of the problem. The root is a *lack of direct, properly handled conflict*. As already mentioned, communication is key in conflict management; it can also be thought of as the key to conflict prevention.

Be prepared to handle conflict. It is inevitable, and you should not be surprised when one comes your way. By preparing and thinking ahead of situations, you might be able to foresee a conflict before it happens. Conflicts arise in any situation that involves a decision being made that affects other people. If you think one might be brewing, talk to each of the individual parties. This might mean taking time out and putting other things that need to be done on the back burner, but if it results in the conflict being diffused, it will be well worth it in the long run and you will not have to deal with the impact the conflict would have had on the overall work environment.

As a manager, you should *pay close attention* to your employees. By paying attention, you might be able to diffuse a conflict before it actually takes place. If you do not pay close attention, you'll probably never see that a conflict exists until your employees are infuriated with each other; at this point, it's too late to diffuse it before it begins. Now you must manage it!

After becoming an active, responsive, and empathetic listener and learning to speak and act with commitment and integrity, the next challenge in resolving conflict is to work through the powerful, intense, negative emotions that keep you from listening with an open heart and mind.[16]

Prevent conflict by *listening actively*. The easier you are to talk to, the more likely employees will come to you with their problems. Always take the time to see the conflict from every perspective. Never side with one person before hearing everyone's side of the story. This is the worst thing a supervisor could ever do. Remember, there are always three stories; your story, my story, and the actual story!

If it seems like a situation may lead to a conflict, you should *speak up* before the situation gets out of hand. Don't just stand on the sideline listening; diffuse the situation. Express concern before circumstances become intolerable. This may lead to the parties stepping back and reassessing the situation.

Always remember to *keep a sense of humor*. Once again, the more approachable you are, the more likely you will hear about or notice a problem before it begins. So remember, lighten up! Everyone in the organization will benefit from the implementation of these conflict prevention techniques. Conflict in the workplace has many negative effects; dealing with it early can prevent these effects from escalating and possibly creating more conflict. In many organizations, conflict is unidentified and never dealt with, and these organizations suffer. Identification and resolution result in success!

Check Your Knowledge

1. What is groupthink?
2. Describe three ways of preventing conflict.

KEY POINTS

1. Conflict happens, because we are human. Conflict is bound to arise in any atmosphere that requires interdependency between people and work.
2. As a supervisor, the conflict is not the real issue. How the conflict is dealt with is.
3. A conflict is a disagreement resulting from individuals or groups that differ in opinions, attitudes, beliefs, needs, values, or perceptions.
4. The main ingredients or sources of conflict include desires, needs, perceptions, power, values, and feelings.
5. Communication is the key to resolving and preventing most workplace conflicts.
6. Conflict management is application of strategies to settle opposing ideas, goals, and/or objectives in a positive manner.
7. The first step in conflict management is to analyze what is at the center of the conflict.
8. The second step to managing conflict is to determine the strategy to resolve the conflict; common strategies are collaboration, compromise, competition, accommodation, or avoidance.
9. The third step to managing conflict is prenegotiation.

10. The fourth step to managing conflict is to negotiate.

11. The fifth step to managing conflict is to implement the negotiations agreed on.

12. There are six guiding principles for handling conflict.

13. Supervisors are on the front line in preventing or identifying workplace violence.

14. Preventing conflict is substantially more effective than having to manage it after the fact.

15. Identification and resolution of conflict result in success.

KEY TERMS

Accommodation

Alternative dispute
  resolution (ADR)

Anger

Avoidance

Collaboration

Competition

Compromise

Conflict

Conflict management

Desires

Diversify

Diversity

Feelings

Groupthink

Needs

Perceptions

Power

Values

Workplace violence

REVIEW QUESTIONS

Answer each of the questions in complete sentences. Read each question carefully and make sure you answer all parts of the question. Organize your answer using more than one paragraph when appropriate.

1. What is conflict?

2. How is conflict caused?

3. How can employers manage conflict?

4. How can conflicts be resolved?

5. Can conflicts be prevented?

ACTIVITIES AND APPLICATIONS

1. Discussion Questions

- Can workplace violence be avoided? If so, how?
- Is there good conflict? If so, what?
- As an employee, what should you do if you notice another employee acting in a weird manner?

2. Group Activity: Workplace Violence

Develop a plan and a policy for the prevention of workplace violence at a hospitality company.

3. **Group Activity: Conflict Management**

Do a quick survey of your classmates to find out what their employers are doing in the area of conflict management. Report on your findings and compare them with those in the text.

4. **Case Study: Conflict Management**

At Cool, the new restaurant in town, Jim is the closing manager. He observes two of the kitchen staff having a loud verbal interaction with two of the servers. Stepping in to stop the argument, he tells them all to report to the office after their shift. When the four employees arrive, they are still arguing. Jim says, "OK, sit down and write down exactly what happened and how it can be fixed." One hour later, all four of them had an account of the incident and some suggestions for dealing with the problem.

Case Study Questions

1. Is this a good approach to conflict management? Give reasons.
2. What should Jim do next?
3. Do you think the situation can be resolved in this manner?

WEB ACTIVITY

- Go to the following website: www.abetterworkplace.com/conflicts.html.
- Answer the following questions:
  1. Go to the article "Waging Peace in the Workplace." How does the article say that ADR applies in the workplace?
  2. Go to the article "Resources for Keeping the Peace." Define negotiation and mediation.
  3. Go to the article "When to Engage, When Not to Engage." According to this article, describe when *not* to engage.

RELATED WEBSITES

Federal Mediation and Conciliation Service—offers mediation dispute resolution, and conflict management services	www.fmcs.gov
National Labor Relations Board—administers the law governing relations between unions and employers in the private sector	www.nlrb.gov
National Mediation Board—a resource for alternative dispute resolution services including training	www.nmb.gov
U.S. Equal Employment Opportunity Commission Mediation Program	www.eeoc.gov
American Arbitration Association—offers several arbitration services	www.adr.org
Association for Conflict Resolution—offers conflict resolution services	www.acrnet.org

ENDNOTES

1. Craig Runde and Tim Flanagan, *Becoming a Conflict Competent Leader: How You and Your Organization Can Manage Conflict Effectively* (San Francisco: Jossey-Boss [a John Wiley & Sons Imprint], 2007), p. 7.
2. *Merriam Webster Dictionary: Home and Office Edition*, (Springfield, MA: 1955), pp. 20,110.
3. Anita Naves, *Power Principles for Peaceful Living* (Bloomington, IN: Author House, 2006), p. 19.
4. Vicki Hess, "Conflict Management Contributes to Communication," Society for Human Resource Management: Workplace Diversity Library—Employment Issues. January 2007.
5. Ibid.
6. Morton Deutsch, Peter Coleman, and Eric Marcus, *The Handbook of Conflict Resolution: Theory and Practice* (San Francisco: Jossey-Boss [a John Wiley & Sons Imprint], 2006), p. 161.
7. This section was adapted from: Herb Kindler, *Conflict Management: Resolving Disagreements in the Workplace* (Boston: Thomson, 2006), pp. 3–4.
8. Robert Friedman, "Knock Out On-the-Job Conflicts, Complaints with Six Simple Steps," *Nation's Restaurant News*, vol. 40, no. 37 (September 11, 2006), p. 30.
9. *Webster's*, s.v. diversity.
10. Stephen Barth, "Why In-house Dispute Resolution Makes Sense," *Lodging Hospitality*, vol. 58, no. 7 (May 15, 2002), p. 19.
11. Nancy R. Lockwood, SPHR, "Alternative Dispute Resolution," *Society for Human Resource Management*, SHRM Research, February 2004.
12. Ibid.
13. USDA, "The USDA Handbook on Workplace Violence Preventions and Response" (December 1998), www.usda.gov/news/pubs/violence/wpv.htm. Retrieved on March 28, 2011.
14. Allen Smith, "Browne Sanders Scores Big in Harassment Lawsuit Against Knicks," *Society for Human Resource Management Workplace Law Library—Employee Relations*, October 5, 2007.
15. U.S. Equal Employment Opportunity Commission, "McDonald's Franchise to Pay $90,000 to Settle EEOC Disability Discrimination Lawsuit," Press release March 2, 2010. eeoc.gov/eeoc/newsroom/release/3-2-10.cfm. Retrieved April 28, 2011.
16. Adapted from: Kenneth Cloke and Joan Goldsmith, *Resolving Conflicts at Work* (San Francisco: Jossey-Boss [a John Wiley & Sons Imprint], 2005), p. 74.

Chapter 13

Decision Making and Control

Overview

Making decisions is a built-in requirement of a supervisor's job. When associates run into problems, they bring them to you and you decide what they should do. When crises arise—equipment breakdowns, supplies that don't arrive, people calling in sick or hurting themselves or fighting or walking off the job—you decide what should be done. When employees can't or won't do their jobs as they should, you decide whether to retrain them, motivate them, discipline them, or fire them.

When things are not going well in your department, you are the one who decides what to do about it. Sometimes your entire day consists of one decision after another, and it seems to you that there is no time left to get any work done.

For a supervisor in this fast-paced, time-pressured industry, decision making is your work, like it or not. It is not you but the people you supervise who make the products or deliver the services. You plan their work, hire and fire them, solve their problems, settle their arguments, grant or deny requests, deal with the unexpected, troubleshoot, and—by making countless small decisions you may not even think of as decisions—you see that the work gets done. How well the work gets done depends a great deal on how good your decisions are.

In this chapter, we explore the kinds of down-to-earth decision making that supervisors in the hospitality industry are faced with day by day. After completion of this chapter you should be able to:

- **Identify the three essential elements of a managerial decision, and explain how they help to clarify the decision-making process.**
- **List and describe common approaches to decision making.**

423

■ **Describe the steps to making good decisions and how to apply them.**

■ **Explain the relationship between problem solving and decision making, and apply decision-making techniques in solving problems.**

■ **Discuss the pros and cons of participative problem solving and state an example of when it would be appropriate to use.**

■ **List guidelines for approaching various kinds of people problems.**

■ **Build good decision-making skills.**

■ **List ways hospitality supervisors control the work being done.**

Decision Making

Human beings are constantly making decisions of one sort or another as they go about their daily lives. How do they do this, and what is special about a supervisor's decisions?

✳ ELEMENTS IN A MANAGERIAL DECISION

decision

A choice among alternative courses of action directed toward a specific purpose.

Human resources and management decisions derive from the role and responsibility of being a manager. A manager's *decision* should be a choice among alternative courses of action directed toward a specific purpose. There are three key phrases in this definition that describe three essential elements in the decision-making process:

1. The first phrase is a *choice among alternatives*. If there is no alternative, if there is only one way to go, there is no decision to make: You do the only thing you can. Choice is the primary essential in decision making. You deliberately choose one course of action over others. You are not swept along by events or habit or the influence of others; you don't just go with the flow. You are making it happen, not just letting it happen.
2. The second essential of a managerial decision is a *specific purpose*. The decision has a goal or objective: to solve a specific problem, to accomplish a specific result. Like a performance-based objective, a decision has a *what* and a *how*. The specific purpose is the what.
3. The third essential is a *course of action*. The decision is to do something or have something done in a particular way. This is the *how*. Making a decision requires seeing that the decision is carried out.

A good decision is one in which the course of action chosen meets the objective in the best possible way—usually, the one with the least risk and the most benefit to the enterprise.

A manager and a supervisor considering decision alternatives.
Photo courtesy of the author.

✳ APPROACHES TO DECISION MAKING

Different people approach decision making in different ways. One way is to go deliberately through a series of logical steps based on the scientific method. You formulate your objectives and rank them, gather all the relevant facts, examine and weigh all the alternative courses of action and their consequences, and choose the one that best meets the objectives.

Management scientists recommend this *logical approach to decision making* (with variations). It takes time, something busy hospitality supervisors do not have, and it is probably foreign to their habits: Most people in operations tend to be doers rather than deliberators. It is better suited to weighty top management problems than to the day-in, day-out decisions of hotel and foodservice supervisors. Nevertheless, it can be adapted for solving their important problems, as we shall see.

At the opposite extreme is the *intuitive approach to decision making*: the hunch, the gut reaction, the decision that *feels* right. People who take this approach to decisions tend to be creative, intelligent people with strong egos and high aspirations. They draw on life experience to give them insight into what would work in another situation. Some entrepreneurs are like this: They may be driving around and suddenly they will say, "There's a perfect location for a restaurant," and they buy it, build a restaurant, and make it a big success.

But this approach does not work for everybody; much of the time it does not work for the people who practice it. When it does, there is bound to be a lot of knowledge, experience, and subconscious reasoning behind the hunches and the gut reactions.

logical approach to decision making
Going deliberately through a series of logical steps based on the scientific method.

intuitive approach to decision making
Acting on a hunch or gut feeling based on life experience to make a decision.

Most people would do about as well flipping a coin: You have a 50 percent chance of being right.

Your biases, habits, preconceptions, preferences, and self-interest are all at work right along with your knowledge, experience, and subconscious reasoning. It is almost impossible to see things clearly in a flash, even with extensive background and experience.

Many people have no particular approach to decision making. Some are *indecisive* and afraid of it: They worry a lot, procrastinate, ask other people's advice, and never quite come to the point of making up their minds. Others make *impulsive,* off-the-cuff decisions based on whim or the mood of the moment rather than on facts or even intuition.

Both the ***indecisive*** and ***impulsive approaches to decision making*** have trouble distinguishing important from unimportant decisions, and they confuse and frustrate their superiors and the people they supervise. Both types have a poor batting average in making good decisions and tend to be plagued with problems and frustrations.

indecisive approach to decision making
Fearing to make decisions and thus procrastinating or deferring the decision making to someone else.

impulsive approach to decision making
Making off-the-cuff decisions based on a whim.

✳ RATIONAL VERSUS EMOTIONAL DECISION MAKING

On occasion, all decision makers use too much emotion in making a decision. For example, consider a couple who spent a fortune in fancy decor when opening up a new restaurant. The rational part of decision making would question the amount being spent because it does not make sense if the restaurant cannot pay back the amount spent preopening. As managers it is important to weigh the consequences of our actions before we react purely on emotion. In the hospitality field, managers need to learn how to approach decision making using both emotion and rationality.

✳ KINDS OF DECISIONS

The decisions a hospitality supervisor is called on to make range from deciding how many gallons of cleaning compound to buy, up to solving problems that are affecting production, people, and profit. Some decisions are easy to make; others are more difficult.

Routine decisions are easier: what supplies to order and whether to take advantage of special prices; number of portions to prepare; weekly schedule assignments; assigning rooms to be made up; granting or denying employee requests for time off or schedule changes; what time to schedule an interview; whether to confirm a reservation in writing or by telephone; and number of banquet servers to bring in for a special event, for instance. All these decisions are simple to make because you have the historical data or the know-how on which to base your decision.

Sometimes you have a set routine or formula for finding answers to recurring decisions, and if there is nothing new to affect today's decision, you just follow the routine of what has been done before and you don't have anything to decide. This is really a standard operating procedure that may have been established by usage or may be spelled out in your policy and procedures manual.

Many decisions are less clear-cut and more complicated. They may affect many people. There may be many factors to consider. The wrong decision may have serious consequences. Among such decisions are hiring and firing, delegating, and making changes in the work environment or in the work itself, such as introducing a new menu, redecorating a dining room, and changing work procedures. Such decisions require time and thought.

Complicated time-pressure decisions arise when emergencies occur: from equipment breakdowns to accidents, fights, people not showing up, and food that does not meet your quality standards. Even if you have established routines for meeting emergencies, you must still make critical decisions, and one decision may require a whole string of other decisions to adjust to new circumstances.

If, for example, you pull a busperson off the floor to substitute for an injured kitchen worker, you have to provide for the busing, and when you ask servers to bus their own tables, you know that guest service will be affected and you have to handle that situation. A single incident thus demands one split-second decision after another.

This kind of decision making requires a clear grasp of what is going on plus quick thinking and quick action: **decisiveness**. These are qualities that you develop on the job. You develop them by knowing your operation and your people well, by watching your superiors handle emergencies and analyzing what they do, and by building your own self-confidence and skill as you make decisions on everyday problems.

decisiveness
The ability to reach a firm conclusion.

Perhaps the most difficult decisions are those necessary to resolve problem situations. In a sense, all decision making is problem solving. But in some situations you cannot choose an appropriate course of action because you do not know what is causing the problem. For example, you discover that guest complaints about room service have increased during the last few weeks, but you do not know why.

The problem you are aware of (guest complaints) is really a symptom of a deeper problem, and you cannot choose a course of action until you know what that problem is and what is causing it. You need a quick study to isolate the problem: Is it in order taking, preparation, or delivery where the system or procedure has failed? This is a far more complicated decision than, for example, deciding what to do about a stopped-up drain.

Some of the decisions that come up in your job are not yours to make. Sometimes the decision is made for you by company policy, such as prescribed penalties for absenteeism or improper food portioning or smoking on the job. In such instances, the only thing you decide is whether the incident fits the policy specifications—was this the second or third time it happened, and does it deserve the penalty if the clock was fast and she thought it was closing time when she stepped outside to light up her cigarette?

You may have other problems that you do not have the authority to do anything about. If you supervise the dining room and your servers complain about one of the cooks, you do not have authority to discipline that cook. You can work with the head cook, who is on the same level you are, to resolve the problem. If this fails, you can send the problem up through channels to the food and beverage director. But you cannot give orders anywhere but in your own department. It is important never to make decisions or take action where you do not have authority and responsibility.

Since time is probably your biggest problem, it is essential to recognize which decisions are important and which are unimportant, which decisions you must make now and which can wait. As a rule of thumb, unimportant decisions are those that have little effect on the work or on people: Nothing serious will happen if you make the wrong choice.

Should you put tonight's specials on menu fliers or let the servers describe them when they take orders? What kind of centerpiece should you use on the chamber of commerce lunch table? What color paper should you have the new guest checks printed on? Such decisions are worth little more than a few seconds' thought: What is the problem? Who is involved? What are your choices? Is there a clear choice?

If there is no clear choice, make one anyway and move on. Getting hung up on unimportant decisions can be a disaster. It impedes the work, your boss and your people lose confidence in you, and you lose your own perspective, your conceptual grasp of your job.

The opposite mistake—giving too little time to an important decision—can also have serious consequences. An important decision is one that has a pronounced impact on the work or the employees, such as a change in policy or procedures, what to do about a drop in productivity, or how to deal with friction between workers. In such situations the most serious mistake is not taking the time needed to consider the decision carefully. The wrong decision is hard to undo. It may cause serious consequences or increase the problem you are trying to solve.

In another interesting decision-making situation a restaurant owner might seriously consider forming an advisory board because it can enhance both the individual and collective performances of the leadership team. Over time, the board will potentially help perform four key functions:[1]

1. Develop and implement a strategic plan.
2. Steer clear of potential "avoidable" problems.
3. Create optimal solutions to issues and challenges as they arise.
4. Hold yourself accountable over time.

An advisory board does not replace the owner's primary role of leadership; rather, it is a mechanism to enhance results.

How to Make Good Decisions[2]

When making decisions, six steps will lead to improved decision-making capabilities (see Figure 13.1). The following six steps are a simple version of the logical approach. The procedure is elastic and can be expanded or shortened to fit circumstances:

1. Define the problem and set objectives. (What do you want to happen?)
2. Analyze the problem: get the facts: the relevant who, what, when, where, how, why.
3. Develop alternative solutions.
4. Decide on the best solution.
5. Convert the decision into action.
6. Follow up.

When you are out there on the job coping with an emergency, think about taking these steps. But chances are that you actually will without thinking, and this is as it should be. Suppose that the dishwasher breaks down suddenly at noon on one of the busiest days in the year. You don't think about defining the problem and the objective; they define themselves: you need enough plates, silverware, and glasses to get the food out to customers until you can get the machine fixed.

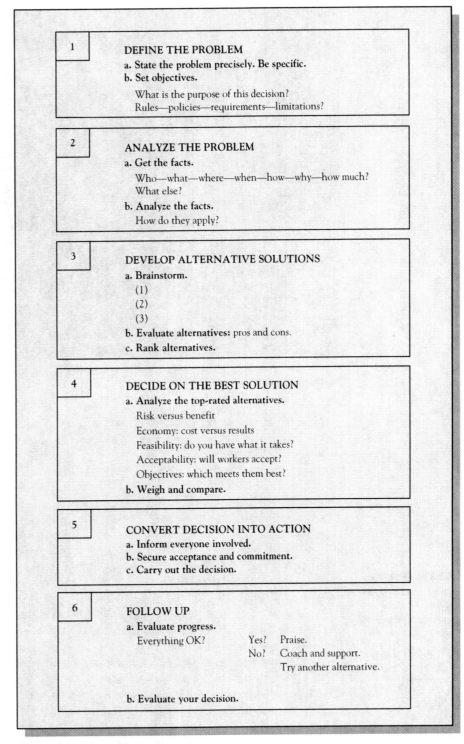

1 DEFINE THE PROBLEM
a. State the problem precisely. Be specific.
b. Set objectives.

What is the purpose of this decision?
Rules—policies—requirements—limitations?

2 ANALYZE THE PROBLEM
a. Get the facts.
Who—what—where—when—how—why—how much?
What else?
b. Analyze the facts.
How do they apply?

3 DEVELOP ALTERNATIVE SOLUTIONS
a. Brainstorm.
(1)
(2)
(3)
b. Evaluate alternatives: pros and cons.
c. Rank alternatives.

4 DECIDE ON THE BEST SOLUTION
a. Analyze the top-rated alternatives.
Risk versus benefit
Economy: cost versus results
Feasibility: do you have what it takes?
Acceptability: will workers accept?
Objectives: which meets them best?
b. Weigh and compare.

5 CONVERT DECISION INTO ACTION
a. Inform everyone involved.
b. Secure acceptance and commitment.
c. Carry out the decision.

6 FOLLOW UP
a. Evaluate progress.
Everything OK?   Yes? Praise.
No?   Coach and support.
Try another alternative.

b. Evaluate your decision.

FIGURE 13.1: Pattern for making decisions.

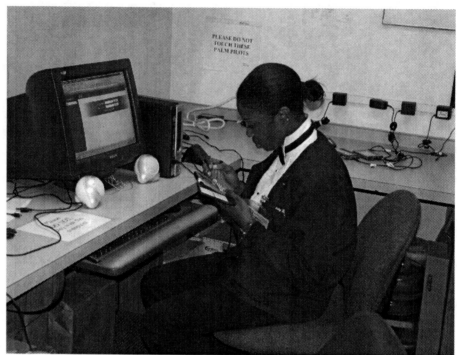

Making good decisions can sometimes take a team effort.
Photo courtesy of the author.

You might ask how many clean dishes there are—or you might not even stop for this—you know you are going to run out. You generate alternatives at lightning speed: Wash by hand in the bar sinks? Use the bar glasses? Ask the restaurant next door (a friendly competitor) for help (borrow dishes or share their dishwashing machine)? Use paper and plastic? You don't have time to figure out the pros and cons of each choice: You make a judgment on which is best, and you might use all of them.

You take action immediately by directing your employees and doing some of the work yourself. This requires more split-second decisions. Some won't work out, but you can work with what you have. In fact, what you did was to move logically through the six steps, but you also utilized one of the most critical success factors in decision making: *timing*. In many on-the-spot decisions of a supervisor's job, timing may be the overriding factor: A decision is necessary *now*.

The need to make hundreds of quick decisions every day might make you forget that there is any other way to make a decision. Quick decision making becomes a habit. Yet a quick decision is *bad* timing if it is something you need to think through. In the dish machine breakdown you knew the necessary facts and the available alternatives, and you recognized the problem at once.

But in other circumstances you might not know all the facts. You might not recognize the real problem. You might jump in with the first solution that comes to mind. You may not realize the consequences it could have. If your decision affects your people and their work, it is worth taking the time to ensure the best possible outcome.

timing
Selecting the time when taking action will be most effective; making a decision at the moment it is most needed.

Let us take an example and run through the decision-making process using our six-step method. You have just hired a new server, Cindy, to replace Gary. She will work a split shift, 11 to 3 and 7 to 11 Tuesday through Saturday, which is Gary's last day. Cindy must be trained well enough to start work on Tuesday. She is an experienced server, having worked in a restaurant similar to yours. In the next five sections we follow this decision through to its solution.

✳ DEFINING THE PROBLEM

The first step has two parts: *State the problem precisely* and *formulate your objectives*: what you want to happen as a result of your decision. You start out by writing down *Who will train Cindy?* Then you realize that there is more to the problem than *who*; there are *when* and *what*: How much training does Cindy need? You restate your problem: *Give Cindy enough training to start on the noon shift Tuesday*. This statement broadens your approach: You begin to include the training itself in your thinking. Figure 13.2 shows your worksheet as you develop your decisions.

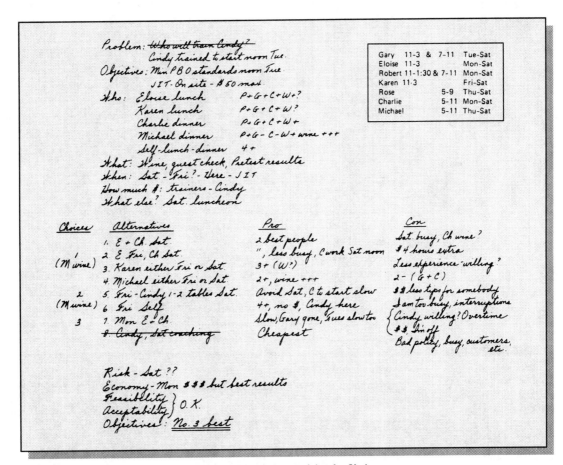

FIGURE 13.2: Decision making: manager's worksheet on training for Cindy.

Your objectives should restate your problem in terms of the results you expect. They should also include any rules or policies that apply, any requirements as to where, when, how, and so on, and any limiting factors such as time and money. These things are sometimes referred to collectively as **conditions and limitations**.

For your objective, then, you write down: Cindy is to meet minimum performance standards by noon shift Tuesday. JIT method, on site. Training expenses $50 maximum.

✳ ANALYZING THE PROBLEM

The next step is to assemble the relevant data, but don't overdo it: Keep the goal clear. It is easy to tell people more than they need to know, yourself included, so don't confuse yourself with too many facts. You can get more as you need them—and you probably will.

The easiest way to organize the **fact finding** is to go through the who–what–when–where–how–why routine. The first question is who. After studying the weekly schedule, you put down: *Ashley or Karen (lunch), Charlie or Luis l (dinner).* Some of these servers would make better trainers than others, but you do not eliminate anyone at this point. You want to keep your mind open and your thinking positive. Besides, you need all the possibilities you can get because you might have to settle for a less than perfect solution. Then, reluctantly, you add *Self.* You really don't have the time.

The next question is *what.* You start to write *Server procedures,* and then you think, "Wait a minute, Cindy has been a waitress before; we don't need to train her from scratch." Then you think, "Just what does she know?" and right away, you pick up the phone and call her to come in on Friday at 9 A.M. for a pretest.

You know that she doesn't know wine service; they serve wine only by the glass where she worked before. She won't know your guest check system, either. But a lot of things will be the same. She's bright, and it shouldn't take long to train her. You make a few notes: *wine, guest check, pretest results.*

The next question is *when.* You put down *Saturday* and then you think, Well, maybe part of Friday, too, since she's coming for the pretest anyway. And Saturday is so busy—you have that bridal luncheon for the mayor's daughter. You put down *Friday?*

The next question is *where,* and the answer is *Here,* with your equipment and your setup, just as though she were working.

The next question is *how.* You write *JIT, show and tell.* You will have to coach your trainers on this, but since they were trained this way themselves and you have performance standards to go by, it shouldn't take long, maybe an hour on Thursday.

The last question is *why,* and you have answered that in your objective. Next you analyze the data you have gathered. Which server would make the best trainer? You rate them plus or minus on performance, guest relationships, communication, and willingness. What about costs? A few extra hours for the trainers and maybe an extra half day for Cindy. It shouldn't go over your $50 limit.

Anything else? That luncheon on Saturday.

✳ DEVELOPING ALTERNATIVE SOLUTIONS

Now that you have all the facts, your next step is to develop as many alternatives as you can. The first stage should be uninhibited **brainstorming**: You give free rein to your

---

conditions and limitations
Factors such as rules, policies, specific requirements, and limiting factors (e.g., time) that may apply when a problem is being defined.

fact finding
The process of collecting all the facts about a certain situation.

brainstorming
Generating ideas without considering their drawbacks, limitations, or consequences (typically), a group activity.

imagination and put down every possibility that you can think of without regard to its drawbacks or limitations. You do not want any negative thoughts to inhibit your creativity. Sometimes a totally impractical idea will suggest a really good solution or a way of adapting another solution for a better result. Sometimes an entirely new idea will suddenly emerge. Ideas spark other ideas, so keep them coming.

You jot down the following:

1. Ashley and Charlie on Saturday.
2. Ashley Friday and Charlie Saturday.
3. Substitute Karen for Ashley either day.
4. Substitute Luis for Charlie either day.

After a moment's thought, you add:

5. Train Friday (Ashley or Karen and Charlie or Luis).
6. Yourself Friday.

And then, since the idea of training on busy days is beginning to really bother you, you add:

7. Train Monday (Ashley and Charlie—Luis and Karen off).

Finally, in case all else fails, you add:

8. Let Cindy start working Saturday and assign someone to coach her.

At this point you run dry. You think you have some good possibilities.

You now move to the second stage of developing alternatives: You weigh the pros and cons of each. You consider the good and bad points, keeping in mind how these would help or hinder the outcome and whether there would be side effects or bad consequences. It is very easy, in concentrating on achieving your objectives, to overlook other results that a course of action might have (the operation is a success but the patient dies).

The larger the problem, the more important this step is. In a major problem affecting production and people, thinking through the consequences is one of the most important steps of all. In our example, some alternatives might produce poor training quality, which could result in problems of service and cost. Or a personality clash might start a good server off on the wrong foot.

You start by listing the pros and cons. As you do this, you discover some things you hadn't thought of before. Here are your thoughts:

1. Ashley and Charlie on Saturday.
   Pro: Ashley probably 4+ (willing?). Charlie definitely 4+ except on wine.
   Con: Very busy day, Charlie wine?
2. Ashley Friday, Charlie Saturday.
   Pro: Best trainers. Friday not as busy, Cindy coming in Friday anyway. Cindy can work bridal luncheon Saturday.
   Con: Extra cost (Cindy 4 hours Friday).

3. Substitute Karen for Ashley.
   Pro: 3+ trainer (willing?).
   Con: Less experienced than Ashley, probably less interested.
4. Substitute Luis for Charlie.
   Pro: 2+ (excellent performer, willing), superb on wine.
   Con: 2+ (goes too fast, condescending).
5. Train Friday, Cindy work 1 or 2 tables both shifts Saturday.
   Pro: Avoid training on Saturday. Break Cindy in on job gradually.
   Con: Extra cost, 1 or 2 fewer tables and tips for someone Saturday dinner—resentment?
6. Yourself Friday.
   Pro: 4+ as trainer. No training cost. Cindy coming in anyway.
   Con: Important morning appointments. Off 2 to 5. Interruptions.
7. Train Monday, Ashley and Charlie.
   Pro: Slow day. Best trainers. Gary gone. Tuesday good for first workday (slow dinner).
   Con: Will Cindy trade Saturday for Monday? Six-day week for Cindy. Your day off. Slightly over budget (overtime for Cindy).
8. Cindy to work Saturday with someone coaching.
   Pro: Cheapest.
   Con: Bad policy. Poor training, bad start, hidden costs. Too busy on Saturday. Guest confusion.
9. Luis to do separate wine training before a shift with anyone who needs training in this skill (like Charlie).
   Pro: Inexpensive.
   Con: Need to make time—might need more than one time.

The final step of this stage is to weigh the pros and cons and rank your alternatives. When you are making a very important decision with momentous consequences and you have plenty of time, you will rank all alternatives carefully. But if you have several feasible alternatives and limited decision time, you should pick out the top three or four alternatives and rank them. Don't throw the others out; you may have to come back to them.

Moving on, then, here is what you end up with:

- **First choice:** No. 2. Ashley train for lunch Friday, Charlie for dinner Saturday. Use Luis for wine training Saturday.
- **Second choice:** No. 5. Cindy to pretest and train Friday with Ashley and Charlie and work her regular hours Saturday. Luis to teach wine Saturday. Cindy to work bridal luncheon and one or two of Gary's dinner tables.
- **Third choice:** No. 7. Train Monday, Ashley and Charlie. (Must shave cost a bit further.)

You now have three alternatives that will meet your objectives reasonably well. Of the five remaining, you cross off Number 8: After weighing the pros and cons, you find it unacceptable. The rest are feasible alternatives, but you should not bother with them at this point. At least one of your three choices is bound to work.

✳ DECIDING ON THE BEST SOLUTION

Before making any decision of consequence, the decision maker should test the top-rated alternatives by asking five questions:

1. *Risk.* Which course of action provides the most benefit with the least risk?
2. *Economy.* Which course of action will give the best results with the least expenditure of time, money, and effort?
3. *Feasibility.* Is each course of action feasible? Do you have the people and resources to carry it out?
4. *Acceptability.* Will each course of action be acceptable to the people it will affect?
5. *Objectives.* Which course of action meets your objectives best?

These questions require you to do some more analysis. You must analyze benefits and risks and weigh one against the other. You must figure time, money, and effort and weigh cost against results. You must determine whether you have the people and resources needed in each case and whether it will be acceptable to the people concerned. Finally, you must weigh one course of action against another and decide which meets your objectives best.

You can run through this pretty quickly.

1. *Risk.* There isn't much risk anywhere. The biggest risk is probably in your first choice—Saturday being such a hectic day and leaving the dinner training until Saturday night. Charlie might come in late or things might get busy early. And there really isn't time for Luis to teach wine. So there *is* some risk in training quality that might make trouble later. Now, how about Monday? Monday is your day off; is there a risk there? You could stop in to see how things are going, and with your best trainers, little could go wrong and there's time to deal with it.
2. *Economy.* Monday is definitely the most expensive, but it would probably give the best results, and it's not *that* much more; you could shave it down to budget some way.
3. *Feasibility and acceptability.* Those are definitely the big questions; they may decide the whole thing. You pick up the phone and call Cindy. You find that Monday is okay with her; in fact, she'd like the overtime. She could also meet the other two schedules, but they sound a little confusing. You check with Ashley and Charlie. They can both meet all three arrangements and would like to do the training. They both think Monday sounds best.
4. *Objectives.* Which solution meets them best? You decide on Monday, largely on the basis of risk and, in the end, economy. Although it costs a bit more, you think the training quality will be much the best, and Cindy will have a good start. It is a decision you are not likely to regret, and it will pay for itself in the long run.

✳ ACTION AND FOLLOW-UP

The next step in decision making is to hand the decision over to the people who will carry it out. At this point, good communication is the key to success. The people who will carry out the decision must fully understand it, and everyone affected must be informed. Every effort must be made to gain acceptance and commitment. If the people who must carry out a decision are involved in developing the alternatives, it usually pays off, but in our industry this often isn't practical.

You have already involved Cindy and Ashley and Charlie; you had to involve them before you could come to a decision. You know that they are committed. You pick up the phone again and tell the three of them that the plan for Monday is on. You give them the details of the Monday schedule and set a time on Thursday for training the trainers. You will give Cindy the pretest on Friday and pass along the necessary information to Ashley and Charlie. Luis will do a separate wine training before a shift for those who need it. You inform the assistant manager, who will be in charge on Monday. The decision is complete.

Altogether, this decision took you 15 minutes or less from beginning to end. Was it worth the time? You think so, definitely. You will start Cindy off on the right foot. She will know what to do and how to do it, she will be confident instead of confused and anxious, and she will feel good about the trouble you have taken to provide her training.

She will probably stay beyond the critical first seven days and turn into a good, productive worker. You have probably saved yourself a lot of grief by not making a snap decision for Saturday training.

You also have a lot of new insights on making decisions and on training. You might decide later to delegate training on a regular basis to Eloise and Charlie and give them more training than the quickie things that you can give them in an hour. The last step in decision making is to follow up—keep tabs on how things are going. It is an important step for several reasons. If problems develop, you can catch them early or even fall back on another alternative. If questions arise, you can answer them. Follow-up supports the people carrying out your decision: It reassures them and gives them confidence.

It also gives you a chance to evaluate your decision making. Is everything working out? Did you think of everything? Could you have done a better job in the time you had? Should you have given it more time? What have you learned from this decision? Such a review will help you develop skills and confidence.

Check Your Knowledge

1. How should a supervisor make his or her own decisions?
2. Describe three essential elements in the decision-making process.

Problem Solving

Problem solving is a special kind of decision making that involves more than a choice between courses of action: It involves identifying the cause of a problem and developing ways to correct or remove the cause. Usually you become aware of the problem through a symptom such as customer complaints, below-standard performance, or substandard food product or room cleanliness—some sort of gap between what is and what should be.

problem solving
Using a logical
process to identify
causes and solutions
to problems or to
make decisions.

As a supervisor, it is important to have follow-up training for employees to see how they are progressing.
Photo courtesy of the author.

Do you know?

What are the pros
and cons of group
decision making?

✳ PATTERN FOR SOLVING PROBLEMS

The chief difference between solving this kind of problem and simple decision making is that there are extra steps you must take before you can begin to generate alternative courses of action. The pattern goes like this:

1. Describe the problem.
2. Search out the cause (get the facts).
3. Define the real problem and set objectives.
4. Develop alternative solutions.
5. Decide on the best solution.
6. Implement the decision.
7. Follow up.

As you can see, the last four steps are the same as in any decision-making process. The difference is in the first three steps. You do your digging for data before you attempt to define the problem and set objectives for solving it. If you try to develop decisions on the basis of your first impression of the problem, you might take the wrong action and the problem will recur. You will have mistaken a symptom for the real cause.

219

✳ PROBLEM-SOLVING EXAMPLE

To illustrate the problem-solving method, let us run quickly through an example. You are the manager of an independent restaurant and you have recently hired a new cook, a young graduate of a fine culinary school. This is her first full-time job. Your problem is that she is too slow. You think you will have to fire her; she is just too inexperienced. But the food has never been better, especially the daily "cook's specials" you asked her to develop. The customers are raving about the food but complaining about the service. What a dilemma! Where do you start?

The first step is to *describe the problem as you see it now*. This description should include not only what you see at this point as the primary problem but any other problem it is causing. You write down the following: *The cook is too slow; the food isn't ready at pickup time. Servers are angry because customers are blaming them for poor service. Customers are angry, too.*

The second step is to *search out the cause of the problem*. This involves getting all the relevant facts: the who, what, when, where, how, and why, the ongoing story of what is and is not happening, and any other relevant data.

It is obvious that you must get the cook's side of the story. When you first talk to her, she is very defensive. She says that the servers are harassing her and it makes her nervous and she can't work efficiently. You are sure there is more to it than that. That night you spend half an hour in the kitchen observing.

Naturally, the servers do not heckle while you are there, but the cook still has problems. You are surprised at how quickly she works. But she cooks the special at the last minute and she can't do that and plate and garnish everything at the same time. She gets farther and farther behind, so you step in and help her plate the orders.

You make a date to talk to her tomorrow. She is almost in tears and obviously thinks you are going to fire her. You reassure her of your desire to help and you compliment her on the food.

The food is fantastically good. You talk to the guests and they rave about it, not only the special but also the regular menu items. It occurs to you that if you can solve this problem and keep this cook, the word will get around about the good food and your business will grow.

One of the ways to get at the basic problem is to ask a lot of comparison questions. What is being done that was not done before? What is different now, and what is the same? Let's see:

- The cook is different.
- The food is better, all of it.
- The menu is the same except for the specials.
- You also noticed that she is doing some special garnishes.
- The old cook cooked everything ahead except hamburgers and steaks. The new cook cooks the specials to order as well as the hamburgers and steaks.

The next day you talk to the new cook about the problem. You tell her how pleased you are with the food and you make it very clear that you want to solve this situation, which affects both of you. Can she help you analyze it? Finally, she says that she has been afraid to mention it, but the cook's special is a lot of extra work. She is really doing more work than your last cook. You acknowledge that this is true. (Is this a piece of the problem?)

Besides, she says, more specials are being ordered than any other item on the menu, so that makes still more work, especially at dish-up time. You ask her if she could cook the specials ahead and hold them, and she says "No, it's the sauce made in the pan at the last minute that makes the difference." (Aha! Another clue!)

And the garnishes? She prepares them ahead, but it's true that you can't just plunk them onto the plate; you have to handle them carefully. You found this out last night. (Still another clue.)

You talk with various servers, and they verify that it seems to be the last-minute cooking that slows things up, and maybe the garnishes. Two waitresses confirm that some waiters are loud and nasty in their complaints while they wait for their orders and that the atmosphere gets very unpleasant.

As a stopgap solution to this aspect of your basic problem, you speak to the offenders, pointing out that they are only making their own problem worse. You believe that you have identified the real problem, and if you can resolve it, this side issue will disappear.

The third step in problem solving is to *define the real problem precisely and set objectives*. This corresponds to step 1 of the decision-making formula.

You have decided that you definitely want to keep this cook. But that does not solve any part of the problem. You write down what you now see as the real problem and state your objectives as follows:

> Problem: Time between order and pickup is too long. Can't afford to lose this cook.
> Objectives: To reduce the time between order and pickup to the standards specified in the cook performance standards, retaining the present cook. Present menu must be retained for the next four months. (You have just had it printed.) Cook's specials concept is to be retained if possible. Extra help may be hired if cost-effective. The cook must agree to the final decision (but not make it).

You start to add: *Long-range objective: to expand business*. Then you come to your senses. Building a business around the skills of a particular cook is an entirely different ball game. You have to solve your present problem within its own frame of reference.

You are now in a position to generate and evaluate alternatives, decide on the best solution, and put it to work, as in the basic decision-making formula.

✳ PARTICIPATIVE PROBLEM SOLVING

In the case we have been following, it is logical for the manager at this point to consider bringing the cook into the next three steps of the problem-solving process. Is this a good idea in general? What are the pros and cons? In management theory, there is a school of thought with a strong following that believes in *group decision making*. They argue that many heads are better than one because:

1. You get more information and expertise relevant to the decision.
2. You get more good ideas and can generate more and better alternatives.
3. People thinking together can arrive at better decisions because of the stimulation and interplay of different points of view.

group decision making

A process in which a group of people work together to come to a decision.

PROFILE Eric Walker

Courtesy of
Eric Walker.

Eric grew up in Kansas City and later moved to several cities in his career with the Ritz-Carlton, including Naples, Atlanta, and St. Thomas.

Currently, Eric is catering and conference services floor manager, The Ritz-Carlton, Sarasota, where his general manager has high expectations of the newly created position. That's a challenge he likes. Having worked as a valet parker, doorperson, bellperson, and concierge, Eric has seen both sides of the supervision equation and knows that everything is not black and white. One of the secrets to his success is to empathize with people and to put himself in their shoes. He will do anything to make a guest happy so long as it will not harm the hotel.

Eric leads by example and would not ask any of his associates to do something he would not or could not do. An example of this is when he "jumps in" to help the setup team during the meeting room cleanups while the guests are having a coffee break. He recognizes that the setup team is the most important group in his area and helps them whenever possible. As a supervisor, Eric also has high expectations and holds his associates accountable.

Eric's workday begins 6 A.M. when he goes over the day with his staff and he checks that breakfasts are ready. He then goes over the day with the client and monitors all the functions and meetings to ensure perfect guest service. In his role as the catering and conference services manager, Eric has to take care of all the meeting planners and their VIP's requests.

This means he communicates with virtually all departments. Eric is ranked number one, two, or three in all the guest surveys with an average guest satisfaction score of 97 percent. Recently, Eric's general manager asked him which position he was eyeing next. Eric's reply was that he wanted to be the best in the company in his position before he moved to another position. Now that's commitment and dedication for you! No wonder the general manager and the executive committee, in view of his meritorious performance, nominated Eric for the J. W. Marriott employee of the year award.

When not working, Eric loves to spend quality time with his wife, five children, and grandchildren.

They also argue that in practice:

4. People who have participated in making the decision are generally committed to carrying it out.
5. The coordination and communication necessary to carrying out the decision are simpler and better because everyone already understands what is happening.

This school of thought is associated with Theory Y management style. The experience of many managers who practice group decision making bears out that the theory can and does work.

Other people take a dim view of group decision making and find the following problems with it:

1. It takes longer for a group to decide something than it does for one person to make the decision. Furthermore, it takes everybody away from his or her other work. (The decision may be better, but is it worth the total work hours required to make it?)

2. Groups are often dominated by one person—usually the boss—because people want to please or are afraid to speak up or disagree, so there really is no advantage. (Here there is really no group decision.)

3. Group participants often get involved in winning arguments or showing off rather than in getting the best decision. (Groups often don't work the way they are supposed to.)

4. If consensus (general agreement of all participants) is required, people may go along with a decision they don't like just to get the meeting over with. (This is not a true consensus.)

5. Consensus leads to mediocre decisions that will appease everyone rather than the best decision. It can also lead to *groupthink* or conformity rather than to the creativity that is supposed to happen. (Groups may produce worse decisions.)

6. Self-seeking managers can use groups for their own purposes to shift blame in case of mistakes or to manipulate people into agreeing to a decision they do not want to carry out. (Here, again, there is no group decision.)

Clearly, group decision making is not a panacea. It works better in some types of organizations than it does in others, and it is more suitable to some problems, some leaders, and some groups than it is to others. Generally, groups work best when:

- Members are accustomed to working together as a team and have differing expertise and points of view but common goals.
- The leader is skillful at keeping meetings on target without dominating or manipulating (or allowing others to do so).
- The group is rewarded for making good decisions.

A group works at participative problem solving.
Courtesy of the Hyatt Hotel and Marina Sarasota.

This combination of conditions is found more often at high corporate levels, but teams of hourly employees are becoming more involved in group decision making. There are times when including workers at some stages of problem solving makes a lot of sense.

This is especially true when the problem or decision involves specialized skills or experience that the supervisor does not have or when participation will motivate workers to accept the decision and carry it out. In our example, both conditions are present: The cook knows more than you do about cooking and about the particular problem, and you need her commitment to the decision.

The degree of participation in problem solving and decision making may also vary. This is similar to variations in leadership style running from autocratic to democratic (Chapter 2). Figure 13.3 illustrates such variations of participative problem solving. At one end of the scale the autocratic manager will make the decision alone and tell the workers how to carry it out. For example, a manager will decide on a menu item for tomorrow and order the cook to make it. There is no participation whatever.

Toward the middle of the scale, the manager will originate an idea and put it out for comment: "As a server, as a cook, what do you think of this menu item—will it sell?" The workers participate in the evaluation, but they do not take part in generating alternatives. Farther along the scale, the manager says, "Give me some ideas for menu items and let's discuss them."

Here the cook takes part in everything but the decision. Still farther to the right is the manager who says to the cook, "I want you to come up with a couple of new menu items by next Monday; anything you choose within reason is okay with me." Here, the manager delegates the decision with merely a precautionary restriction. At the extreme right is the group decision—clearly inappropriate to this simple problem.

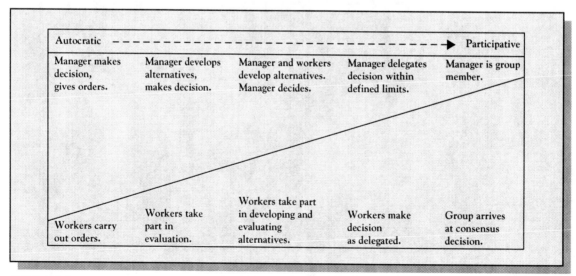

FIGURE 13.3:   Range of participation in problem solving and decision making.

Continuing our example, you as the manager invite the cook to help generate alternatives for solving the time-lag problem. The two of you come up with the following alternatives:

- Develop specials that can be prepared ahead and simplify the garnishes.
- Keep the current cooked-to-order specials the customers like so well and hire a part-timer to cook hamburgers and to plate and garnish each order.
- Keep the current specials, simplify the garnishes, and have the servers plate and garnish the orders.

The cook thinks that she can handle any of the three. Although she will still be doing more work than your former cook, she likes the challenge of developing specials. She wants to work with you on the details of carrying out the decision.

Since your budget and the servers are involved, you will not include the cook in making the decision. You decide to have the servers participate in evaluating the third alternative. You hope they will see that the popularity of the current specials probably means increased business and higher tips in the future. But if they do not agree willingly to the extra work for them, this course of action will cause nothing but trouble. You need their commitment.

✳ SOLVING PEOPLE PROBLEMS[3]

Usually, your most difficult problems have to do with people. Problems about the work focus on products, procedures, schedules, time, costs, and other tangible things. Problems centered on people involve emotions, expectations, needs, motivation, and all the other intangibles associated with being human. The problem-solving steps are the same, but people problems require the sensitive practice of human skills.

Suppose that a cook comes in very late for the second time in a week and you slap a penalty on him, as your company procedure requires. He messes up everything all morning: scorches the soup, leaves the herbs and garlic out of the stew, drops an entire crate of eggs, and walks off the job. Two days later, you learn that his wife had walked out on him that day, leaving him with two little children to care for. You didn't get the facts. You didn't find the real problem. You made the wrong decision. You lost the worker.

A festering problem in many operations is the continuous antagonism between servers and cooks. Perhaps the underlying problem is unsolvable, since it probably has to do with self-image and professional jealousy. Often, each side looks down on the other.

Cooks are proud of their skills and their salaries, and they think of themselves as artists. They look down on serving tables, and they resent it when servers try to order them around. Servers, by contrast, look down on cooks for very similar reasons. In some instances, male-female rivalries are also involved. These are psychological conflicts that no manager has the skills to resolve.

Problems involving conflicts between people who work together surface quickly because most people don't hesitate to complain about each other. The usual problem-solving pattern is very appropriate here. But getting to the real problem might take time because of the number of people involved, their emotions, and probably their disagreement about the facts.

Yet identifying the real problem and solving it is more important than ever. The more people are affected, the more it affects the work. And if people's emotions are running high, they will carry them to the front desk, the lobby, the dining room, the kitchen, or the hospital bed. Guests and patients will not get the treatment they expect and deserve.

Guidelines in Solving Personal Problems

People problems flag you with symptoms—a drop in output, substandard quality, absenteeism, customer complaints—any gap between standards and performance. The first thing to do is get the facts and dig for the real problem. Don't make a hasty decision.

Personal problems are not yours to resolve, of course, but listening when people need to talk can help them to solve their own problems, or at least relieve their tensions enough to get on with their work. Advice is appropriate only if it helps to steer someone toward professional help. You might be able to help your distraught cook find a day-care center, or you might need to refer the person to an employee assistance program (see Chapter 12).

It is important to keep your own emotions out of your workers' problems and to maintain your supervisory role. Dependent people often try to manipulate the boss into telling them how to live their lives. Active but neutral listening, as described in Chapter 4, is the best approach to such problems. The time this takes is appropriate only if the problem is interfering with the work.

There are, however, ways to eliminate the friction. Sometimes the best decision is to choose not to solve the real problem but to bypass it. Some managers have made the decision to use a food expediter to receive the orders from the servers and transmit them to the cooks, so the rivals have no contact at all.

Win/Win Problem Solving[4]

For dealing with problems involving one person, an interesting participative approach includes the worker from the beginning to the end of the problem-solving process. It is known as *win/win problem solving* because everybody wins. People who have used it say that it solves the problem 75 percent of the time.

The win/win concept is difficult for many supervisors to accept. When a supervisor is dealing with a worker who is causing a problem, it is very natural to think of the situation as a contest that the supervisor must win. Win/lose is a competitive concept that pervades our culture: ball game, tennis match, arm wrestling, election, war—whatever the contest, there is a winner and a loser; that's what it's all about.

In win-or-lose terms, you as a supervisor have four possible ways of approaching the problem solving. The first is a *win/lose* stance: You say to the worker, "You've gotta shape up or else; if you don't shape up, you're fired." You win, the employee loses. Of course, you win the battle, but you lose the war: You either have to hire a new employee or, with a different penalty, put up with a continuation of the conflict on the guerrilla level.

The second approach is a *lose/win* posture: retreat and appeasement. You don't take a stand, you let the worker get away with things, and you back away from any

win/win problem solving
A method of solving problems in which supervisor and employee discuss a problem together and arrive at a mutually acceptable solution.

decision. You lose and the employee wins. And soon you lose not only the battle but also your job.

The third approach is *lose/lose*: compromise. You give up something in exchange for the employee's giving up something, and each of you has less than before. You both lose. Neither of you is satisfied and the problem is likely to reappear, perhaps in another form.

The fourth approach is *win/win*: You collaborate to find a solution that satisfies both of you. You include the employee from the beginning of the problem-solving process, and you go through the following steps:

1. Together, you establish the facts and identify and define the problem. As the supervisor you make it clear that both you and the employee will benefit from getting the problem solved. You pull out all your interviewing skills; you listen, encourage, and let the worker vent feelings and complaints. Finally, you agree on the definition of the problem.
2. Together, you generate all possible alternative solutions—no vetos at this point. You keep going until neither of you can think of any more.
3. Together, you evaluate the alternatives and pick the one that is best for both of you.
4. Together, you carry out the agreement. You follow up at intervals to see how the solution is working.

Suppose, for example, that you have a desk clerk who does not get to work on time. After considerable discussion you agree that the problem is that her starting hour of 7 A.M. is incompatible with her home situation. She has two young children to get ready for school.

You generate alternatives: Let her husband deal with the children. Have her pay someone to come. Put her on a different shift. Have her work 9 to 5 instead of 7 to 3. Terminate her. Put her in a different job: the office, payroll clerk. And so on.

You go over the alternatives and finally agree that she will work the evening shift starting an hour late. She is happy that she can handle both ends of the school day and still make almost as much money. You are happy that you will not have to hire and train a new desk clerk. You already have someone on the evening shift who would like to trade shifts. You both win.

For many supervisors, the win/win approach represents a major shift in attitude. It denies the traditional assumption that problem employees are adversaries in a contest, replacing it with the far healthier assumption that both parties to the problem are in it together.

It goes right along with the Theory Y idea that jobs can be structured to fulfill personal goals and company goals at the same time. And it fits perfectly with the humanistic approach to management that seeks to build a positive work climate and an atmosphere of cooperation and trust. For supervisors who can make that shift in attitude, it is certainly another string to one's bow.

Check Your Knowledge

1. What does problem solving involve?
2. What is the difference between problem solving and simple decision making?

Building Decision-Making Skills

The ability to make good, sound, timely decisions is one of the most important qualities on which a manager is judged. It is essential to running a tight ship and to being a good manager of people. You can learn a great deal about making decisions from books and from observing people who are good decision makers. But the only way to build a skill is to practice it. Here are some guidelines to help you along the way:

- Make sure that the decision is yours to make, that you have both the authority and the responsibility. Make each decision in the best interest of your employer, not your own interests.
- Accept your responsibility fully: Face decisions promptly. Be ready to take unpopular stands when they are necessary.
- Sort out the important decisions from the inconsequential ones. Make minor decisions quickly. Make major decisions deliberately, seeking out the basic problem and considering consequences before you take action.
- Calculate the risks, and do not be afraid to take them if they are worth the benefits.
- Timing is important; often, it is everything. Adapt your decision making to this overriding requirement.
- Be alert to signs of problems. If you let a situation become a crisis, it may be too late for a good decision.
- Keep an open mind when investigating a problem. Avoid jumping to conclusions, and stay away from your own biases, prejudices, and self-interest. Remember, too, that the easiest solution is not necessarily the best.
- Do consult your supervisor when a problem is truly beyond your ability or experience.
- Make sure that you are not part of the problem yourself.
- You will make some bad decisions along the way—everyone does. Don't brood over them; learn from them.
- Follow up on your important decisions to see how they are working out. Were they good decisions? What would you do differently next time?
- Look at each situation from its own unique perspective. When presented with a situation similar to an earlier one, some supervisors will make the same decision as that used earlier. Although this sometimes works, it is best to examine each situation individually.

Controlling

Controlling is a process by which managers measure, evaluate, and compare results to goals and standards previously agreed on, such as performance standards, and take corrective action when necessary to stay on course. There are visible controls throughout your workplace: door locks, time clocks, the bartender's measuring device, keys to the cash register.

✳ THE CONTROL PROCESS

A major area of control for hospitality supervisors is cost: food cost, beverage cost, labor cost, supply cost, energy cost. Cost control is a process by which managers try to regulate costs and guard against excessive costs in order to have a profitable business. It is an ongoing process and involves every step in the chain of purchasing, receiving, storing, issuing, and preparing food and beverages for sale, scheduling employees, and using supplies and energy.

On a daily basis you will be involved in cost-control techniques such as checking vendors' invoices and counting cash. The exact methods you use will vary from place to place, depending in part on the nature and scope of your business, but the principle of sparing your employer excessive costs remains the same.

In the hospitality industry, excessive costs are often due to inefficiency, theft, and waste—factors that you can influence. For instance, you may check production records against recorded sales to ensure that all quantities produced are accounted for. Figure 13.4 displays various control tools that can be used, depending on the department (e.g.,

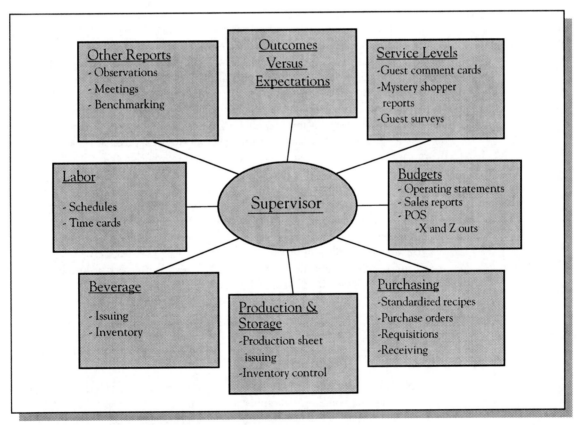

FIGURE 13.4: Examples of control tools for various departments.

comment cards to access quality of service, purchase orders to control purchasing expenditures). As a supervisor, you can use the following control techniques:

- Require records and reports (such as production reports, food, beverage, and labor costs and income statements).
- Develop and enforce performance standards.
- Develop and enforce productivity standards.
- Develop and enforce departmental policies and procedures.
- Observe and correct employee actions.
- Train and retrain employees.
- Discipline employees when appropriate.
- Be a good role model.

productivity standards
A definition of the acceptable quantity of work that an employee is expected to do (e.g., the number of rooms that can be cleaned in a day).

As discussed in Chapter 7, performance standards define how well a job is to be done (the quality aspect); *productivity standards* define the acceptable quantity of work an employee is expected to do (following performance standards, of course). For example, you may determine that it is a reasonable expectation for a housekeeping employee to complete cleaning a guest room according to your performance standards in 30 minutes, for a server to be able to serve four tables at a time, or for a hospital tray line to produce three trays per minute.

Control in the hospitality industry means providing information to management for decision-making purposes. A good example is the food cost percentage. Let's say we have a casual Italian restaurant and its food cost percentage is budgeted to be 28 percent, but the inventory just taken and calculated shows it to be 33 percent. Then at least you know it and can begin the fun part of figuring out what is going on!

An old Swiss chef once told the author that "before you can stop someone stealing the chicken—you first must know how to steal the chicken." Control in a situation like a difference in the actual result from what was expected looks at each step in the process—ordering, receiving, storage, issuing, prepping, cooking, holding, serving, and billing.

Taking another common situation in hospitality, if kitchen labor costs are budgeted to be 14 percent of sales, but turn out to be 18 percent, then we know we must impose a better control and not wait for the end of the month for the result. We would need to monitor labor costs on a daily basis, so as to avoid a repeat situation.

productivity
How effectively an operation converts an input (e.g., food) into an output (e.g., a meal).

Productivity is the output of employees' services and products in a given time period. In a restaurant, inputs such as food and service are used to produce outputs such as meals. Productivity can generally be thought of as a ratio:

$$\text{Productivity} = \frac{\text{Outputs (products or services: quantity and quality)}}{\text{Inputs (resources to produce outputs such as food, labour, and supply costs)}}$$

Productivity measurements tell much about an operation's efficiency and performance and are the common denominator for comparing your operation with others. They also help when developing budgets and allocating resources. Productivity in the hospitality industry is as much a matter of quantity as it is quality.

For example, a server might be able to handle six tables in 20 minutes, but the quality of the service is inferior to that of another server who takes care of fewer guests in the same period of time. Figure 13.5 lists common foodservice productivity measures.

It's amazing to think that a high proportion of employees will likely steal if given the chance. The trick is to prevent that from happening. It begins with the Swiss chef's words: "Before you can stop someone stealing the chicken, you must first know how to steal the chicken."

This was borne out when Julian E. Montoya, founder of the Burrito King chain of restaurants, saw his chain go from success to near disaster in just a few years due to increasing competition and employee theft. Montoya recalls the difficulty of monitoring all of his stores at the height of expansion.

One night he went to one of his restaurants unannounced, donned an apron, and went up front to cover the cash register. "The cook took me aside and said, 'Here's how it works: You take the order; you take the cash and don't put it in the register. At the end of the night, we split it.'"[5]

❋ ADDITIONAL TYPES OF CONTROL

feedforward control
Control measures designed to prevent problems before the activity begins.

concurrent control
Control measures conducted during the activity.

feedback
Giving information about the performance of an individual or group back to them during or after performing a task or job.

Other types of control are *feedforward control*, *concurrent control*, and *feedback*. With *feedforward* control, the idea is to prevent problems before the activity. When McDonald's opened in Moscow, it sent a team of experts to show the Russians how to grow potatoes, how to make and bake the buns, and how to ensure the quality of the beef so it would make a burger that tastes the same as one in the United States.

Concurrent control is control that is conducted during the activity. Supervisors practice concurrent control by walking around and observing the work in their areas.

Productivity Measures

Sales Per Employee: $$\frac{\text{Sales}}{\text{Number of Employees}}$$

Labor Cost Percentage: $$\frac{\text{Labor Costs \$}}{\text{Sales}}$$

Departmental Labor Cost Percentage: $$\frac{\text{Department Labor Cost}}{\text{Departmental Sales}}$$

FIGURE 13.5: Common foodservice productivity measures.

This is known as *management by walking around*. The manager can immediately see if something is being done wrong and can show the associate how to do it the correct way.

Feedback is the most-used control. It provides accurate information after the fact. Management uses such information in a variety of ways. Daily reports on operations provide feedback on how well the operation performed. The information provided on the daily report can help managers and supervisors compare the results with what was forecast.

Feedback can, when shared with associates, motivate them to even better performance. A guest survey or a positive write-up in a newspaper or popular blog encourages most associates to strive for even better results. People generally want and welcome feedback on their performance, and this form of control provides it.

Finally, control provides information necessary for management to make informed decisions. Control is the last element of the management functions and should interface with planning to make for a continuous process.

 # KEY POINTS

1. A supervisor's or manager's decision should be a conscious choice among alternative courses of action directed toward a specific purpose.

2. Different people approach decision making in different ways. Examples include logical, intuitive, indecisive, and impulsive approaches.

3. The decisions that a hospitality supervisor is called on to make range from those that are easy to make to complicated time-pressure decisions to problem solving.

4. It is essential to recognize which decisions are important and which are unimportant, which decisions you must make now and which can wait.

5. The following six steps are a simple version of the logical approach to decision making: Define the problem and set objectives; get the facts (who–what–when–where–how–why); develop and rank alternative solutions; decide on the best solution by examining risk, economy, feasibility, acceptability, and objectives; convert the decision into action; and follow up.

6. When making decisions, your timing can be very important.

7. Problem solving is a special kind of decision making that involves more than a choice between courses of action. It involves identifying the cause of a problem and developing ways to correct or remove the cause.

8. The chief difference between problem solving and simple decision making is that there are extra steps that you must take before you can begin to generate alternative courses of action. The pattern goes like this: describe the problem, search out the cause, define the real problem and set objectives, develop alternative solutions, decide on the best solution, implement the decision, and follow up.

9. Group decision making is advantageous because you get more information relevant to the decision as well as more good ideas. People thinking together can arrive at better decisions, and people who have participated in making the decision are generally committed to carrying it out. Critics of group decision making say that the process takes too much time and tends to be dominated by one person (usually, the boss). If consensus is required, critics say that it leads to mediocre decisions that will appease everyone rather than the best decision.

10. Group decision making is not a panacea. It works best when members are accustomed to working together as a team and have differing expertise and points of view but common goals, when the leader is skillful at keeping meetings on target without dominating or manipulating, and when the group is rewarded for making good decisions.

11. The degree of participation in problem solving and decision making may also vary.

12. For dealing with problems involving one person, an interesting participative approach, win/win problem solving, means that you find a solution that satisfies both of you. You include the worker from the beginning of the problem-solving process, from defining the problem through to carrying out the agreement.

13. Some important decision-making skills include: make sure the decision is yours to make, face decisions promptly, sort out the important decisions from the inconsequential ones, calculate the risks, think about timing, be alert to signs of problems, keep an open mind when investigating a problem, consult your supervisor when necessary, make sure that you are not part of the problem, learn from your decisions, and follow up on your decisions.

14. Controlling is a process by which supervisors measure, evaluate, and compare results to goals and standards previously agreed upon, and take corrective action when necessary to stay on course. Figure 13.5 gives examples of controls commonly found in the hospitality industry.

KEY TERMS

brainstorming
concurrent control
conditions and limitations
controlling
decision
decisiveness
fact finding
feedback
feedforward control
group decision making

impulsive approach to decision making
indecisive approach to decision making
intuitive approach to decision making
logical approach to decision making
problem solving
productivity
productivity standards
timing
win/win problem solving

REVIEW QUESTIONS

Answer each question in complete sentences. Read each question carefully and make sure that you answer all parts of the question. Organize your answer using more than one paragraph when appropriate.

1. What are the three essential elements in a managerial decision?
2. Describe four different approaches to decision making.
3. What is decisiveness?
4. Describe the six steps in decision making.
5. What is *brainstorming,* and what are its pros and cons?
6. How can you test which alternative is best?
7. Explain the relationship between decision making and problem solving. Why would you group them together? Why would you consider them separately?
8. Describe the pattern for solving patterns.
9. What are the pros and cons of group decision making?
10. What are the steps involved in win/win problem solving?
11. List ten tips for making good decisions.
12. Give five examples of controls commonly found in hospitality operations.

 # ACTIVITIES AND APPLICATIONS

1. Discussion Questions

- What is the difference between decisiveness and decision making? What is their relationship?
- What kind of decision maker are you: logical, intuitive, impulsive, indecisive? Do your decisions usually turn out well? How can you improve them?
- What relationships do you see between decision making and responsibility, authority, and accountability? What supervisory responsibilities discussed earlier in this book involve decision making? Give examples of the kinds of decisions required.
- What situations do you see in the hospitality industry where participative decision making would be useful? Explain. Where would it be detrimental or impossible? Explain. If possible, give instances from your own experience where workers participated in some phase of decision making, and comment on the process and outcome.

2. Group Activity: Decision Making

In a group of two, each person presents a work or school problem to work through in the group. Using the pattern in Figure 13.1, go through the steps for each problem. The person who brought up the problem should write down the results of the discussion on his or her problem.

3. Brainstorming

Brainstorming is a technique that can be useful in a variety of training and other supervisory situations. It requires a few ground rules to promote participation: All ideas must be accepted, the pace needs to be fast, ideas need to be recorded, and some of the ideas must be used.

To learn more about brainstorming, take part in a brainstorming session in which you need ideas on (1) the advantages of participative problem solving, and (2) the disadvantages of participative problem solving. Were the ground rules met?

4. Case Study: Who's Managing This Place?

Leon has been head chef at the Elite Cafe since it opened 25 years ago. This little restaurant has been a landmark in a small seaside resort town and up to a year or so ago had always been crowded with customers who came back to enjoy the same fresh seafood dishes they remembered from years before.

In the past year, however, there has been a noticeable drop in its business, owing to competition from several new restaurants that feature nouvelle cuisine, health food, and ethnic cuisines.

Leon's boss, Dennis, the restaurant manager, is an eager young man fresh out of a college hospitality program. He sees what is happening and wants Leon to change the menu, but Leon flatly refuses. He says that the food is as good as it ever was—the best food in town—and that Dennis simply isn't promoting it properly and is probably making a lot of other mistakes, too.

Leon makes it clear that he has no respect for college graduates who haven't paid their dues and gotten their hands dirty—a figure of speech that is all too appropriate for Leon, whose sanitation practices are old-fashioned, too.

The other employees are aware of this ongoing situation between Leon and Dennis and are beginning to take sides. Dennis is aware that he must do something quickly. But what? Dennis sees his main problem as regaining the cafe's share of the market and putting it out front, where it has always been. He can see only the following alternatives:

1. Fire Leon for insubordination. This is what he would like to do. But Leon is an excellent cook and no one on his staff can duplicate his chowder, his lobster bisque, and some of the other classics, and there are no recipes to follow. Also, it would be difficult to hire someone who could develop a new menu quickly. There is also the problem that it is mainly a summer market; How do you hire a chef for six months of the year?

2. Try it Leon's way—a marketing program emphasizing an old-timey image and ambience—the good old days, tradition. Dennis's heart is not in this approach—he can't believe that Leon is right. He also thinks that giving in to Leon will put Leon in charge—which he very nearly is now—and will make it impossible for Dennis to maintain his authority with his other employees.

3. Discuss the problem with his boss, the owner of the cafe. She is an older woman who really doesn't understand the restaurant business—and besides, Dennis doesn't want to admit to her that he has this problem.

4. Get some expert advice on market trends and how to make a market study: Hire a consultant or pay a visit to his favorite professor at the Hospitality Institute. Dennis has made a preliminary decision. He visits his former teacher and comes back with a new perspective. He still has not made his decision, but he is making headway.

Case Study Questions

1. What do you think of Dennis's four alternatives? What are the pros and cons of each? What are the consequences?
2. What do you think is the real problem? How would you define it?
3. What should Dennis's objectives be?
4. Is Dennis himself part of the problem? If so, does this make it harder or easier to solve?
5. Are there other alternatives besides those Dennis has listed? Suggest as many as you can, and give pros and cons for each.
6. Who do you think is right about the menu: Dennis or Leon?
7. Is it possible for Dennis to change Leon's opinion of him? If so, how?
8. Do you think Dennis and Leon might ever get together using the win/win problem-solving method? Would it be appropriate in this situation?

WEB ACTIVITY

- Go to the following website: www.mindtools.com/pages/article/newTED_00.htm.
- What is the systematic approach to decision making? Apply it to a decision of yours.

RELATED WEBSITES

Mind Tools—a great decision-making information website   www.mindtools.com/pages/main/newMN_TED.htm

Free Management Library—good decision-making tools and techniques   managementhelp.org/prsn_prd/decision.htm

ENDNOTES

1. Bradley S. Schneider, *Restaurant Hospitality Cleveland*, vol. 91, no. 2 (February 2007), p. 62.
2. This section is adapted from Michael Tsonton, "New Line Order," *Restaurants and Institutions*, vol. 110, no. 12 (May 1, 2000).
3. This section (including the guidelines but not the win/win strategies) is adapted from John Walsh, "Reservations Manager Maintains Steady Business Stream," *Hotel and Motel Management*, vol. 215, no. 19 (November 6, 2000).
4. This section is adapted from Barbara Young, "Profitable Partnership," *National Provisioner*, vol. 214, no. 10 (October 2000).
5. Stephen P. Robbins and Mary Coulter, *Management*, 8th ed. (Upper Saddle River, NJ: Prentice Hall, 2005), p. 477.

Chapter 5

Equal Opportunity Laws and Diversity

Overview

Promoting equal opportunity, *diversity*, and *inclusion* in the workplace sounds simple enough, but we all know it simply isn't. For years, women and minorities were not—and in some cases, still are not—treated equally. Lack of equal opportunity was such a pressing concern that in June 1963, President John F. Kennedy sent comprehensive civil rights legislation to Congress. Later that summer, in front of the Lincoln Memorial, Dr. Martin Luther King Jr. gave his famous "I Have a Dream" speech that came to symbolize the insistence for meaningful legislation to address the demand for racial equality and justice.[1]

The *Equal Employment Opportunity Commission (EEOC)* was established in 1978 as a central authority, responsible for leading and coordinating the efforts of federal departments and agencies to enforce all laws relating to equal employment opportunity without regard to race, color, religion, sex, national origin, age, or disability.

Today, a visit to the Equal Employment Opportunity Commission's website at www.eeoc.gov will likely have an example of a hospitality company being sued by the EEOC for violation of equal opportunity laws. As a hospitality leader, you will be responsible for equal opportunity in the workplace, for employing and supervising people from cultures different from your own. Applying a "standard" approach to employees—one that does not consider each employee's cultural background—will often create communication barriers. Culturally appropriate communication strategies are needed. But how does that conform to equal opportunity in the

diversity
Physical and cultural dimensions that separate and distinguish individuals and groups: age, gender, physical abilities and qualities, ethnicity, race, sexual preference.

inclusion
To include, to make a person feel welcome.

141

Equal Employment Opportunity Commission (EEOC)
A federal office responsible for enforcing the employment-related provisions of the Civil Rights Act of 1964 as well as other EEO laws.

culture
The socially transmitted behavior patterns, art, beliefs, institutions, and all other products of human work or thought characteristic of a community or population.

workplace? What role does culture play? What is diversity? Why should we want equal opportunity, diversity, and inclusiveness?

Our *culture* is defined as our values, which are manifested in the way we behave, speak, think, and dress; our religious beliefs; the music we like and food we eat; and the way we interact. Culture strongly influences behavior. On the one hand, failure to understand and respect the diverse cultural backgrounds of your employees, and the differences among them, can result in misunderstandings, tension, poor performance, poor employee morale, and higher rates of absenteeism and turnover. On the other hand, when differences are respected, the working environment is richer, much more fun, and even more interesting. Employee satisfaction and performance improve because of this. Equal opportunity, diversity, and inclusiveness in the workplace are critically important in the hospitality industry.

In this chapter you will learn to:

- **Define equal opportunity in the workplace.**
- **Describe the equal opportunity laws.**
- **Explain what every leader needs to know.**
- **Outline EEO and the hiring process.**
- **Apply principles of diversity to the workplace.**
- **Describe steps that increase positive cross-cultural interaction.**
- **Give examples of leading diversity issues positively.**

Equal Opportunity in the Workplace

Today, whenever a job is advertised and candidates are recruited, interviewed, tested, and selected, it is necessary to take equal opportunity into account. Progressive corporations create offices and programs responsible for planning, developing, implementing, and evaluating a comprehensive equal opportunity and diversity program with multifaceted initiatives to support the company's commitment to equal opportunity, diversity, and inclusiveness. Many large hospitality companies have an office of equal opportunity and diversity (EO&D). They may also be called by similar names, such as diversity and equal opportunity (DEO).

✳ EEO AND DIVERSITY

The equal opportunity and diversity office provides effective leadership to ensure that diversity and equal opportunity are a thriving part of the fabric of your company. This department provides an array of services:

- Education and training the public about equal opportunity and diversity
- Advocacy for diversity

- Support for companies' initiatives toward equal opportunity and diversity
- Consultation on best strategies for equal opportunity and diversity recruitment
- Conflict mediation and resolution
- Monitoring employers' equity and affirmative action goals
- Reviewing compliance with state and federal regulations
- Processing and resolving complaints

Applebee's is one of the restaurant industry's progressive companies. Former CEO Lloyd Hill took a stand on racial and sexual orientation issues by saying, "There have been too many 'no comments' on these matters." Operations, finance, and marketing have been the "big three" of the industry for years and something crucial has been left out of the equation—human resources. Applebee's, for example, has a chief people officer, Lou Kaucic, who says that it is critical for human resources to have a seat around the executive table.[2]

Sodexo, which is rated one of the top 50 employers for diversity, says that it is committed to respecting, leveraging, and celebrating the diversity of its workforce, its clientele, and the community in which they live, work, and serve.[3]

Marriott International, one of *Fortune* magazine's 100 best companies to work for, says that its commitment to diversity is absolute. It is the only way to attract, develop, and retain the best talent available.[4]

✳ INCLUSION

Inclusion in the workplace means exactly what it says: to include everyone regardless of gender, marital status, race, national origin, religion, age, disability, sexual orientation, weight, or physical appearance:[5] People who are overweight or less beautiful should not be discriminated against—the only employment criterion should be the ability to do the job. Likewise, a person's sexual orientation should be immaterial: the person's job performance is the only factor that matters.

The restaurant industry's ten-year effort to improve diversity and inclusion in all aspects of the business has been average at best and failing in some areas according to Garry Fernandez, president of the MultiCultural Foodservice Alliance. Fernandez urges the pursuit of diversity in four areas: workforce, customer, community, and suppliers.[6]

Equal Employment Opportunity Laws

A number of laws have been passed to ensure that no individual or group is denied the respect deserved. Understanding the legal requirements of equal opportunity in the workplace is important for three reasons. It will help leaders to (1) do the right thing; (2) realize the limitations of your company's HR and legal departments; and (3) minimize your company's potential liability. Equal employment opportunity is a concept that means that people should be treated equally in all employment matters. Figure 5.1 lists important federal laws commonly referred to as equal employment opportunity (EEO) laws. In general, EEO laws make it unlawful for you to discriminate against

Federal Laws	Type of Employment Discrimination Prohibited	Employers Covered
Equal Pay Act of 1963	Gender differences in pay, benefits, and pension for substantially equal work	Almost all companies, private and government
Title VII, 1964 Civil Rights Act (amended in 1991)	Discrimination in all human resource activities based on race, color, gender, religion, or national origin; established Equal Employment Opportunity Commission to administer the law	Companies with 15 or more employees
Age Discrimination in Employment Act of 1967 (amended in 1986)	Age discrimination against those 40 years of age or older	Companies with 20 or more employees
Pregnancy Discrimination Act of 1978	Prohibits discrimination in hiring, promoting, or terminating because of pregnancy; pregnancy to be treated as medical disability	Same as Title VII
Immigration Reform and Control Act (1986 and 1990)	Prohibits discrimination on the basis of citizenship status and nationality	Companies with 4 or more employees
Americans with Disabilities Act of 1990	Bars discrimination against disabled persons in hiring and employment	Businesses with 15 or more employees
Family and Medical Leave Act of 1993	Mandates 12 workweeks of leave for husband or wife upon birth or adoption of a child or sickness in the family	Companies with 50 or more employees
Fair employment practice acts of states and local governments	Bars discrimination; varies	Varies

FIGURE 5.1:   Equal employment opportunity laws.

applicants or employees with respect to recruiting, hiring, firing, promotions, compensation, or other employment-related activities, on the basis of race, color, religion, gender, nationality, age, or disability. Discrimination in the workplace can be thought of as making employment decisions based on factors that have nothing to do with a person's ability to do the job.

Diversity in the workplace is on the increase.
Photo courtesy of the author.

Equal Pay Act of 1963
A law that requires equal pay and benefits for men and women working in jobs requiring substantially equal skills, effort, and responsibilities under similar working conditions.

Civil Rights Act of 1964, Title VII
An act that makes it unlawful to discriminate against applicants or employees with respect to recruiting, hiring, firing, promotions, or other employment-related activities, on the basis of race, color, religion, gender, or national origin.

Age Discrimination in Employment Act of 1967 (ADEA)
An act that makes it unlawful to discriminate in compensation, terms, or conditions of employment based on a person's age. The ADEA applies to everyone 40 years of age or older.

The starting point for EEO laws was probably passage of the *Equal Pay Act of 1963*. This law requires equal pay and benefits for men and women working in jobs requiring substantially equal skills, effort, and responsibilities under similar working conditions. Congress passed the *Civil Rights Act of 1964, Title VII* (amended in 1991), to bring about equality in employment decisions. The act makes it unlawful for you to discriminate against applicants or employees with respect to recruiting, hiring, firing, promotions, or other employment-related activities, on the basis of race, color, religion, gender, or national origin. Other employment-related activities include, but are not limited to, wages, overtime pay, job assignments, training opportunities, leaves of absence, and retirement plans. Title VII does not require you to hire, promote, or retain employees who are not qualified. The law does provide for you to hire a person of a particular gender if it is based on what is called a bona fide occupational qualification (BFOQ). For instance, it is permissible to hire a man to clean lounges and restrooms reserved for men. The Equal Employment Opportunity Commission (EEOC) was created by the Civil Rights Act of 1964, and it is responsible for enforcing the employment-related provisions of the Civil Rights Act of 1964 as well as other EEO laws. Employees with the EEOC, which also develops and issues guidelines to enforce EEO laws, can file complaints of discrimination.

Age discrimination was addressed in the *Age Discrimination in Employment Act of 1967 (ADEA)*, amended in 1978 and 1986, which makes it unlawful for you to discriminate in compensation, terms, or conditions of employment because of a person's age. The ADEA applies to all people 40 years of age and older. This act also bans forced

The Pregnancy Discrimination Act of 1978
An act that makes it unlawful to discriminate against a woman on the basis of pregnancy, childbirth, or related medical conditions.

Immigration Reform and Control Act (IRCA)
A federal law that requires employers to verify the identity and employment eligibility of all applicants and prohibits discrimination in hiring or firing due to a person's national origin.

Americans with Disabilities Act (ADA)
An act that makes it unlawful to discriminate in employment matters against the estimated 43 million Americans who have a disability.

retirement. *The Pregnancy Discrimination Act of 1978* makes it unlawful to discriminate against a woman on the basis of pregnancy, childbirth, or related medical conditions. You cannot refuse to hire (or promote) a woman just because she is pregnant. According to this law, pregnancy is a temporary disability and women must be permitted to work as long as they are physically able to perform their jobs. Employers cannot determine the beginning and ending dates of a pregnant employee's maternity leave.

The *Immigration Reform and Control Act* (IRCA, written in 1986 and amended in 1990) was prompted by problems associated with the increasing numbers of immigrants living in the United States. This act makes it illegal to discriminate in recruiting, hiring, or terminating based on a person's national origin or citizenship status. In these kinds of cases, fines can be charged and judges can order employers to provide back pay, pay court charges, and reinstate an employee. Although Title VII of the Civil Rights Act of 1964 has long prohibited this type of discrimination, IRCA covers employers with 4 or more employees, and Title VII covers employers with 15 or more employees.

The only people you can discriminate against are those you are not legally allowed to hire (or continue to employ): illegal aliens. IRCA imposes penalties for hiring unauthorized aliens. To help ensure that you don't hire an illegal alien, IRCA requires employers to verify that the people they hire are eligible to work in the United States. This is done by completing an I-9 Employment Eligibility Verification form within three days after hire. Using this form, the employer may ask for certain documents that establish the person's identity (such as a driver's license) and employment eligibility (such as a U.S. birth certificate or valid Immigration and Naturalization Services' Employment Authorization Card). To be fair and nondiscriminatory, you cannot request certain work status documentation from some applicants but not others.

The *Americans with Disabilities Act of 1990 (ADA)* makes it unlawful to discriminate in employment matters against the estimated 43 million Americans who have a disability. Under the ADA, a person has a disability if he or she has a physical or mental impairment that substantially limits one or more major life activities, such as hearing, seeing, speaking, or walking. It also covers recovering alcohol and drug abusers (as long as they are in a supervised treatment program) and people infected with the HIV virus.

It is unlawful to ask an applicant whether he or she is disabled or about the disability itself. You can ask an applicant questions about his or her ability to perform job-related functions as long as the questions are not phrased in terms of a disability. You can also ask the applicant to describe or demonstrate how (with or without reasonable accommodation) he or she will perform job duties. The ADA does not interfere with your right to hire the best-qualified applicant, and a disabled applicant must satisfy your job requirements and be able to perform essential job functions.

Reasonable accommodation, which is legally required, refers to any change or adjustment to a job or the work environment that will enable someone with a disability to perform essential job functions. For example, a worktable might be lowered to enable someone to work while seated, a work schedule might be modified, or a job might be restructured. Employers are not required to lower quality or quantity standards to provide an accommodation, nor are they required to make an accommodation if it would impose an undue hardship on the operation of the business. Undue hardship is defined as an "action requiring significant difficulty or expense" and is determined on a case-by-case basis.

In addition to the federal EEO laws, state and local governments have fair employment practice acts (FEPs) that often include further conditions. For example, some states forbid employment discrimination on the basis of marital status. It is important to learn about EEO laws because you need to be able to select applicants in a fair and nondiscriminatory manner.

The *Family and Medical Leave Act of 1993* allows employees to take an unpaid leave of absence from work for up to 12 weeks per year for any of the following reasons:

Family and Medical Leave Act of 1993
An act that allows employees to take an unpaid leave of absence from work for up to 12 weeks per year for the birth or adoption of a child or a serious health condition of the employee or his or her spouse, child, or parent.

- Birth or adoption of a child
- Serious health condition of a child
- Serious health condition of a spouse or parent
- Employee's own serious health condition

When the employee returns from leave, he or she is entitled to his or her former position or an equivalent position. To be eligible for a leave of absence, the employee must have worked for the employer for at least 12 months. If it was provided before the leave was taken, the employer is obligated to maintain group health insurance during the leave.

Do You Know?

Are EEO laws effective?

EEO Laws and the Hiring Process

Figure 5.2 lists recommended ways to ask questions of job applicants, whether on job applications or during interviews, to avoid charges of discrimination. The kinds of questions that are not allowed relate to race, gender, age (except to make sure that the applicant's age meets labor laws), family and marital status, religion, national origin, appearance, and disabilities unrelated to the job.

Job requirements or qualifications, such as those regarding education and work experience, must be relevant to the job, nondiscriminatory, and predictive of future job performance. Although requiring a high school diploma for an entry-level food-service job, such as server, seems to be acceptable, there are certainly many servers who do their jobs well without the diploma. The requirement of a high school diploma when it is not related to successful performance of the job can be viewed as discriminatory.

Any type of preemployment test must be valid, reliable, and relevant to the job. To be valid, tests must be related to successful performance on the job. To be reliable, tests must yield consistent results. Tests should be given to all applicants, with a single standard for rating scores, and must be given under the same conditions. Even when a test is given to all concerned, it might be considered discriminatory if the test eliminates members of protected groups (the groups protected or covered by EEO laws) more frequently than members of nonprotected groups.

Subject	Inappropriate Questions (May Not Ask or Require)	Appropriate Questions (May Ask or Require)
Gender or marital status	• Gender (on application form) • Mr., Miss, Mrs., Ms.? • Married, divorced, single, separated? • Number and ages of children • Pregnancy, actual or intended • Maiden name, former name	• In checking your work record, do we need another name for identification?
Race	• Race? • Color of skin, eyes, hair, etc. • Request for photograph	
National origin	• Questions about place of birth, ancestry, mother tongue, national origin of parents or spouse • What is your native language? • How did you learn to speak [language] fluently?	• If job-related, what foreign languages do you speak?
Citizenship, immigration status	• Of what country are you a citizen? • Are you a native-born U.S. citizen? • Questions about naturalization of applicant, spouse, or parents	• If selected, are you able to start work with us on a specific date? If not, when would you be able to start? • If hired, can you show proof that you are eligible to work in the United States?
Religion	• Religious affiliation or preference • Religious holidays observed • Membership in religious organizations	• Can you observe regularly required days and hours of work? • Are there any days or hours of the week that you are not able to work? • Are there any holidays that you are not able to work?

FIGURE 5.2: Equal employment opportunity: Appropriate and inappropriate questions sometimes used in hiring a new employee.

Age	• How old are you? • Date of birth	• Are you 21 or older? (for positions serving alcohol)
Disability	• Do you have any disabilities? • Have you ever been treated for (certain) diseases? • Are you healthy?	
Questions that may discriminate against minorities	• Have you ever been arrested? • List all clubs, societies, and lodges to which you belong. • Do you own a car? (unless required for the job) • Type of military discharge • Questions regarding credit ratings, financial status, wage garnishment, home ownership	• Have you ever been convicted of a crime? If yes, give details. (If crime is job-related, as embezzlement is to handling money, you may refuse to hire.) • List membership in professional organizations relevant to job performance. • Military service: dates, branch of service, education, and experience (if job-related)

FIGURE 5.2:   *(continued)*

A good way to check yourself to ensure that you are not discriminating when evaluating job applicants is to be sure you can answer yes to the following five questions:

1. Are the qualifications based on the actual duties and needs of the job, not on personal preferences or a wish list?
2. Will the information requested from the applicant help me to judge his or her ability to do the job?
3. Will each part of the selection process, including job descriptions, applications, advertising, and interviews, prevent screening out those groups covered by EEO laws?
4. Can I judge an applicant's ability to do the job successfully without regard to how he or she is different from me in terms of age, gender, race, color, nationality, religion, or disability?
5. Is the selection process the same for all applicants?

Check Your Knowledge

1. Define equal employment opportunity.
2. List four important federal laws commonly referred to as equal employment opportunity laws.
3. What is the function of equal employment opportunity laws?

Equal Opportunity in the Workplace: What Leaders Need to Know

The following is excerpted from the U.S. Equal Employment Opportunity Commission "Training and Technical Assistance Program."[7]

✳ Q & A: RACE, ETHNICITY, COLOR—WHAT PRACTICES ARE DISCRIMINATORY?

Title VII of the Civil Rights Act of 1964 prohibits employment discrimination based on race, color, religion, sex, or national origin. It is illegal to discriminate in any aspect of employment including:

- Hiring and firing
- Compensation, assignment, or classification of employees
- Transfer, promotion, layoff, or recall
- Job advertisements
- Recruitment
- Use of company facilities
- Training and apprenticeship programs
- Pay, retirement plans, and disability leave
- Terms and conditions of employment

✳ INTERVIEWING

Questions you can and cannot ask at an interview are discussed in more detail in Chapter 6 on recruiting and selecting applicants. But we should mention here that there are several inappropriate questions that should be avoided (also refer back to Figure 5.2): How many children do you have? What country do your parents come from? What is your height? What is your weight? What church do you go to? Are you a U.S. citizen? Do you have any disabilities? Are you dating anyone right now? When did you graduate from high school? A simple rule to follow is if it's not job related—don't ask. When facing charges of discrimination, the employer bears the burden of proving that answers to all questions on application forms or in oral interviews are not used in making hiring and placement decisions in a discriminatory manner prohibited by law. The guiding principle behind any question to a job applicant is: "Can the employer demonstrate a legitimate job-related or business necessity for asking the question?" Both the intent behind the question and how the information is to be used by the employer are important for determining whether a question is an appropriate preemployment inquiry.[8]

Diversity

One of the biggest business drivers is the changing demographics. The ever-changing face of the U.S. population continues to reflect an increase in women, racial and ethnic groups, immigrants, older workers, and individuals with disabilities, as well as changing family structures and religious diversity.[9]

Understanding and embracing diversity is of critical importance in today's increasingly multicultural and diverse society. The term *diversity* is often used when discussing people of different cultures. Diversity refers to the following cultural as well as physical dimensions, which separate and distinguish us both as individuals and as groups. This list is not meant to be all-inclusive of all groups. Diversity is so much more than just what is listed:[10]

- Culture
- Ethnic group
- Race
- Religion
- Language
- Age
- Gender
- Physical abilities and qualities
- Sexual orientation

Culture, ethnic group, and *race* are related terms. Culture is a learned behavior consisting of a unique set of beliefs, values, attitudes, habits, customs, traditions, and other forms of behavior. Culture influences the way that people behave. Cultural behavior varies from culture to culture. *Culture* refers to the behaviors, beliefs, and characteristics of a particular group, such as an ethnic group. *Ethnic groups* share a common and distinctive culture, including elements such as religion and language. *Race* refers to a group of people related by common descent.

The population of the United States is becoming more multicultural, and diverse, every day. Almost one in four Americans has African, Asian, Hispanic, or Native American ancestry. It is estimated that by 2020, the number will rise to almost one in three, and by 2050, the number will be almost one in two.

As the United States becomes more diverse, so does the workplace. The hospitality workplace employs a particularly diverse group of employees. A restaurant's staff often resembles a miniature United Nations, with employees from all around the globe. According to the U.S. Department of Labor, 12 percent of foodservice employees are foreign-born, compared to 8 percent in other occupations. Foodservice also employs many more Hispanics and African Americans than other industries. The National Restaurant Association's website states the following:[11]

- Restaurants employ more minority managers than any other industry.
- More than two-thirds of the supervisors in the foodservice industry are women; 16 percent are African American; and 13 percent are Hispanic.

Up until the late 1980s, white males made up the majority of the U.S. workforce. Many of the workers now entering the labor force are minorities, such as Hispanics, Latinos, and Asians, and many are immigrants. The reasons behind these trends include a young, growing minority population and a continuing high rate of immigration.

PROFILE Gerry Fernandez

Courtesy of
Gerry Fernandez.

Gerry Fernandez began working as a cook at Royal's Healthside Restaurant in Rutland, Vermont. Ernest Royal, owner of the restaurant and a noted New England restaurateur, was the first African American board member of the National Restaurant Association. Royal had experienced considerable racism, and in his honor, Gerry Fernandez conceived the Multicultural Foodservice and Hospitality Alliance (MFHA), www.mfha.net. The MFHA is dedicated to promoting diversity within the foodservice industry.

Since his first position as cook at Royal's, Gerry has had a successful career, beginning with earning a bachelor of science in food service management from Johnson and Wales University, where he also earned a degree in culinary arts. His stint as a cook was followed by terms as sous chef, manager, and general manager of various New England restaurants. Gerry spent more than ten years as a senior manager opening and operating fine-dining restaurants.

In 1995, Gerry moved to General Mills as a technical service specialist in foodservice research and development. He provided support and training to sales, marketing, and product development teams. Additionally, he evaluated current new competitor products, and he conducted recipe development, concept testing, tolerance testing, photo shots, and product presentations. Gerry has received numerous awards, including the General Mills "Champion's Award" and *Nation's Restaurant News* "50 Power Players."

In a recent interview, Fernandez spoke about the vision of the MFHA organization and its intended impact on foodservice operations worldwide.

How does diversity affect foodservice in general? "Comprehensive diversity issues exist in many large companies, and they are asking foodservice operators, 'Where do you stand?' It is coming, whether or not you like it. Diversity is not simply a social agenda issue; it

The market-savvy businesses of today are responding to the changing demographics by targeting diverse consumers, employees, and supply partners in ways that build meaningful and reciprocal relationships. If companies' marketers and service providers do not reach out to minority communities in a holistic way, they're setting themselves up for failure in the long run.

Promote inclusion in the supply chain by partnering with minority-owned firms that support our businesses as patrons. This demonstrates a commitment to inclusion and creates jobs in the very communities that support our businesses as patrons. If companies' marketers and service providers do not reach out to minority communities in a holistic way, they're setting themselves up for failure in the long run. The market-savvy businesses of today are responding to the changing demographics by targeting diverse consumers, employees, and supply partners in ways that build meaningful and reciprocal relationships.[12]

In the hospitality workforce it is vital that multicultural management recognizes and respects cultural differences among employees and allows and encourages them. Cross-cultural awareness in today's hospitality industry promotes harmonizing with other cultures and prevents misunderstandings. By allowing and encouraging variation, blends of people from all different kinds of backgrounds are able to learn from one another and grow in aspects of the workplace.[13]

(continued)

is a bottom-line issue. When people talk about diversity, they think about inclusion of more women and more people of color. They tend to think only about the soft issues, the green issues. Diversity really is a green discussion more than it is any other color. MFHA is striving to make this an economic discussion rather than a social discussion."

What is the object of MFHA? "To be the solutions bridge for multiculturalism in the foodservice industry so that operators can leverage diversity as a positive influence on the bottom line. We think of multicultural diversity as a way to improve the foodservice business in all aspects: human resources, marketing, training, community relations, and so on. We are the multicultural Yellow Pages for the industry. We are solution focused: a connector of people to issues and people to information."

What does MFHA offer operators? "This is a place to start the diversity process. If operators are looking for opportunities, recipes, programs, or qualified diversity experts, they can call on us. Whether you are an on-site operator—self-op or contract managed—there is a concern regarding bids for city, state, and federal contracts. These potential clients are inquiring directly as to what percentage of your business purchases are from women and minority-owned businesses. Companies are realizing that they need a way to address this issue. We offer a context in which such issues can be explored constructively."

What kinds of services does MFHA have available? "We help identify qualified women and minority-owned business operators who can do business with the big boys. Additionally, MFHA can provide in-house solutions in the form of awareness and skills training, recruiting and retention, marketing, purchasing, and referral services."

How is MFHA evolving? "The last three years have been internally focused as we have developed the infrastructure. Now we are focused externally on our members. We will be able to provide more research and, through focus groups and benchmarking, help operators by training in ways to be more strategic in their diversity effort and to recruit better talent. It's not about one company or one ethnic segment, it's about our industry as a whole reaching out and recruiting from and to every segment of the population."[14]

ARAMARK's definition of diversity is, "The mosaic of people who bring a variety of backgrounds, styles, perspectives, values, and beliefs as assets to ARAMARK and our partners." Kaleidoscope Vision states that ARAMARK is composed of unique individuals who, together, make the company what it is and can be in the future. Only when all individuals contribute fully can the strength and vision of ARAMARK be realized. Here are ARAMARK's guiding principles for diversity:

> Because we are committed to being a company where the best people want to work, we champion a comprehensive diversity initiative. Because we thrive on growth, we recruit, retain, and develop a diverse workforce. Because we succeed through performance, we create an environment that allows all employees to contribute to their fullest potential.[15]

Why Does Cultural Diversity Matter?

Cultural diversity matters to every single one of us, both professionally and personally. When a group or segment is excluded or oppressed, all of us are denied. For businesses and communities not only to survive but to thrive, each of us must be aware and sensitive to all members of the community. Our communities are rich in resources. When all segments are respected and utilized, it benefits everyone involved. America is the most diverse nation in the world. Our ethnicity, religion, life experience, and so on make each one of us unique.

Developing Cross-Cultural Interaction

Diversity in itself is not a challenge but, in fact, an opportunity. It is an opportunity for us to build diverse teams, diverse knowledge perspective, and experiences that can solve business problems and create value for our shareholders and guests. The main thrust of the initiative is moving beyond awareness training and toward diversity skills training, which helps to enhance the skills of managers and supervisors in communication across lines of difference. This enhances the ability to recognize and respond to the needs of our diverse customers. Every successful business needs to practice sensitivity to diversity.

By developing cross-cultural interaction skills, you will be better equipped to do your job and to motivate diverse employees to accomplish company goals. But don't think you will be able to develop these skills overnight or, for that matter, even over a few months. By considering the major steps listed in Figure 5.3, you will better appreciate that this process is complex and will take time to master. The effective supervisor is aware that employees come from different cultural backgrounds, and so the supervisor learns about how their cultures differ and works with employees without passing judgment about their cultures.

Shifting demographics make practicing diversity more than just a politically correct idea in the hospitality industry. Diversity is anything that makes people different from each other, such as gender, race, ethnicity, income, religion, and disabilities. Foodservice has welcomed minorities for a long time, and minorities make up the largest percentage of workers in the foodservice industry. For supervisors in the hospitality industry it is important to encourage minority talent. Promoting people based solely on their abilities, skills, and job performance into supervisory positions helps promote minority advancement in the foodservice industry.

1. Increase personal awareness.
2. Learn about other cultures.
3. Recognize and practice cross-cultural interaction skills.
4. Maintain awareness, knowledge, and skills.

FIGURE 5.3: Developing cross-cultural interaction skills.

How to Increase Personal Awareness

Without realizing it, it is possible to become culture bound, meaning that you believe that your culture and value system are the best, the one and only. You think your way of talking, perceiving, thinking, valuing, and behaving are normal and right. For example, when you hear someone talking with an accent, you are likely to think how strange it sounds, or even how wrong or abnormal it is. How many of us realize that each of us has an accent, which probably sounds strange to those of different backgrounds? The first step in developing your cross-cultural skills is to examine how your own culture has influenced who you are. Consider, for example, how your culture has influenced your attitudes toward the following:

- Education
- Work
- Family
- Self-sufficiency
- Money
- Authority
- Expression of emotions

An activity at the end of this chapter will help you look more deeply at your own cultural attitudes and compare them to others.

After becoming more aware of your own culture, the next step is to learn various facts of other cultures. As a supervisor, it is crucial to see other cultures as objectively as possible and not pass judgment. By learning about another culture, it is hoped that you will be better able to understand people from that culture, as well as to be understood better in turn. Some aspects of another culture that are interesting to learn include verbal and nonverbal language differences, values, customs, work habits, and attitudes toward work.

A danger in learning about any culture is that the information may be overgeneralized, thereby promoting stereotypes. It is important to keep in mind that regardless of cultural background, a person is still an individual and needs to be treated and respected as someone with a unique personality, wants, and needs.

You can learn about other cultures in various ways: reading about them in books and magazines, attending cultural fairs and festivals, and interacting with individuals from other cultures. By learning about other cultures and interacting with people of varying backgrounds, you can work on valuing your differences as well as uncovering and overcoming any of your own fears, stereotypes, and prejudices.

How to Recognize and Practice Cross-Cultural Interaction

A person's nationality, culture, race, and gender affect how he or she communicates. However, communication between people of different cultures can often be difficult when neither person is familiar with the other's style of communicating. There are three specific problem areas that supervisors must take steps to overcome:

1. The tendency not to listen carefully or pay attention to what others are saying
2. Speaking or addressing others in ways that alienate them or make them feel uncomfortable
3. Using or falling back on inappropriate stereotypes to communicate with people from other cultures

To be an effective supervisor in a culturally diverse workforce, you must be able to recognize the different ways that people communicate, be sensitive to your own employees' cultural values, and adapt your own supervisory style accordingly.

For example, in some cultures, people rely primarily on verbal communication. In other cultures, the spoken word is only part of communication; people express themselves "in context"—language, body language, the physical setting, and past relationships are all parts of communication.

The use of personal space is another important culture difference. If you step into someone's personal space, he or she will often step back, in order to maintain personal space. People from Latin America, Africa, the Middle East, and South America often prefer to communicate at much closer distances than would seem comfortable for

Creating opportunities to learn about other cultures is helpful in creating cultural harmony.
Courtesy of PhotoDisc/Getty Images.

people from Canada or the United States. Asians, by contrast, sometimes prefer even more personal space. As a supervisor, if an employee steps into your personal space and you step back, your action may be seen as being aloof or not wanting to talk. To adjust to situations when talking with someone, stay put and let the other person stand where he or she is comfortable.

Eye contact and facial expressions are two other nonverbal communication techniques that vary among cultures. Whereas in North America it is common to maintain good eye contact and employ facial cues such as nodding the head when listening to someone speak, not all cultures share those practices. In many Asian and African cultures, people will make greater eye contact when speaking, but when listening, make infrequent eye contact. They also might not use facial expressions when listening to others. These nonverbal communication differences may lead to misunderstanding. A supervisor may wrongly misinterpret that an employee who does not make eye contact or nod in response is simply not listening or doesn't care, when, in fact, the employee is listening in a respectful manner.

Cultural differences also affect other areas of communication, such as the rate at which people speak, the volume, speech inflections, and the use of pauses and silence when speaking. It is common in Europe and North America to speak whenever there is silence in a conversation, and to speak loudly. This is not always the case in other cultures. In Asian cultures, silence is not regarded as an interruption or indication that the conversation has ended but is often considered as much a part of conversation as speaking is. Silence is also often used as a sign of politeness and respect for elders rather than a lack of desire to keep talking. Whereas a North American's loud speech in many Asian countries is often interpreted as being aggressive or even angry, an Asian's soft-spoken voice in the United States might be seen as a sign of weakness or shyness.

Another communication difference is the tendency in Europe and the United States to be direct in conversation and get to the point. In many other cultures, this practice is considered impolite and rude. To an Asian American, being direct might be interpreted as being insensitive to the feelings of others. Native Americans, Asian Americans, and some Hispanic Americans value respect and harmony and will use indirect speaking methods to achieve those ends.

It is also important to remember that not everyone from one culture will act the same. Even though it is a common perception that Asian people are soft-spoken, it is not uncommon for Asian people to speak loudly. Furthermore, not all people who look like they are of certain cultures are. For example, someone who "looks" Hispanic might have been born and raised a few blocks away from your establishment, right next door to another employee.

As a leader, you should be sensitive to your employees' cultural values and understand their different communication styles. Always be open for feedback when communicating. Feedback can tell you how you are perceived by others as well as how well you are getting your point across. Also, keep in mind that it is only natural that people from other cultures speak with a different tone of voice, rhythm, and pace. Finally, as a supervisor, you can also focus on core values that transcend cultural boundaries by creating a workplace where all employees feel valued, safe, and respected.

Check Your Knowledge

1. Describe the process of developing cross-cultural interaction skills.
2. Define culture bound.

Leading Cultural Diversity in the Workplace

In the twenty-first century supervisors and managers, in order to be effective, have to handle greater cultural diversity. Supervisors and managers who are not able to handle diversity in the workforce are a liability. Poor supervision can cost companies dearly in the following ways:

- Discrimination lawsuits
- Litigation time and money
- Legal fees/settlements
- High employee turnover rates
- Negative community image

Understanding what cultural diversity is, why it matters, and how to effectively manage your diverse team of associates can minimize risks.

Leading diversity in the workplace means to recognize, respect, and capitalize on the different backgrounds in our society in terms of race, ethnicity, gender, and sexual orientation. Different cultural groups have different values, styles, and personalities, each of which may have a substantial effect on the way they perform in the workplace.

More women are members of the executive committee or guidance team.
Courtesy of Digital Vision.

Rather than punishing or stifling these different management styles because they do not conform to the traditional white (male) management methods, employers should recognize these differences as benefits. Not only can diverse leadership styles achieve the same results as traditional methods, but a diverse workforce can also help improve the company's competitive position in the marketplace.

Diversity, or sensitivity, training is now commonplace in the corporate world. However, small businesses need to be aware of these issues just as well. As a small business owner, your awareness and respect of diversity truly matters to your employees and client base.

You must create a balance of respect and understanding in the workplace to have happy and optimally productive workers. In addition to this, it is important that you and your employees are aware of the importance of respecting diversity when dealing with your clients. When you work effectively with your community, both you and the community benefit.[16]

Rohini Anand, senior vice president and chief diversity officer, Sodexo USA, says that diversity has an extremely broad definition at Sodexo. It includes all those differences that make us unique, including race and gender, ethnicity, sexual orientation, religion, class, physical and mental abilities, language abilities, and so on. We also have a very clear mission statement about diversity being the right thing to do and making business sense for our company. It's about creating a work environment for our employees as well as giving back to the community and providing socially responsible services to our clients.

There must be a real commitment for top management to "walk their talk." Plus, senior management must establish goals and monitor their accomplishment; otherwise, they won't be met. In some companies people only do things because the president says so, but what if the president leaves? The next president may not have the same agenda. It is better to have diversity, inclusion, and multiculturalism in the mission statement and in the departmental goals with objectives as to how the goals will be met.

Sodexo strives to be the best in class in the hospitality industry and is rapidly becoming a benchmark for corporate America. This is being achieved by six strategic imperatives, diversity being one of them. Alongside financial results the company reports on how it is doing on diversity and inclusion. The company also has an incentive program where bonuses of 10 to 15 percent are linked to the diversity scorecard. Twenty-five percent of the executive team's bonus is linked, and the CEO has guaranteed that this bonus will be paid out regardless of the financial performance of the company. Now that's putting your money where your mouth is!

Sodexo recommends having someone whose sole job is to attend to diversity and inclusion because it has such a broad scope in terms of the kinds of things that are involved in a diversity effort. Plus, it really shows the commitment. The symbolic aspect is as important as the actual work. According to Anand:

There are so many pieces included in a diversity effort. It ranges from recruiting and sourcing to retention . . . my recommendation is that somebody be responsible for diversity and inclusion and report to senior management—preferably the president. You want to have influence at the top. A diversity effort can only be successful if you get top level buy-in along with grass roots efforts.[17]

An example of managing cultural diversity in the workplace is that many hospitality organizations are hiring more Hispanics because they have proven themselves capable and enthusiastic. However, this is often accompanied by new communications problems. Whatever your approach, patience is a virtue—and a necessity. Establish workplace policies and resources, then recognize and encourage a family mentality. Provide easy and affordable access to make long-distance calls home; supply phone cards as incentives and gifts; ask about the well-being of their relatives; arrange for easy and affordable transmission of money home.[18]

Hospitality human resource professionals and leaders should be careful to avoid problems associated with requiring employees to speak English at all times in the workplace. This is in conflict with Title VII, which prohibits workplace discrimination based on national origin. Clearly, it is important for hotel owners, operators, and managers to balance how to best deliver a unique brand experience along with the rights of their workforce. The increasingly diverse U.S. workforce makes English-only a difficult question. This potential conflict is best reflected in a recent settlement between the EEOC and The Melrose Hotel Co. of New York. In that case, 13 employees received an $800,000 settlement for complaints of a hostile work environment—which included allegations that Hispanic employees were subjected to an English-only rule.[19]

Establishing a Diversity and Inclusion Program

The following five steps are the how-tos for establishing a diversity and inclusion program:

1. Develop a mission statement that includes diversity and inclusion.
2. Develop goals for diversity and inclusion for each key operating area.
3. Develop objectives/strategies to show how the goals will be met.
4. Develop measurements to monitor progress toward the goals.
5. Monitor progress toward goal accomplishment.

Gerry Fernandez, president of the Multicultural Foodservice and Hospitality Alliance (MFHA), says that with more than $1 trillion in buying power, minorities of today will be the majority of tomorrow. That's not a philosophical argument; it's based purely on facts and data found in the U.S. Census. Focusing on multiculturalism isn't about doing the right thing; it is about doing the right thing for your business.[20]

Hotel corporations are also reaching out to minority groups to help them become hotel owners. For example, Hilton says it has picked all the low-hanging fruit by approaching minority athletes and entertainers, and now it's going after people who are pooling their money.[21]

Some might be concerned about the costs of promoting diversity and education about other cultures. According to Salvador Mendoza, director of diversity at Hyatt Hotels, it is possible to leverage diversity to the bottom line. Multicultural initiatives are bottom-line issues. You have to be sensitive to the needs of employees, and you have to make money. There's a way to do both while promoting a multicultural environment.[22]

Many of the larger, well-known hotel and restaurant corporations have a diversity initiative to encourage minority ownership of franchised hotels and restaurants as well as becoming suppliers to those companies. Cendant's Keys to Success program aims to give minorities a leg up in the hotel business by offering an allowance of $1,000 per room for properties up to 74 rooms and $1,500 per room for larger ones. At Starwood Hotels and Resorts, which *Fortune* magazine recently named among the top 50 companies for minority employees, 80 percent of the associates are women and minorities.[23]

The W Hotel on Union Square in New York celebrates the holidays of many religions and countries, theme days in the employee recreation room and coffee breaks, and provides opportunities for more formal communication by an employee survey index, which measures how successful it was in creating a multicultural workplace of excellence. Supervisors and managers take this seriously because one-third of their bonus is based on the survey results.[24]

Managing Diversity Issues Positively

The following list of tips and suggestions will help you to remember that your staff is made up of individuals, which is important to keep in mind, no matter how diverse your staff.

✳ GENERAL GUIDELINES

- Get to know your employees, what they like about their jobs, what they do not like, where they are from, what holidays they celebrate. Listen to their opinions. Help to meet their needs.
- Treat your employees equitably but not uniformly. Do not treat everyone the same when, after all, they are all different. Of course, there must be some consistency to what you do, but as long as you apply the same set of goals and values to each situation, you can treat each employee individually and consistently.
- Watch for any signs of harassment, such as employees telling jokes that make fun of a person's cultural background, race, sexual orientation, religion, and so on. Know your company's policies on harassment.
- Foster a work climate of mutual respect.
- Encourage the contributions of diverse employees at meetings, in conversations, in training. Recognize their valuable contributions. Also, allow differences to be discussed rather than suppressed.

✳ GENDER ISSUES

- Make sure that you are not showing favoritism to males or females, by, for instance, granting time off more readily or allowing certain employees to come in late or leave early.
- Show the same amount of respect and listen actively to both genders.
- Know your company's policy on sexual harassment and take seriously any charge of misconduct.

✳ CULTURAL ISSUES

- Learn some of the foreign language phrases that are used by your employees. It shows respect for the employees who speak that language and improves communication.
- Find out how your employees want to be addressed in their own language and how to pronounce their names correctly. Avoid using slang names such as "Honey," "Sweetheart," "Dear," "Fella," and so on. They are disrespectful and annoying.
- Give rewards that are meaningful and appropriate to all employees.
- If employees are having trouble with English, be careful when speaking to them. Speaking a little more slowly than usual might be helpful, but speaking too slowly might make your employees feel that you think they're stupid. Speaking very loudly will not make things easier to understand. Make sure that slang terms and idioms are understood. It's always important that employees (even those who speak English well) know and are comfortable enough to tell you when they don't understand what you're saying.
- Be cautious about the use and interpretation of gestures. Gestures such as thumbs up are by no means universal. For example, in the United States, a customer may gesture "one" to a server in a restaurant by putting up an index finger. In some European countries, this gesture means "two." If you are not sure what someone's gesture means, ask for the meaning.

✳ RELIGIOUS ISSUES

- Be consistent in allowing time off for religious reasons.

✳ AGE ISSUES

- Both the young and the old sometimes feel that they do not get the respect they deserve. They need to know what is going on in the department and how well they are doing their jobs, just like anyone else. Make them feel like part of the team.
- Young workers want to do work they consider worthwhile and to have fun doing it. They want their supervisors to listen to them, to let them participate in decision making. Not surprisingly, they do not want supervisors to bark orders military-style. They like to have time and money invested into their training and development.
- Do not have higher expectations of older adults than of their younger coworkers, and don't patronize them.

✳ PHYSICALLY AND OR MENTALLY CHALLENGED ISSUES

About 43 million Americans have a physical disability. At work, people with disabilities often feel that supervisors do not see beyond their disabilities and do not think they are capable. Coworkers may seem to patronize them and, because of embarrassment, may avoid speaking directly to them.

- Look at the differently abled employee the same way you look at other employees, as a whole person with likes, dislikes, hobbies, and so on, and encourage the employee's coworkers to do so.
- Speak directly to the differently abled employee.
- Hiring of handicapped workers does have a positive effect on the economy.
- Disabled workers are good for the community and for employers.
- The hospitality industry has a responsibility to provide job opportunities for all.
- Employees with disabilities are just as productive as other employees. You might have to make some adjustments for disabled employees, but this does not affect the quality of their work.

Even with great cross-cultural interaction skills, you will occasionally do something that offends an employee. When this happens, do the commonsense thing: Apologize sincerely.

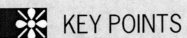 # KEY POINTS

1. Equal employment opportunity was denied to so many for so long that eventually in 1963 Congress passed the Equal Pay Act and, in 1964, the Civil Rights Act, Title VII, which established the Equal Employment Commission.
2. Progressive companies embrace equal opportunity, diversity, and inclusiveness. Many have EEO/diversity officers who plan, develop, implement, and monitor EEO, diversity, and inclusion programs.
3. The equal employment opportunity laws are reviewed.
4. When hiring, it is important to know the questions you can or cannot ask and an outline of what supervisors need to know.
5. On the one hand, failure to understand and respect the differences, or the diversity, of your employees can result in misunderstandings, tension, poor performance, poor employee morale, and higher rates of employee absenteeism and turnover. On the other hand, when differences are respected, the working environment is richer, more fun, and more interesting, and employee satisfaction and performance improve.
6. Steps to develop cross-cultural interaction skills are:
   - Increasing personal awareness
   - Learning about other cultures
   - Recognizing and practicing cross-cultural interaction skills
   - Maintaining awareness, knowledge, and skills
7. The chapter lists tips that can be used to manage diversity issues positively.

KEY TERMS

Age Discrimination in Employment Act of 1967 (ADEA)
Americans with Disabilities Act (ADA)
Civil Rights Act of 1964, Title VII
culture
diversity
Equal Employment Opportunity Commission
Equal Pay Act of 1963
Family and Medical Leave Act of 1993
Immigration Reform and Control Act (IRCA)
inclusion
Pregnancy Discrimination Act of 1978

REVIEW QUESTIONS

Answer each question in complete sentences. Read each question carefully and make sure that you answer all parts of the question. Organize your answer using more than one paragraph when appropriate.

1. Outline equal opportunity in the workplace.
2. List the laws that affect equal opportunity in the workplace.
3. Identify the important things that every supervisor needs to know about diversity.
4. Describe the process of developing cross-cultural interaction skills.
5. Identify two diversity-related problems that could come up in a day-to-day job scenario, and give tips for managing these situations.

ACTIVITIES AND APPLICATIONS

1. Discussion Questions

- Have you ever been discriminated against in the workplace, or observed when someone else was discriminated against? Describe what happened and how it could have been handled better.
- Do you know a supervisor/manager who handles diverse employees skillfully? If so, what skills does he or she have?
- What are some traditions that are important in your family? After those of several families have been discussed, look for similarities and differences.
- What are some foods and dishes native to your culture?

2. Group Activity

In groups of two (or four) students, each student writes down two adjectives (positive or negative) that come to mind for each of these groups: New Yorkers, Californians, Latinos, lesbians, whites, Asian Americans, women, teenagers, elderly, men, Catholics,

African Americans, and disabled. Discuss your reactions with the group using the following discussion questions.

- Were there any groups you know so little about that you felt uncomfortable writing about them?
- Were any of your adjectives used because you had limited personal experience?
- Were any of your adjectives reflective of stereotypes?
- Do you think the way you described certain groups would affect how you would communicate with them?
- How quick are we to prejudge others when we know little about them?

3. Group Activity: The Cultural You

In groups of two, each student should first write down his or her attitudes toward each of the following: money, expression of emotions, time, religion, education, authority, family, independence, work, children, competition, and use of alcohol. Next, discuss your attitudes with your partner. Identify to what extent your culture has influenced your attitudes.

4. Case Study: Culture Clash

As the new head of housekeeping, Nancy, a white, middle-aged woman, oversees a staff made up of a diverse group, mostly minorities. She is not sure that she is getting her messages through to her staff because they do not respond the way she expects them to when she gives directions. She is starting to wonder if they are really listening. To solve this problem, Nancy decides to spend a half-hour each day supervising the employees directly.

One week later, she comes to the conclusion that just about everyone is doing the job the way they should, but she hears from another department head that housekeepers are grumbling about being watched over. Later that day, one of the housekeepers complains in a very emotional way, and Nancy isn't sure what to do.

Case Study Questions

1. What did Nancy do right?
2. What did Nancy do wrong?
3. In what ways was Nancy insensitive to cultural differences?
4. What should Nancy do now? How can she learn more about the cultures represented in her staff to help her to do her job better?

WEB ACTIVITY

- Go to the following website: www.mfha.net. Click on About Us and scroll down to Mission to read the organization's mission, vision, and values. What do you think about them?

RELATED WEBSITES

Americans with Disabilities Act	www.ada.gov/pubs/ada.htm
Equal Employment Opportunity Commission (EEOC)	www.eeoc.gov

Immigration Reform and Control Act of 1986	www.oig.lsc.gov/legis/irca86.htm
Title VII of the Civil Rights Act of 1964	www.eeoc.gov/laws/statutes/titlevii.cfm
Multicultural Foodservice and Hospitality Alliance	www.mfha.net
Women's Foodservice Forum	www.womensfoodserviceforum.com

 # ENDNOTES

1. www.eeoc.gov/abouteeoc/35th/pre1965/index.html. Retrieved May 18, 2010.
2. Charles Bernstein, "The Missing Piece," *Chain Leader*, vol. 9, no. 7 (June 2004), p. 10.
3. Sodexo, "Workplace Diversity," www.sodexousa.com/usen/citizenship/diversity/workforce/workforce.asp. Retrieved April 29, 2011.
4. www.marriott.com/corporateinfo/culture/diversity. Retrieved May 19, 2010.
5. Personal correspondence with Dr. Chad Gruhl, February 16, 2010.
6. Dina Berta, "MFHA: Industry Gets a Barely Passing Grade on Diversity Issues," *Nation's Restaurant News*, vol. 40, no. 34 (August 21, 2006), p. 14.
7. www.eeoc.gov/facts/qanda.html
8. www.isis.fastmail.usf.edu/eoa/interviewfaq.asp.
9. Cornelia Gamlem in Sharon Armstrong and Barbra Mitchell, *The Essential HR Handbook* (Franklin Lakes, NJ: The Career Press Inc., 2008), p. 140.
10. Personal correspondence with Dr. Chad Gruhl, February 16, 2010.
11. www.restaurantsusa.com.
12. Gerry A. Fernandez, "Multicultural Diversity: It's the Right Thing to Do for Your Business," *Nation's Restaurant News*, vol. 37, no. 20 (May 19, 2003), p. 42.
13. John R. Walker, *Introduction to Hospitality Management*, 3rd ed. (Upper Saddle River, NJ: Prentice Hall, 2009), p. 532.
14. Texas Center for Women's Business Enterprise, Austin, TX. SBA Online, August 10, 2004.
15. www.aramark.com/aboutaramark.asp?topic_diversity. Retrieved May 20, 2010.
16. Diane Ridge, "Diversity Runs Deep," *Food Management*, vol. 35, no. 7 (July 2000), pp. 48–52.
17. Rohini Anand, "Make Diversity Part of the Business Plan," *Restaurants and Institutions*. vol. 114, no. 10 (May 2004), p. 22.
18. Phillip M. Perry, "Culture Clash," *Restaurant Hospitality*, vol. 90, no. 8 (August 2006), p. 74.
19. Davis E. Morrison, & Michael L. Sullivan. English-Only Can Be Discriminatory. *Lodging Hospitality*, vol. 62, no. 13 (September 1, 2006), p. 28.
20. Gerry A. Fernandez, "Multicultural Diversity: It's the Right Thing to Do for Your Business," *Nation's Restaurant News*, vol. 37, no. 20 (May 19, 2003), p. 43.
21. John P. Walsh, "Putting It Together," *Hotel and Motel Management*, vol. 218, no. 15 (September 1, 2003), p. 4.
22. Jeff Higley, "Hospitality Leaders Promote Diversity During Conference," *Hotel and Motel Management*, vol. 215, no. 16 (September 18, 2000), p. 4.
23. Carlo Wolf, "Hotel Companies Diversify their Diversity Targets Even as Growth Lags," *Lodging Hospitality*, vol. 60, no. 10 (July 15, 2004), pp. 46–48.
24. Personal conversation with Arash Azarbarzin, July 23, 2007.

THE
HOSPITALITY
INDUSTRY AND YOU

Courtesy of Four Seasons Hotel, Mexico, D.F.

Chapter

1

THE PURPOSE OF THIS CHAPTER

Your own career choice is probably the most important management decision that you will ever make—at least from your point of view. This chapter has been designed, therefore, to help you analyze a career in the hospitality industry and correlate that analysis with your personal, professional, and educational experiences. It will also help prepare you for the first career decision you make just before or after you graduate. This chapter discusses the career decisions that are ahead of you over the next three to five years.

THIS CHAPTER SHOULD HELP YOU

1. List examples of the kinds of businesses that make up the hospitality industry.
2. Understand the various roles that a hospitality manager serves.
3. Identify the reasons people study hospitality management—and list the advantages these academic programs offer.
4. Describe your career plan in terms of a life's work and not just as an economic means of survival.
5. Identify two key components of the job-benefit mix that allow one to profit from work experience.
6. Appreciate the value of networking and the other strategies for landing a job.
7. Consider the steps necessary in launching your career after graduation.
8. Name three general career goals frequently cited by graduates seeking employment.
9. Identify key trends driving change in employment opportunities in the hospitality industry.

WHAT IS HOSPITALITY MANAGEMENT?

When most people think of the hospitality industry, they usually think of hotels and restaurants. However, the true meaning of **hospitality** is much broader in scope. According to the *Oxford English Dictionary, hospitality* means "the reception and entertainment of guests, visitors or strangers with liberality and good will." The word *hospitality* is derived from *hospice*, the term for a medieval house of rest for travelers and pilgrims. *Hospice*—a word that is clearly related to hospital—also referred to an early form of what we now call a nursing home.

Hospitality, then, not only includes hotels and restaurants but also refers to other kinds of institutions that offer shelter, food, or both to people away from their homes. We can also expand this definition, as many people have, to include those institutions that provide other types of services to people away from home. This might include private clubs, casinos, resorts, attractions, and so on. This wide variety of services will be discussed in later chapters.

These different kinds of operations also have more than a common historical heritage. They share the management problems of providing food and shelter—problems that include erecting a building; providing heat, light, and power; cleaning and maintaining the premises; overseeing employees; and preparing and serving food in a way that pleases the guests. We expect all of this to be done "with liberality and good will" when we stay in a hotel or dine in a restaurant, but we can also rightfully expect the same treatment from the food service department in a health care facility or while enjoying ourselves at an amusement park.

Turning our attention now from the facilities and services associated with the hospitality industry to the people who staff and manage them, let us consider the profession of the hospitality provider. The hospitality professions are among the oldest of the human professions, and they involve making a guest, client, member, or resident (whichever is the appropriate term) feel welcome and comfortable. There is a more important reason, however, that people interested in a career in these fields should think of hospitality as an industry. Today, managers and supervisors, as well as skilled employees, find that opportunities for advancement often mean moving from one part of the hospitality industry to another. For example, a hospitality graduate may begin as a management trainee with a restaurant company, complete the necessary training, and shortly thereafter take a job as an assistant manager in a hotel. The next job offer could come from a hospitality conglomerate, such as ARAMARK. ARAMARK provides food service operations not only to businesses but also in such varied areas as recreation centers, sports stadiums, college and university campuses, health care facilities, convention centers, and gourmet restaurants. Similarly, Holiday Inns is in the hotel business, but it is also one of the largest food service companies in the United States.

A Former Student's Unexpected Change

When one of the authors was an undergraduate student studying hospitality management at a large state university, he heard repeatedly from his professors how important it was that he become active with the student organizations on campus. There were quite a few student chapters of professional hospitality organizations to choose from, including the Hospitality Sales and Marketing Association International, the Travel and Tourism Research Association, and various food service organizations, among others. Partially to satisfy his professors, and partially out of curiosity, he joined the student chapter of the Club Managers Association of America (CMAA), which had a strong presence on campus. When he joined, he was quite confident that he would never have occasion to work in a private club, but he had to admit that it sounded like an interesting segment of the industry. He spent two years with the association and even took an elective course on club management to learn a little bit more about the field. He then promptly began his management career with a food service management company. Much to his surprise, he was offered a job at a private club a few years after graduating. His membership in the student chapter, and the connections that he made while a member, went a long way in helping him secure the club position. He has since enjoyed a long association with the Club Managers Association of America as well as the private club industry. In fact, he was also the faculty advisor to a student chapter of CMAA for ten years. Our own students now share similar stories with us. This just goes to further illustrate how careers can take strange twists and turns and how hospitality graduates can find themselves moving from one sector to another in short order.

The point is that the hospitality industry is tied together as a clearly recognizable unit by more than just a common heritage and a commitment to "liberality and good will." Careers in the industry are such that your big break may come in a part of the industry that is very different from the one you expected. (See Case History 1.1 for a personal example.) Hospitality management is one of the few remaining places in our increasingly specialized world of work that calls for a broadly gauged generalist. The student who understands this principle increases his or her opportunity for a rewarding career in one or more segments that make up the hospitality industry.

THE MANAGER'S ROLE IN THE HOSPITALITY INDUSTRY

As a successful manager in the hospitality industry, you must exhibit many skills and command much specialized knowledge, all directed at achieving a variety of management objectives. The **manager's role** is wide and varied. Let's now

5

Entertainment and attractions, such as the Freemont Street Experience in Las Vegas, play an important part in the hospitality industry. (Courtesy of Las Vegas News Bureau.)

discuss three general kinds of hospitality objectives with which management must be concerned:

1. *A manager wants to make the guest feel welcome.* Doing this requires both a friendly manner on your part toward the guest and an atmosphere of "liberality and good will" among the people who work with you in serving the guest. That almost always translates to an organization in which workers get along well with one another.

2. *A manager wants to make things work for the guest.* Food has to be savory, hot or cold according to design, and on time. Beds must be made and rooms cleaned. Gaming facilities must be service oriented. A hospitality system requires a lot of work, and the manager must see that it is done.

3. *A manager wants to make sure that the operation will continue to provide service while also making a* profit. When we speak of "liberality and good will," we don't mean giving the whole place away! In a restaurant or hotel operated for profit, portion sizes are related to cost, and so menu and room prices must consider building and operating costs. Managing these aspects enables the establishment to recover the cost of its operation and to make enough additional income to pay back any money borrowed as well as to provide a return to the owner (or investor), who risked a good deal of money—and time—to make the establishment a reality. (The unique challenges associated with the operation of subsidized or noncommercial facilities will be discussed later.) The key lies in achieving a controlled profit, loss, or break-even operation. A good term to describe this management concern is "conformance to budget."

6

Simply stated, these objectives suggest that managers must be able to relate successfully to employees and guests, direct the work of their operation, and achieve operating goals within a budget—that is, to run a productive operation within certain constraints.

WHY STUDY IN A HOSPITALITY MANAGEMENT PROGRAM?

One way to learn the hospitality business is to take the direct route: Go to work in it and acquire the necessary skills to operate the business (as has been the traditional route). The trouble with this approach, however, is that the skills that accompany the various line-level workstations (cook, server, etc.) are not the same as those needed by hospitality managers. In earlier times of small operations in a slowly changing society, hospitality education was basically skill-centered. Most hospitality managers learned their work through apprenticeships. The old crafts built on apprenticeships assumed that knowledge—and work—was unchanging. However, this assumption no longer holds true. As Peter Drucker, a noted management consultant whose management observations are virtually timeless, pointed out, "Today the center [of our society's productivity] is the **knowledge worker**, the man or woman who applies to productive work ideas, concepts, and information."[1] In other words, knowledge is crucial to success, and studying is a necessary part of your overall preparation for a career as a supervisor or manager.

Many people argue that a liberal arts education provides an excellent preparation not only for work but also for life. They're quite right. What we've found, however, is that many students just aren't interested in the liberal arts subject matter. Because they are not interested, they are not eager to learn. However, these same people become hardworking students in an applied career-oriented program that interests them, whether that is in the hospitality industry or some other profession. There is no real reason for educational preparation for work to be separate from preparation for life. We spend at least half our waking hours at work. As we will learn shortly, work lies at the heart of a person's life and can lead directly to self-discovery.

Business administration offers one logical route to management preparation. Indeed, many hospitality managers have prepared for their careers in this field. Business administration, however, is principally concerned with the manufacturing and marketing of a physical product in national (and increasingly international) markets. By contrast, the **hospitality industry** is a service industry, and the management of a service institution is vastly different. Food may be the primary product of a restaurant, but most of the "manufacturing" is done right in the same place that offers the service.

High-volume food service depends on a highly skilled team made up of both front-of-the-house and back-of-the-house associates. (Courtesy of Bon Appétit Management Company.)

The market is often local, and the emphasis is on face-to-face contact with the guest. Hospitality operations also tend to be smaller (with some obvious exceptions), so the problems of a large bureaucracy are not as significant as the problems of face-to-face relationships with employees and guests. Moreover, the hospitality industry has a number of unique characteristics. People work weekends and odd hours. We are expected by both guests and fellow workers to be friendly and cheerful. Furthermore, we are expected to care what happens to the guest. Our product, we will discuss in a later chapter, is really the guest's experience. Additionally, the industry has its own unique culture. An important task of both schooling and work experience, then, is that of acculturating people to the work and life of hospitality industry professionals.

Our point is not that there is something wrong with a liberal arts or business administration education. Rather, the point is that programs that are specifically focused on hospitality management are usually made up of students who are interested in the industry that they are studying. There is a clear difference between the hospitality service system and the typical manufacturing company—between the hospitality product and the manufacturer's product. For these reasons, hospitality management programs provide a distinct advantage for such students.

Why do people want to study in a hospitality management program? Perhaps the best answer can be found in the reasons why students before you have chosen this particular course of study. Their reasons fall into three categories: their experience, their interests, and their ambitions. Figure 1.1 lists the various reasons that students cite, in order of frequency. Many students become interested in the industry because a job they once had proved particularly captivating. Others learn of the industry through family or friends working in the field. Others learn about it through their experiences as customers.

8

EXPERIENCE

Personal work experience

Family background in the industry

Contact with other students and faculty in hospitality management programs

INTERESTS

Enjoy working with people

Enjoy working with food

Enjoy dining out, travel, variety

AMBITION

Opportunity for employment and advancement around the world

Desire to operate own business

Desire to travel

Desire to be independent

Figure 1.1
The reasons students select hospitality management programs.

One final consideration for many students is that they like and are genuinely interested in people. Working well with people is a crucial part of a manager's job in our industry. Many students, too, have a natural interest in food, and some are attracted by the glamour of the hospitality industry.

EMPLOYMENT OPPORTUNITIES

Another important consideration when choosing a profession is what the future holds for the industry. In the case of hospitality, the employment outlook is solid in most segments, particularly for managers. For example, in the period 2010 to 2020, employment of lodging managers is expected to grow 9 to 17 percent. This should encourage those students who are attracted to a field in which they can be reasonably sure they will secure employment. Others feel that in a job market with more opportunities than applicants, they will enjoy a good measure of independence, whether in their own businesses or as company employees. Many students are drawn to the hospitality industry because they want to get into their own business. Others, with good reason, suspect that there are opportunities for innovation off the beaten track of the traditional or franchise organizations. There have been many successful examples of the latter throughout the history of the hospitality industry.

CAREERS IN HOSPITALITY

One segment in particular that seems to offer tremendous opportunities is the catering industry. Many young entrepreneurs have chosen catering as a low-investment field that offers opportunities to people with a flair for foods and the ability to provide customized service. Catering is a fast-growing segment of food service and is also a business that students sometimes try while in school, either through student organizations or as a group of students setting up a small catering operation. A related career path is event planning, with many students seeking careers with event planning firms or hotel chains that coordinate large events.

There are ample opportunities in the lodging area as well. One of the areas that provides opportunities for entrepreneurs is the bed-and-breakfast/inn segment. Operators are typically able to enter these segments with lower capital requirements than would be necessary in other lodging segments.

Whichever the segment, the hospitality industry has always attracted its share of entrepreneurs for the simple reason that it offers everything that appeals to small-business owners. One characteristic that very much appeals to independent-minded individuals is being able to be your own boss.

There are many other opportunities as well. For instance, people with chef's training may open their own business, especially if they feel that they have a sufficient management background. In the health care area, home care organizations are expanding in response to the needs of our growing senior-citizen population and offer a wide range of opportunities to entrepreneurs.

Whether you're studying hospitality management because you want to start a business of your own or because you found your past work experience in the business especially interesting—or perhaps just because the need for managers in the area makes the job prospects attractive—management studies are an important preparation for budding entrepreneurs. Hospitality management students tend to be highly motivated, lively people who take pride in their future in a career of service. Starting positions that hospitality, tourism, and culinary students typically accept upon graduation are presented in Figure 1.2.

PLANNING A CAREER

THE MEANING OF WORK

We all have several motives for going to work. We work to live—to provide food, clothing, and shelter. Psychologists and sociologists tell us, however, that our work also provides a sense of who we are and binds us to the community in which we live. The ancient Greeks, who had slaves to perform menial tasks, saw work as a curse. Their Hebrew

LODGING

Sales Managers

Front Office Managers

Guest Services Managers

Revenue Managers

FOOD SERVICE

Restaurant Managers

Banquet Managers

Food Service Managers

Bar Managers

CULINARY

Chef Supervisor

Banquet Cook

Station Cook

TRAVEL AND TOURISM

Meeting and Convention Planner

Festival Manager

Market Researcher

Figure 1.2

Potential starting positions for hospitality and tourism management graduates.

contemporaries saw it as punishment. Early Christians, too, saw work for profit as offensive. By the time of the Middle Ages, however, people began to accept **work as a vocation**, that is, as a calling from God. Gradually, as working conditions improved and work became something that all social classes did, it became a necessary part of maturation and self-fulfillment in our society.

Today, workers at all levels demand more than just a job. Indeed, work has been defined as "an activity that produces something of value for other people."[2] This definition puts work into a social context. That is, it implies that there is a social purpose to work as well as the crude purpose of survival. It is an important achievement in human history that the majority of North Americans can define their own approach to a life of work as something more than mere survival.

Work contributes to our self-esteem in two ways. First, by doing our work well, we prove our own competence to ourselves. Psychologists tell us that this is essential to a healthy life, as this information gives us a sense of control over both our environment and ourselves. Second, by working, we contribute to others—others come to depend on us. Human beings, as social animals, need this sense of involvement. For these reasons, what happens at work becomes a large part of our sense of self-worth.

Education, too, is clearly important. Indeed, education has become essential in most walks of life. There is, moreover, a clear connection among education, work, and income. Studies have shown that workers with a postsecondary education earn much more annually than workers with just a high school education. This difference is expected to grow as the demand for "knowledge workers" continues to increase. The evidence, then, is that your commitment to education will pay off.

The next section explores career planning in regard to employment decisions that you must make while you are still in school. We will also discuss selecting your first employer when you leave school. If you've chosen the hospitality industry as your career, this section will help you map out your job plans. If you are still undecided, the section should help you think about this field in a more concrete way and give you some ideas about exploring your career through part-time employment. A large number of those reading this text already have significant **work experience**, many in hospitality fields. Because not everyone has such experience in his or her background, however, this is a subject that does need to be covered. Perhaps those with more experience will find this a useful opportunity to review plans they've already made. Taking a fresh look at your commitments is always worthwhile.

It's hard to overstate the importance of career planning.

EMPLOYMENT AS AN IMPORTANT PART OF YOUR EDUCATION

Profit in a business is treated in two ways. Some is paid out to the owner or shareholders as dividends (return on their investment). Some of the profit, however, is retained by the business to provide funds for future growth. This portion of profit that is not paid out is called retained earnings. We can apply the concept of retained earnings to consider the real place of work experience in career development.

PROFITING FROM WORK EXPERIENCE

The most obvious profit you earn from work is the income paid to you by an employer. In the early years of your career, however, there are other kinds of benefits that are at least as important as income. The key to understanding this statement is the idea of a lifetime income. You'll obviously need income over your entire life span, but giving up some income now may gain you income (and, we ought to note, enjoyment, a sense of satisfaction, and independence) just a few years later. There is, then, a **job-benefit mix** made up of both money and knowledge to be gained from any job. Knowledge gained today can be traded with an employer for income tomorrow: a better salary for a more qualified person. The decision to take a job that will add to your knowledge and experience base is thus a decision for retained earnings and for acquiring knowledge that you can use later. Many graduates choose their first job on the basis of salary without concern for the potential long-term advantages that one job may offer over another.

Every job, therefore, has to be weighed according to its benefit mix, not just in terms of the dollar income it provides. A part-time job at a retail store might seem attractive

Hospitality takes many forms, including fast-growing areas such as takeout and delivery. (Courtesy of Domino's Pizza, Inc.)

because it pays more than a job busing dishes does. However, if you think about the learning portion of the benefit mix and your total income, including what you learn, your decision may—and probably should—be for the job that will add to your professional education.

There is another important point to consider about retained earnings and the benefit mix. Often the only part-time jobs in the industry available to students are unskilled ones. Many people find these jobs dull, and they often pay poorly. If you think about these jobs in terms of their total income, however, you may change your perspective. Although the work of a busperson or a dishwasher may not be very challenging, you can improve your total profits from such a job by resolving to learn all you can about the operation. In this way, you can build your retained earnings—the bank of skills and knowledge that nobody can ever take away from you.

LEARNING STRATEGIES FOR WORK EXPERIENCE

When you go to work, regardless of the position you take, you can learn a good deal through careful observation. Look first at how the operation is organized. More specifically, look at both its **managerial organization** and its physical organization.

MANAGERIAL ORGANIZATION.

Who is the boss? Who reports to (or works directly with) him or her? Is the work divided into definite departments or sections? Is one person responsible for each department? To whom do the department staff members report? If you can answer these questions, you will have figured out the formal managerial organization of the operation. Indeed, most large companies will have an organization

13

chart. If your employer doesn't have such a chart, ask him or her to explain the organization to you. You'll be surprised at how helpful to hospitality management students most employers and supervisors are.

While you're thinking about organization, it is also important to notice the **informal organization**, also known as the social organization, of the group with which you are working. Which of the workers are influential? Who seem to be the informal leaders? Why? Most work groups are made up of cliques with informal leaders. After you identify this informal structure, ask yourself how management deals with it. Remember that someday the management of these informal organizations will be your challenge; in time, you will be helping to manage the organization, and you will need their cooperation. In the meantime, this firsthand experience will help you both in your studies and in sizing up the real world of work.

THE PHYSICAL PLANT.   You can learn a great deal about a **physical plant** by making a simple drawing of your workplace, such as the one shown in Figure 1.3. On this drawing, identify the main work areas and major pieces of equipment. Then begin to note on it where you see problems resulting from cross traffic or bottlenecks. For example, if you're working in the back of the house, you can chart the flow of products from the back door (receiver) to storage and from there to preparation. You should also trace the flow of dishes. Dirty dishes come to the dish room window and go to the clean-supply area after washing. How are they transported to the line or to the pantry people for use in service? If you are working in the back of the house, you will be looking mostly at the flow of kitchen workers and dishes from the viewpoint of the kitchen, dish room, or pantry. A similar flow analysis of guests and servers (and plates) can also be made from the front of the house (i.e., the dining room).

A study of guest flow in a hotel lobby can also be educational. Trace the flow of room guests, restaurant guests, banquet department guests, and service employees arriving through the lobby. Where do you observe congestion?

These simple charting activities will give you some practical experience that will be useful for later courses in layout and design and in food service operations and analysis and, more important, for decisions that you will make while on the job later in your career. Sometimes simple observations can lead to improvements in workflow patterns.

LEARNING FROM THE BACK OF THE HOUSE.   Things to look for in the **back of the house** include how quality is ensured in food preparation, menu planning, recipes, cooking methods, supervision, and food holding. (How is lunch prepared in advance? How is it kept hot or cold? How long can food be held?) How are food costs controlled? (Are food portions standardized? Are they measured? How? How is access to storerooms controlled?) These all are points you'll consider a great deal in later courses. From the

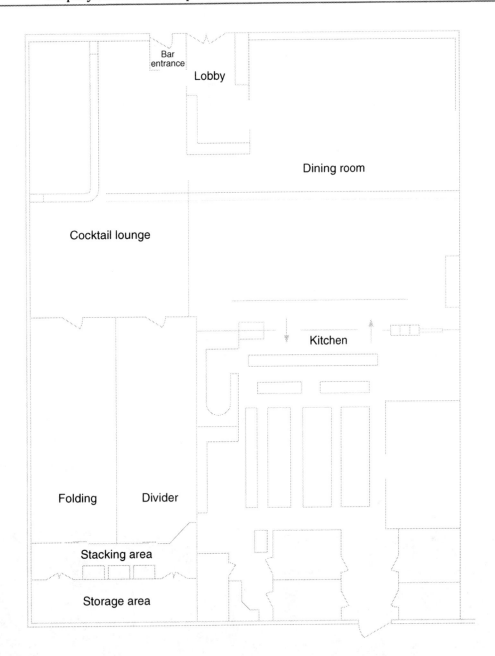

Figure 1.3
A sample layout.

very beginning, however, you can collect information that is invaluable to your studies and your career.

LEARNING FROM THE FRONT OF THE HOUSE. If you are busing dishes or working as a waiter, a waitress, or a server on a cafeteria line, you can learn a great deal about the operation from observing the guests or clients in the **front of the house**. Who are the customers, and what do they value? Peter Drucker called these the two central questions in determining what a business is and what it should be doing.[3] Are the guests or clients satisfied? What, in particular, seems to please them?

In any job you take, your future work lies in managing others and serving people. Wherever you work and whatever you do, you can observe critically the management and guest or client relations of others. Ask yourself, "How would I have handled that problem? Is this an effective management style? In what other ways have I seen this problem handled?" Your development as a manager also means the development of a management style that suits you, and that is a job that will depend, in large part, on your personal experience.

GETTING A JOB

Hospitality jobs can be obtained from several sources. For example, your college may maintain a placement office. Many hospitality management programs receive direct requests for part-time help. Some programs maintain a job bulletin board or file, and some even work with industry to provide internships. There are numerous Web sites devoted to matching employers and job seekers, such as www.hcareers.com and www.monster.com. The help-wanted pages of your newspaper also may offer leads, as may your local employment service office. Sometimes personal contacts established through your fellow students, your instructor, or your family or neighborhood will pay off. Networking is as effective as always, and some would suggest it is still the most important tool.

The New York, New York Casino in Las Vegas captures the feel of the original. (Courtesy of Las Vegas News Bureau.)

Networking occurs both formally and informally—often at industry functions, chapter meetings, and the like. Or you may find it necessary to "pound the pavement," making personal appearances in places where you would like to work.

Some employers may arrange for hospitality management students to rotate through more than one position and even to assume some supervisory responsibility to help them gain broader experience.

GETTING IN THE DOOR

It is not enough just to ask for a job. Careful attention to your appearance is important too. For an interview, this probably means a coat and tie for men, a conservative dress or suit for women. Neatness and cleanliness are the absolute minimum. (Neatness and cleanliness are, after all, major aspects of the hospitality product.) When you apply for or have an interview for a job, if you can, find out who the manager is; then, if the operation is not a large one, ask for him or her by name. In a larger organization, however, you'll deal with a human resources manager. The same basic rules of appearance apply, regardless of the organization's size.

Don't be afraid to check up on the status of your application. Here's an old but worthwhile adage from personal selling: It takes three calls to make a sale. The number three isn't magic, but a certain persistence—letting an employer know that you are interested—often will land you a job. Be sure to identify yourself as a hospitality management student, because this tells an employer that you will be interested in your work. Industry Practice Note 1.1 gives you a recruiter's-eye view of the job placement process.

LEARNING ON THE JOB

Many hospitality managers report that they gained the most useful knowledge on the job, earlier in their careers, on their own time. Let's assume you're working as a dishwasher in the summer and your operation has a person assigned to prep work. You may be allowed to observe and then perhaps help out—as long as you do it on your own time. Your "profit" in such a situation is in the "retained earnings" of increased knowledge. Many job skills can be learned through observation and some unpaid practice: bartending (by a waitress or waiter), clerking on a front desk (by a bellperson), and even some cooking (by a dishwasher or cook's helper). With this kind of experience behind you, it may be possible to win the skilled job part time during the year or for the following summer.

One of the best student jobs, from a learning standpoint, is a relief job. Relief jobs are defined as those that require people to fill in on occasion (such as during a regular employee's day off, sickness, or vacation). The training for this fill-in work can teach you a good deal about every skill in your operation. Although these skills differ from the

An Employer's View of Job Placement—Hyatt

What do you look for in a potential management recruit?

We look for someone who is really thinking about a "long-term" career versus getting a good offer. We take pride in the number of managers who have been rewarded with career growth and opportunities. Another characteristic we evaluate is one's energy level and service skills. We look that they have the desire and are able to align with the company service strategy.

What is your favorite question, the one you ask to get the best "read" on a person?

"Tell me what you have learned from past experiences and what you can offer Hyatt." This is a very open question that allows us to hear more about one's experiences. They have to be able to give specific points and apply them to a new career with Hyatt.

How much does Hyatt depend on formal testing and how much on personal interviews?

The personal interview will always outweigh any testing. However, we are experimenting with pre-employment assessments to ensure certain service characteristics and management aptitude are visible. We feel this is a great way to prescreen applicants and create a more focused interview.

What is the quickest way for an interviewee to take him- or herself out of the running?

Indecisiveness. We really want someone to have thought about a future career and have a general direction or goal. In addition, they must be flexible with relocation. A good hotelier is backed by a variety of experiences.

What skills do today's recruits have that those ten years ago didn't?

Hospitality today means much more than it did ten years ago. Today, recruits are introduced to other avenues such as Revenue Management, Retirement Communities, Casino Operations, Recreation, and Development. Due to technology, recruits know how to get information about companies and opportunities (blogs, message boards, etc.).

What are some of the current opportunities for graduates of hospitality management programs in the lodging sector?

Lodging will always offer the traditional opportunities in Operations, Culinary, Facilities, Catering, Sales, Accounting, and Human Resources. The lodging sector offers much more today including Revenue Management, Spa Operations, and Development.

To what extent does your company employ the Internet in recruiting?

There is no other way to apply for a Hyatt job other than online. We deploy our training program and all career opportunities on the Hyatt career site **explorehyatt.jobs**. However, we do leverage job openings on other Internet sites, but we are selective. We prefer to post on a few large and some niche sites rather

18

than posting on as many as possible. Research and networking through social media is now mainstream. Many have discovered that connecting early and beginning dialogue or relationships may connect them to their future employer early on. Is there anything else that might be helpful for a hospitality management graduate to know before applying for a job with Hyatt?

Before applying to Hyatt, we ask that a graduate be open to movement [relocation]. We are focused on growth and differentiating our brands. Our current processes allow our associates movement among all Hyatt entities, which proves beneficial to one's experiences. There is opportunity for experience across all sectors of the industry including:

Park Hyatt, which provides discerning, affluent individual business and leisure guests with elegant and luxurious accommodations, highly attentive personal service in an intimate environment.

Andaz, a vibrant yet relaxed atmosphere geared toward today's individual business and leisure travelers, designed to reflect the unique cultural scene and spirit of the surrounding neighborhood.

Grand Hyatt, which features large-scale, distinctive hotels in major gateway cities and resort destinations providing sophisticated global business and leisure travelers with upscale accommodations.

Hyatt Regency, which offers a full range of services and facilities tailored to serve the needs of conventions, business travelers, and resort vacationers conveniently located in urban, suburban, airport, convention, and resort destinations around the world.

Hyatt hotels are smaller-size properties conveniently located in secondary markets in the United States offering guests the opportunity to experience our signature service and hospitality even when traveling outside of major gateway markets.

Hyatt Place is designed for the busy lifestyle of today's multitasking business traveler and features a selected range of services aimed at providing casual hospitality in a well-designed, high-tech, and contemporary environment located in urban, airport, and suburban areas.

Hyatt Summerfield Suites is an extended-stay, residential-style hotel that aims to provide individual travelers with the feel of a modern condominium located in urban, airport, and suburban locations.

Hyatt Vacation Club provides members with vacation ownership opportunities in regionally inspired and designed residential-style properties with the quality of the Hyatt brand.

Hyatt Resorts is a collection of vacation properties across our Park Hyatt, Grand Hyatt, and Hyatt Regency brands representing attributes of the individual brand in the more personal context of a vacation environment and are characterized by relaxed, comfortable spaces reflective of the local culture.

Randy Goldberg, Vice President Recruiting
Hyatt Hotels Corporation, August 18, 2009

19

skills a manager uses, they are important for a manager to know, because the structure of the hospitality industry keeps most managers close to the operating level. Knowledge of necessary skills gives managers credibility among their employees, facilitates communication, and equips them to deal confidently with skilled employees. In fact, a good manager ought to be able to pitch in when employees get stuck.[4] For these reasons, one phrase that should never pass your lips is "That's not my job."

OTHER WAYS OF PROFITING FROM A JOB

In addition to income and knowledge, after-school part-time employment has other advantages. For example, your employer might have a full-time job for you upon graduation. This is particularly likely if your employer happens to be a fairly large firm or if you want to remain close to the area of your schooling.

You may choose to take a term or two off from school to pursue a particular interest or just to clarify your longer-term job goals. This does have the advantage of giving you more than "just a summer job" on your résumé—but be sure you don't let the work experience get in the way of acquiring the basic educational requirements for progress into management.

Wherever and for however long you work, remember that through your employment, you may make contacts that will help you after graduation. People with whom you have worked may be able to tell you of interesting opportunities or recommend you for a job.

Global Hospitality Note 1.1 offers some information you may find helpful if you think you might like to work overseas.

EMPLOYMENT AT GRADUATION

Graduation probably seems a long way off right now, but you should already be considering strategies for finding a job when you finish your formal education. Clear goals formed now will direct your work experience plans and, to a lesser degree, the courses you take and the topics you emphasize within those courses. If you have not yet decided on a specific goal, this question deserves prompt but careful consideration as you continue your education. You still have plenty of time. Furthermore, you will never know when or where a job opportunity may arise. For this reason alone, you should always keep your résumé up-to-date.

The rest of this section offers a kind of dry-run postgraduation placement procedure. From this distance, you can view the process objectively. When you come closer to graduation, you may find the subject a tense one: People worry about placement as graduation nears, even if they're quite sure of finding a job.

Career Opportunities Overseas

Companies hire North Americans to work in hospitality positions abroad for several reasons. Some countries do not have a large enough pool of trained managers. Moreover, particularly in responsible positions, a good fit with the rest of the firm's executive staff is important—and often easier for an American firm to achieve with someone from North America. The relevant operating experience may not be available to people living outside the United States and Canada. Many factors are considered, however, including familiarity with other cultures and the ability to speak multiple languages.

North American employees, however, are more expensive to hire for most companies than are local nationals because their salaries are usually supplemented by substantial expatriate benefits. But cost is not the only reason for hiring people from the host country. Local people have an understanding of the culture of the employees in a particular country, to say nothing of fluency in the language. Local managers, moreover, do not arouse the resentment that is directed at a foreign manager. For many of the same reasons, foreign-owned firms operating in the United States seek U.S. managers and supervisors in their U.S. operations.

A final point to consider is that many North American firms are using franchising as the vehicle for their overseas expansion. In this case, the franchisee is most often a local national whose local knowledge and contacts are invaluable to the franchisor. Not surprisingly, however, the franchisee is likely to prefer people from his or her own culture if that is possible.

Although most positions in operations outside the United States are filled with people from those countries, many American companies offer significant opportunities for overseas employment. One of the first obstacles to immediate employment overseas is the immigration restrictions of other countries (similar to the restrictions enforced in the United States). Employment of foreign nationals is usually permitted only if the employer is able to show that the prospective employee has special skills that are not otherwise available in the country. It is not surprising, therefore, that many employees who do receive overseas assignments have been employed by the company for a few years and, thus, have significant operating experience.

Another major problem facing Americans who want to work overseas is a lack of language skills. In fact, many hospitality programs are now requiring students to study at least one foreign language as part of their curriculum and require a global learning experience, preferably in a non–English-speaking country. The ability to adapt to a different culture is critically important, and probably the only way to get it is to have experience living abroad.

Summer or short-term work or study abroad not only gives students experience in living in another culture but also may offer them the opportunity to build up contacts that will help them in securing employment abroad upon graduation. Opportunities to study abroad are plentiful in summer programs offered by many hospitality programs. Some institutions also maintain exchange programs with institutions in foreign countries.

As a student seeking overseas work, you should begin with your own institution's placement office and international center. The consulate or embassy of the country you seek to work in may be aware of

Continues on next page

21

Career Opportunities Overseas

Continues from previous page

exchange programs or other means to obtain a work permit. Probably the best source of information is other students who have worked abroad. Talk with students at your own institution or those you meet at regional or national restaurant or hotel shows. They know the ropes and can give practical advice on getting jobs and what to expect in the way of pay and working conditions. Whether you are interested in overseas work as a career or not, work, travel, and study abroad can all be unique educational experiences that broaden your understanding of other cultures, increase your sophistication, and enhance your résumé.

Don't underestimate a recommendation. Even if your summer employer doesn't have a career opportunity for you, a favorable recommendation can give your career a big boost when you graduate. In addition, many employers may have contacts they will make available to you—perhaps friends of theirs who can offer interesting opportunities. The lesson here is that the record you make on the job now can help shape your career later.

GOALS AND OBJECTIVES: THE STRATEGY OF JOB PLACEMENT

Most hospitality management students have three concerns. They all speak to the decision that is known as the **strategy of job placement**. First, many students are interested in such income issues as starting salary and the possibility of raises and bonuses.

Second, students are concerned with personal satisfaction. They wonder about opportunities for self-expression, creativity, initiative, and independence. This applies particularly to students coming from culinary schools who want to be able to immediately apply what they have learned. Although few starting jobs offer a great deal of independence, some types of work (e.g., employment with a franchising company) can lead quite rapidly to independent ownership. Students also want to know about the number of hours they'll be investing in their work. Many companies expect long hours, especially from junior management. Other sectors, especially on-site operations, make more modest demands (but may offer more modest prospects for advancement). Third, many students, particularly in health care food service, want to achieve such professional goals as competence as a registered dietician or a dietetic technician. Professional goals in the commercial sector are clearly associated with developing a topflight reputation as an operator.

These three sets of interests are obviously related; for example, most personal goals include the elements of income, satisfaction, high ethical standards, and professional

22

status. Although it may be too early to set definite goals, it is not too early to begin evaluating these elements. From the concerns we've just discussed, the following are five elements of the strategy of job placement for your consideration:

1. *Income.* The place to begin your analysis is with the issue of survival. How much will you require to meet your financial needs? If your income needs are modest, you may decide to forgo luxuries to take a lower-paying job that offers superior training. Thus, you would make an investment in retained earnings—the knowledge you hope someday to trade for more income, security, and job satisfaction.

2. *Professional status.* Whether your goal is professional certification (e.g., as a registered dietitian) or a reputation as a topflight hotelier or restaurateur, you should consider the job-benefit mix. In this case, you may choose to accept a lower income (but one on which you can live and in line with what such jobs pay in your region). Although you shouldn't be indifferent to income, you'll want to focus principally on what the job can teach you.

3. *Evaluating an employer.* Students who make snap judgments about a company and act aggressively during an interview often offend potential employers, who, after all, see the interview as an occasion to evaluate a graduating class. Nevertheless, in a quiet way, you should learn about the company's commitment to its employees, often evident through its employee turnover rates and its focus on training. For instance, you might want to explore whether it has a formal training program. If not, how does it translate its entry-level jobs into learning experiences? (Inquiries directed to your acquaintances and the younger management people can help you determine how the company really scores in these areas. Recent graduates from the same hospitality program as yours are good sources of information.) Because training beyond the entry-level basics requires responsibility and access to promotion, you will want to know about the opportunities for advancement. Finally, you need to evaluate the company's operations. Are they quality operations? Can you be proud to work there? If the quality of the facility, the food, or the service is consistently poor, can you help improve things? Or will you be misled into learning the wrong way to do things? A final note with regard to evaluating employers who may be independent operators: Sometimes it can be more difficult to research a small business. In this case, it might be worth asking around the local business community to find out what kind of reputation the prospective employer has.

4. *Determining potential job satisfaction.* Some students study hospitality management only to discover that their real love is food preparation. Such students may decide, late in their student careers, to seek a job that provides skill training in food preparation. Other students may decide they need a high income immediately (e.g., to pay off debts or to do some traveling). These students may decide to trade the skills

they have acquired in their work experiences to gain a high income for a year or two as a server in a topflight operation. Such a goal is highly personal but perfectly reasonable. The key is to form a goal and keep moving toward it. The student who wants eventually to own an operation probably will have to postpone his or her goal while developing the management skills and reputation necessary to attract the needed financial backing.

5. *Accepting skilled jobs.* Students sometimes accept skilled jobs rather than management jobs because that is all they can find. This happens quite often, especially during a period of recession. Younger students, too, are prone to suffer from this problem for a year or two, as are students who choose to live and work in small communities. The concept of retained earnings provides the key to riding out these periods. Learn as much as you can and don't abandon your goals.

A final word is in order on goals, priorities, and opportunities. Hospitality students' top-ten preferences for work upon graduation are summarized in Table 1.1. Hotels have traditionally been the favored sector of the hospitality industry, with luxury operations typically preferred over midmarket or midscale operations among this sample of students. Interestingly, quick-service restaurants and on-site food service was not as common but generally equal in terms of starting salaries. There is an old saying, *De gustibus non disputandem est* (In tastes, there is no disputing), and that certainly should apply to job preferences. Later in this text, we will point out that although work in on-site management is not any easier, its hours are more regular and its pace more predictable, often making for a better work-life balance. In short, there are many excellent career opportunities in the food service industry in general, and it is even better in some specific segments.

Luxury hotels, private clubs, and fine-dining restaurants are undoubtedly more glamorous than many other operations—or at least seem so—and it does appear that they are attracting the greatest interest from graduates as applicants. In the supply-demand equation, they have a plentiful supply of applicants, and yet they are relatively smaller sectors of hospitality employment. That is to say, they have less demand for employees than many other sectors. In economics, you may recall, a large supply met by a modest demand is generally expected to yield a lower price. Of course, there are no dollar signs on job satisfaction, and these are highly personal choices. Still, the truth is that no job offers everything. You have to decide what your highest priorities are and then choose the opportunity that suits you best. If career advancement, achieving a substantial income, and gaining responsibility—or perhaps just having a manageable work life—are priorities for you, you may want to consider at least interviewing with some of the companies that are on this list but that you had not previously considered.

TABLE 1.1

Hospitality Graduates' Career Top Ten Preferences

INDUSTRY SEGMENT

1 Luxury hotels	6 Midscale/family restaurants
2 Event Planning/Catering	7 Economy hotels
3 Fine dining/upscale restaurants	8 Quick-service restaurants
4 Midmarket hotels	9 Gaming/casinos
5 On-site food service	10 Sports and entertainment/recreation

THE OUTLOOK FOR HOSPITALITY

Over the past two generations, the hospitality industry has evolved to accommodate explosive growth, radically changing consumer demand, and a substantially different social and economic environment. We will examine some of the basic forces driving these changes in Chapter 2. The following brief summary points will alert you to some of the key trends discussed in the balance of this text. We can begin with trends closest to the industry and move outward to broader societal developments. Also, no hospitality text can ignore the short- and long-term effects of September 11, 2001.

THE EFFECTS OF SEPTEMBER 11, 2001

The effects of the terrorist attacks in the United States on September 11, 2001, on all aspects of life have been examined extensively. Some high-profile hospitality programs, including those at Johnson and Wales University and Cornell University, have hosted panel discussions and/or conducted studies on the impact that the day had on the industry. Certainly, there have been significant effects, both short- and long-term, on the hospitality and tourism industries. These effects have ranged from the initial reaction during which many people in North America (and elsewhere) stopped traveling anywhere for any reason, to traveling sporadically, and finally to travel patterns reaching some level of normalcy. The airlines were perhaps the most affected industry of all. (This is discussed much further in Chapter 13.) The effects are sure to be felt for a long time to come, but travel, accommodation, and food service have all reached activity levels equal to those prior to September 11. Discussions of the impact of that day will be found throughout the chapters that follow. The text also discusses effects that other terrorist attacks have had (such as in Madrid, London, and Bali) as well as recent natural disasters in Asia.

The outlook for the hospitality industry includes the continued growth of the casual dining segment. (Courtesy of Mimi's Café.)

POLARIZATION IN HOSPITALITY SERVICE ORGANIZATIONS

Hospitality companies are grouping themselves, to a very large extent, either as limited-service organizations or as service-intensive operations. In lodging, although there are price point divisions—budget, economy, midscale, upscale, and upper upscale—the most basic division is between limited-service and full-service properties. In later chapters, we will discuss concerns associated with the possibility of overbuilding and future excess capacity in all but the luxury and extended-stay segments of lodging.

In food service, simpler operations specializing in off-premise service to guests—takeout, drive-through, and delivery—have contributed greatly to the growth in restaurant sales in recent years. Quick-service and—the latest new segment—fast casual, too, continue a healthy growth trend. Table-service restaurant growth in the more economical family restaurant segment has flattened, but within the table-service group a more service-intensive format—casual restaurants—has shown healthy growth.

Restaurants and hotels, then, are tailoring themselves to specialized markets, a practice often referred to as target marketing.

ACCELERATING COMPETITION

One of the major reasons that hotels, restaurants, and other hospitality organizations are increasingly targeting specific market segments is that in most markets, there is more than enough capacity to go around. Competition is likely to be even tougher in the years ahead. In food service, operators are adapting their operations by opening new restaurants and bringing them closer to the customer (i.e., making them more convenient). They are also creating smaller prototypes. Lodging capacity, as we have already noted, offers a highly competitive outlook for all but the luxury sector (and even this is changing). The growth in competition makes tightly controlled operations especially

26

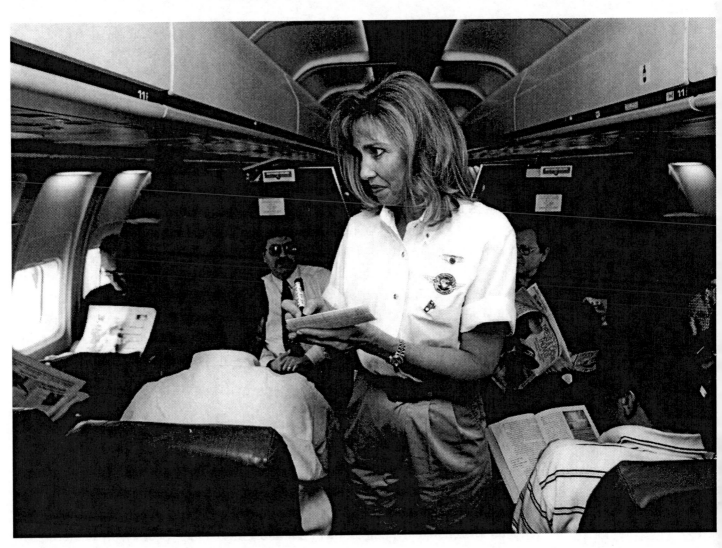

Service is becoming the differentiating factor in all segments of hospitality and tourism. (Courtesy of Southwest Airlines.)

important to survival. Competition also exists in the battle for customers in the convention, resort, and tourist destinations. Competition is no longer just limited to domestic competition either. International competition has become a concern in many markets. We will consider those issues for restaurants in Chapter 6 and for hotels in Chapter 12.

SERVICE IS THE DIFFERENCE

As competing firms expand their menus and amenities and dress up their operations, all operations at a given price level tend to become more like one another. The crucial differentiation becomes service—usually in the form of personal service. Understanding service and how to manage it is so vitally important that the last chapter of this book is devoted to it. In the world of today and tomorrow, service will be the difference between barely surviving (or worse) and achieving success. As Ellsworth Statler, founder of the groundbreaking Statler Hotels, (1893–1928) noted long ago: *Life is service; the one who progresses is the one who gives his fellow men a little more—a little better service.*

27

VALUE CONSCIOUSNESS

An educated, sophisticated customer base is placing increasing emphasis on the value of goods or services received in relation to the price paid in the marketplace. This trend probably originated with the baby boom generation and has continued with subsequent generations. The baby boomers, arguably the best-educated generation in history, has become a generation of careful shoppers. With an intensely competitive industry vying to serve them, consumers are in a position to demand good value for their money. Any discussion of value should also include mention of time and how personal time is valued (as it becomes more precious). For this reason, consumers often strive to balance the price they are willing to pay with a trade-off such as time saved. For example, this helps to partially explain the increasing popularity of the fast-casual dining segment.

TECHNOLOGY

Another driving force the industry has wrestled with for some years is the explosion of technology. Technology has already changed the way work is done in operations through increased automation and computerization. Even more fundamental, how-ever, are the changes in marketing and management made possible by technological advances. Lodging marketing, already shaped by a global computerized reservation network, has been reinvented, so to speak, as the Internet continues to expand the communication capacity of operators, their competitors, and the guest. Restaurants, too, are maintaining Web sites, many of which are interactive rather than simply informational. Even third-party companies, such as OpenTable (www.opentable.com) are changing how we make our restaurant reservations. With greatly improved com-munication and computerized financial and operational reporting, the hierarchy of organizations is collapsing, and a flatter, more integrated organizational structure is emerging.

EMPOWERMENT

As a direct result of the reduced number of middle managers, employees and manag-ers at all levels are being asked to assume more responsibility. For example, they are being empowered to solve many of the guest's service problems on the spot. This is an outgrowth not only of improved communication but of a more educated generation of employees. Bright, well-educated people want to do their own problem solving—and generally are able to do so effectively.

DIVERSITY

The face of North America is changing. Whereas the white male has been the dominant force in the labor market, the majority of people entering the workforce for the foreseeable future will be women and minorities, such as African Americans, Hispanics, and Asians. Managers will need a broad background and an openness to many kinds of people and cultures to prosper in the time ahead.

CONCERN WITH SECURITY

The results of September 11 and other more recent terrorist attacks have only served to underscore the value that travelers put on their personal safety and security. As the perceived incidence of violence increases, people worry about their personal security—and so we see a proliferation of private security forces in hotels and restaurants, marshals on airplanes and other public places, as well as high-tech security measures, such as keyless electronic locks in hotel rooms. Security has become a commodity that some people are willing to pay for—and that hospitality establishments have a responsibility to provide. In some places in the world (such as Israel), security is everywhere, even in local supermarkets.

CONCERN WITH FOOD SAFETY AND SANITATION

The incidence of food-borne illness has increased as the food service system has become more complex and the number of operations has expanded. One case of food poisoning can seriously injure a restaurant's reputation. More than one can endanger an operation's survival. The level of food safety demanded by consumers and regulatory agencies alike has escalated in light of recent cases of food poisoning. That escalation will continue in the years ahead.

SUSTAINABILITY

Another sweeping change affecting hospitality operations is a distinct focus on sustainability. The notion of going "green" is not a new one, but it is one that reflects corporate responsibility and smart business practices. Today, almost all hotels encourage guests to reuse towels, and most have already embraced low-cost changes such as using energy efficient lighting. Customers also like to know that they are supporting businesses that are concerned about the environment. Industry Practice Note 1.2 illustrates how hotels are changing in this respect.

Leading the Charge in Going Green—Orchard Hotels

Why are hotels going green?

It makes sense from both a business perspective and a human perspective. "Green" buildings perform better, so they operate very efficiently and positively impact the triple bottom line—socially, environmentally, and economically. "Green" buildings are healthier for employees and guests—making for happier employees and guests. Finally, it's part of our responsibility to the environment to make our footprint as soft and small as possible—"green" buildings are a part of meeting that responsibility.

For the hotel industry, cost cutting can lead naturally to green solutions. Since it's hard to raise room rates in economically challenging times, the best way to increase profit is to cut costs, but it must be done without harming the guest experience. Working with partners such as electric and water utilities is very important for hotels.

What makes Orchard Hotels different in this respect?

Inspiration for meeting the LEED guidelines comes from our octogenarian owner, Mrs. S. C. Huang. She is passionate about clean environments, after the untimely cancer-related deaths of three family members, and has devoted herself to creating environmentally safe and sustainable hotels.

Mrs. S.C. Huang pursued a LEED certification for her hotels for several important reasons. Studies prove that LEED-certified buildings have lower operating costs, higher employee productivity, and happier, healthier occupants. We're extremely proud to lead the hospitality industry in our dedication to our environment and our guests' and employees' quality of life.

The Orchard Garden Hotel debuted California's first guestroom key card energy control system—after opening the guestroom door with the key card, the guest places the card in a discreet box in order to turn on the lights and other room systems. When exiting the room, the guest simply takes the key card, automatically "turning off" the entire room, with the exception of an outlet that guests can use to charge laptops, cell phones, and other battery-powered devices. This system saves nearly 25 percent in energy consumption, having paid for itself in around two years.

The Orchard Garden Hotel was built "green"—eco-friendly construction materials included using concrete made from fly ash, a by-product of recycling coal, and wood certified by the Forest Stewardship Council as harvested in a sustainable manner. One environmentally sustainable building practice used during construction diverts debris from landfill disposal by redirecting recyclable material back to the manufacturing process.

In 2002, as it became increasingly important to control expenses ever so tightly in the post-9/11 business climate, we wanted to change our cleaning products in Housekeeping. We were taking the first steps to go green. And—yes—these green cleaning products, if used properly, would actually save us valuable dollars! So, we called a meeting with all housekeeping staff members and told them the "good news." To our surprise, the message was greeted with distrust as most of the crew did not believe that green cleaning products would do the job. My argument for a "healthier work environment" was met with very little enthusiasm as the predominantly Chinese housekeeping team was much more focused on getting rooms cleaned quickly and efficiently—no matter the (environmental) price. Potential health benefits? Not much interest either.

At that point, it would have been easy to simply issue a memo and force the team to comply. Realizing, however, that employees look at senior management for inspiration (and not just direction), we decided to ask everyone to participate in an experiment assigning room attendants into two groups—one outfitted with traditional chemicals, and one equipped with green products—for one week initially. During that first week, much training was given to the green team as employees learned how to properly dilute, mix and match, and apply specific surface cleaners. Since the products were nontoxic, fear of mishandling evaporated quickly, but product performance remained a hotly debated point of contention. After another week, the green group slowly began to see the benefits of using the product properly. Two more weeks went by (all the while asking for daily feedback), and then we rotated groups. Those employees having used the new product now had to revert to using chemicals, and the other team now couldn't wait to experience the green items that, in the interim, had generated lots of buzz among those who had been using them for the past month.

The results were astonishing. Not only did our employees overwhelming select the green cleaning products, but the "experiment" created a tremendous boost of confidence among staff members in a very challenging business environment. They had become part of the decision-making process!

Now, seven years later, this story still inspires.

Do customers make buying decisions based on a hotel's decision to be environmentally sensitive?

The typical factors still apply to buying decisions—price, location, service, amenities, and so forth. But we find that our "greenness" makes more people pay attention to our small hotels and will tip them in our favor. So travelers choose a hotel *only* because it's green? Probably not. Will they choose a hotel *also* because it's green? Much more likely!

Example:

How many of you would prefer to stay in a green hotel over a convention property? Probably most or all of you, I would guess. Now, how many of you would stay at that green property if it didn't have Internet connectivity? Not many, I reckon. Does this mean Internet access is more important to you than the environment?

You mention "LEED certified"—what does that mean?

In 2007, the Orchard Garden Hotel was awarded LEED® (Leadership in Energy & Environmental Design) certification by the U.S. Green Building Council (USGBC). San Francisco's first hotel to earn this honor, the Orchard Garden was only the third hotel in the United States and fourth hotel in the world with this certification. LEED is the USGBC's leading-edge system for designing and constructing the world's greenest, energy-efficient, high-performing buildings.

Continues on next page

Leading the Charge in Going Green—Orchard Hotels

Continues from previous page

In 2009, San Francisco's Orchard Hotel joined its sister property, the Orchard Garden Hotel, in "green" certification, earning LEED-EB® (Leadership in Energy & Environmental Design—Existing Building) certification for an existing building by the USGBC. San Francisco's first hotel to earn this honor, the Orchard Hotel is the second hotel in California. LEED-EB is the USGBC's system for operating high-performance buildings dedicated to whole-building cleaning and maintenance issues, recycling programs, exterior maintenance programs, and systems upgrades.

Is this trend going to stay?

In the near future it will be not be a trend, but a part of how business is done. "Green" is here to stay.

What does this mean for future hotel managers?

Get on board now—don't wait. Develop intimate understanding of "green" hospitality, and make it a part of the hotel's everyday life.

Stefan Mühle
Portfolio Hotels & Resorts
Regional Director and General Manager
The Orchard Hotels
August 26, 2009

GLOBALIZATION

In a sense, globalization has already become old news. With the falling of trade barriers such as that brought on by the North American Free Trade Agreement and the European Community, borders have become less important. The ease of financial transactions and information flow means that some of the largest "U.S. firms" are owned abroad—and that U.S. firms are major players overseas as well. Holiday Inn, for example, is owned by a British company, and Motel 6 by a French firm. McDonald's is the largest restaurant chain in Europe and has restaurants in more countries than any other food service company in the world (currently at 119 and counting). Forecasters are expecting tremendous growth opportunities in both China and India, which are positioned to greatly influence global commerce in the coming years. With all of the dynamism that the hospitality industry offers, an exciting future beckons as you begin this study of the industry and what makes it tick.

32

SUMMARY

As we have seen, the hospitality industry includes hotels and restaurants as well as many other types of operations that offer shelter and/or food (and entertainment, etc.) to people away from home. A manager in the hospitality industry, therefore, must keep in mind these three objectives: (1) making the guest welcome personally, (2) making things work for the guest, and (3) making sure that the operation will continue to provide service and meet its budget.

We mentioned the many reasons for studying in a hospitality management or culinary management program, including past experiences working in the field, interests in the field, and ambitions in the field.

We also discussed the meaning of work and how to get the most from a job, including weighing both retained earnings and the job-benefit mix. We pointed out that in the hospitality industry, you can learn a lot from studying the physical plant and from how the front and the back of the house are managed.

We then turned to ways to get a job—including always having a résumé ready and preparing for an interview—and how to gain the most from whatever job you do find. We also talked about what you should consider in regard to a more permanent job: income, professional status, your employer, potential job satisfaction, and accepting an interim less-skilled job. We noted as well that supply and demand work in the hospitality job market as they do elsewhere, suggesting that what is most popular in terms of employment may not necessarily translate into the best opportunity.

Finally, we began our continuing discussion of the outlook for the hospitality industry, which we found to be bright but full of change and competition.

Key Words and Concepts

Hospitality	Job-benefit mix
Manager's role	Managerial organization
Profit	Informal organization
Knowledge worker	Physical plant
Hospitality industry	Back of the house
Work as a vocation	Front of the house
Work experience	Strategy of job placement

Review Questions

1. What kinds of institutions or establishments does the hospitality industry include besides hotels and restaurants?

2. What is the role of a manager in the hospitality industry?

3. Why did you choose to study in a hospitality management program? What alternatives were available to you?

4. What are some of the reasons that people work?

5. What does the concept of retained earnings mean as it relates to a career?

6. Describe the concept of the job-benefit mix. Give examples from your experience or from that of your classmates.

7. What are some things to observe in both the front of the house and the back of the house in the early stages of your career?

8. What kinds of things can you learn from a part-time (or summer) job that are not strictly part of the job?

9. What are three principal concerns in regard to a job after graduation?

10. What are the five elements of the strategy of job placement?

Internet Exercises

1. **Site name:** Résumés and Cover Letters

   URL: www.wku.edu/~hrtm/resumes.htm

   Background information: This site provides a listing of Internet resources for writing résumés and cover letters.

   Exercises:

   a. Surf the résumé and cover letter Web sites for information on writing résumés and cover letters. Write a simple résumé and cover letter for an entry-level hotel, restaurant, or tourism position for which you are interested and qualified. Use only experience that you have already acquired.

   b. After writing the résumé and cover letter, describe the experiences you will need to acquire in the future to obtain an entry-level management position in the hospitality industry.

2. **Site name:** Hotel, Restaurant, and Tourism Management Career Opportunities

   URL: www.wku.edu/~hrtm/hrtmjobs.htm

   Background information: This site is a launch pad for hospitality management career Web sites. The site provides links to generic hospitality Web sites such as Hcareers. com, HospitalityLink.com, and HospitalityJobOnline.com as well as Web sites that specialize in hotels, food service/restaurants, casinos, and travel.

   Exercises:

   a. Explore at least two of the Web sites listed. Look through the job opportunities in your area of interest.

      i.   What job opportunities are available for entry-level management positions (recent graduates of a hospitality management program)?

      ii. Are there abundant job opportunities in a location where you would like to be after graduation?

b. Which support/career services does the Web site provide candidates to assist them with their job search (for example: résumé, cover letter, electronic résumé help, etc.)?

c. Explore the "Career Services" Web site at the college or university you are currently attending.

    i. What types of services does your career services office offer to students (résumé and cover letters, job search assistance, etc.)?

    ii. Is there a person in your career services office who has been specifically designated to assist hospitality management students? If so, what is the name of this person?

    iii. Does the career services office hold job/career fairs for students on your campus? If so, when are these job fairs typically held and do they include potential hospitality employers as exhibitors?

    iv. Does your career services office maintain a database of current job opportunities for students? If so, how do they make this information available to students?

3. **Site name:** Council on International Educational Exchange

URL: www.ciee.org

Background information: Study abroad or work abroad opportunities—CIEE provides quality programs and services.

Site name: Hospitality Internships Abroad

URL: www.internabroad.com/listings.cfm/interntypeID/1 10

Background information: GoAbroad.com was launched to fill an information void in the area of international student travel. GoAbroad.com was conceptualized to provide a one-stop information center for students wishing to travel internationally. The site was created to link prospective travelers with organizations providing international opportunities.

Site name: Idealist.org

URL: www.idealist.org/

Background information: Search for worldwide internship opportunities by location, dates, and required skills.

Exercises:

a. Browse through all three Web sites and describe the countries that are represented and the hospitality job opportunities available on each Web site.

b. Choose an international internship Web site and select an internship that you might be interested in pursuing. Describe the benefits and drawbacks of pursuing an international internship.

Notes

1. Peter F. Drucker, *The Age of Discontinuity* (New York: Harper & Row, 1968), p. 264.
2. *Work in America* (Cambridge, MA: MIT Press, 1973), p. 3.
3. Peter F. Drucker, *Management: Tasks, Responsibilities, Practices* (New York: Harper & Row, 1974), pp. 80–86.
4. If they get stuck too often, of course, management must find out why and correct the problem. If a manager has to pitch in frequently, it can be a sign of an inefficient organization.

Chapter 6

Reducing Stress, and Improving Health and Wellbeing

The 1970s heralded major industrial relations problems, with many confrontations between unions and management. Then came the enterprise culture of the 1980s with major industrial and organisational change. The 1990s and early 2000s saw the Americanisation of most of the UK and Europe, with major restructurings, such as mergers/acquisitions, downsizings, outsourcing of functions, and the undermining of the concept of jobs for life. These activities transformed the UK economy, but at substantial personal cost for many individual employees. You can encapsulate this cost in a single word: *stress*. The problem, of course, has become much worse with the recession and post-recession period, with major job and resource cuts in the public and private sector, and more outsourcing of activities and functions now endemic to most workplaces.

Stress, then, has found as firm a place in the modern life as iPads, tsunamis, and frequent flyer miles. Although a little stress can be positive and motivating, even increasing performance, when levels become too high, detrimental effects can result.

This chapter focuses on the negative outcomes of stress and explores the many causes of workplace stress. We explore the cost of stress to individuals and organisations, as well as how both individuals and organisations can manage and reduce stress.

Understanding the Causes of Stress

People use the word *stress* casually to describe a wide range of health outcomes resulting from the hectic pace of work and life. You've probably heard someone say, 'I feel really stressed' or explain away someone's irritating behaviour because 'he's under a lot of stress'. Indeed, people even use the word to award an odd sort of prestige to a job: 'It's a high-stress job.'

The word *stress* is now in common vocabulary because the ability of people to cope with day-to-day problems is gradually depleting, leading to a range of behaviours that lead to ill health. An enormous amount of research has explored the main sources of stress at work. In this section, we look at the key causes of stress at work, and how people can experience stress differently depending on their personality.

The word *stress* can relate to both causes ('she's under stress') and outcomes of pressure at work ('I feel stressed'). Those who study organisational behaviour call the causes of stress the *stressors* and the effects of stress the *strain*.

Factors intrinsic to the job

Every job is different, so you need to identify which factors intrinsic to that job are different from all others and how they affect the health and wellbeing of the occupants of that role. For example, being a neurosurgeon is very different from being a bomb disposal officer in Afghanistan, although you may describe both jobs as stressful!

Every job has unique factors that may be very stressful and don't translate to other jobs. For example, a neurosurgeon has the stress of the risk of making a mistake, which may cost the patient's life. A bomb disposal officer has the stress of risking her own life.

Understand the stresses that are intrinsic to a job when you hire employees. You want to ensure a person-job fit so that you can select the most resilient people to do what may be a very stressful job. (We discuss person-job fit in Chapter 13. You can find out more about recruiting the right people in Chapter 17.)

Examples of some intrinsic job characteristics that can increase stress are

- **Long hours:** Not having free time and working excessively long hours, particularly over long periods of time, can be incredibly stressful.

- **Poor working conditions:** Working in high or low temperatures or simply not having the right tools to do your job properly can cause stress.

- ✔ **Risk and danger:** A job that involves risk and danger – for example, you work with potentially aggressive or violent people – can raise your stress levels.

- ✔ **Shift work:** Much evidence shows that *shift work* (work activity outside standard daytime hours where an employee, or group, hands over a work task to others) can be stressful and have a detrimental effect on your health.

- ✔ **Work overload and underload:** Simply having too much, or not enough, work to do can cause stress. Have you ever been unable to complete a task because you simply had too much work to do? Remember how it made you feel?

Job role

The role you play in your organisation is vital for your health and wellbeing. If you've a well-defined role, without much built-in conflict, with clear-cut organisational boundaries and a great deal of autonomy and control, then the likelihood is that you don't suffer from much stress.

Research seems to suggest that the key issue is control. The more people feel valued and trusted by their bosses, and the more they can exercise autonomy over their job, the less likely they are to suffer ill health outcomes, and the more likely they are to be satisfied. (Chapter 12 gives you the low-down on effective job design.)

Three job role factors are major sources of stress. Think about how having control over your work can help in each of these areas:

- ✔ **Role ambiguity:** You've inadequate information about your work role. You aren't clear about the scope and responsibilities of your job. If you don't know what your objectives are, how can you achieve them?

- ✔ **Role conflict:** You're given conflicting job demands. For example. a customer service worker is told to keep all customers happy and also to spend only five minutes with each customer. The employee can't always do both, so a conflict emerges. Other role conflict demands include being asked to do tasks you dislike or that aren't within your job specification.

- ✔ **Role responsibility:** Generally, having more responsibility can lead to higher stress at work. Having responsibility for people can be more stressful than having responsibility for things.

Relationships at work

Probably the most important relationship you have at work in terms of your own wellbeing and stress is the relationship you have with your boss. The better this relationship, the more you get along with your boss, and the more beneficial to your job satisfaction and health. A poor relationship can cause ill health effects.

In his humorous book *Something Happened* (Vintage), Joseph Heller's opening page illustrates the significance of work relationships:

> *In the office in which I work there are five people of whom I am afraid. Each of these people is afraid of four people, for a total of twenty, and each of these twenty people is afraid of six people, making a total of one hundred people who are feared by at least one person. . . . In my department, there are six people who are afraid of me, and one small secretary who is afraid of all of us. I have one other person working for me who is not afraid of anyone, not even me, and I would fire him quickly, but I'm afraid of him.*

 Bosses aren't the only relationship that can cause problems; colleagues, customers, and suppliers can as well. The primary relationship stressors are the ones in your own workplace, though, because you interact with these people a lot.

Poor relationships at work can make your job harder and less enjoyable. You may have a boss who expects you to work harder than you feel possible, or an unhelpful, unsupportive colleague. Studies of workplace stress have shown that

- ✔ Bad relationships make stress worse.
- ✔ Supportive relationships reduce pressure and levels of stress.

We talk about fairness at work in Chapter 11, so check it out for discussion of extreme relationship problems at work, such as discrimination and bullying, and consideration of the stress that can be caused if you're unfortunate enough to experience it. Also check out Chapter 8 for more on leadership and how to be a good boss.

Career development

Career-driven issues, such as being overpromoted or underpromoted or fearing job loss or early retirement, can be stressful. These career events are now more common because people are much more mobile between employers and sectors.

Some areas relating to career development that can affect stress levels are

- ✔ **Fear of redundancy:** Especially important post-recession, fearing you may lose your job can be highly stressful.

- ✔ **Performance appraisals:** Stress can increase if you feel that you're unfairly appraised. (Chapter 18 covers appraisals.)

- ✔ **Reaching a career ceiling:** Not progressing in your career can be frustrating.

- ✔ **Retirement:** Worrying about retirement can cause stress. (See Chapter 11 for more on retirement.)

Job security

As we are entering an era of leaner organisations, intrinsic job insecurity and a culture of longer working hours, adverse stress effects on employee attitudes and behaviour are emerging. In 2001, the Chartered Management Institute's Quality of Working Life survey of 5,000 managers found that downsizing, outsourcing, and delayering in the workplace led to substantially increased levels of job insecurity, decreased morale, and eroded motivation and loyalty.

In addition, substantial research shows that job insecurity leads to ill health. Between 1985 and 2000, job security among British workers dropped from 70 per cent feeling secure to only 45 per cent feeling secure. In 2007, 66 per cent of 10,000 managers reported that as a result of all the structural changes in their organisation, they now felt significantly less secure. This trend of intrinsic job insecurity is of great concern for two reasons:

- ✔ A person's sense of job security is related to job satisfaction.

- ✔ A strong link exists between job dissatisfaction and mental and physical ill health.

We talk more about job satisfaction and dissatisfaction in Chapter 9.

Related to job security is the issue of short-term contracts. Many organisations are moving toward creating a short-term *contract culture* where people are hired in for the short term, or they outsource work to outside agencies or freelancers. This move has enhanced the stress levels of staff, as the permanence of their job is under threat. The insecurity of a short-term contract, as well as the more tenuous relationship an agency worker has with the organisation, is a real problem in these settings.

A survey in 2006 of a cohort of 10,000 UK managers compared the years 2000 with 2005 and discovered the following:

- ✔ The use of short-term contract staff rose from 41 per cent to 57 per cent.

- ✔ Cost-reduction programs went from 47 per cent to 63 per cent.

- ✔ Twenty-five per cent of managers reported that their organisations were engaged in major outsourcing.

And these figures were before the recession! Are we going to see greater use of contract staff and outsourcing post-recession as organisations seek to cut manpower and reduce costs?

Culture and climate

The organisation you work for has its own culture and climate, which can make work life pleasant or unpleasant and stressful. Some cultures are more bureaucratic or restrictive, but others may have effective consultations and be more engaging. A great deal of research has shown that work environments that create a culture of engagement produce greater productivity and health and therefore support a more trusting climate.

Check out Chapter 13 for more on organisational culture. There we discuss the importance of values and attitudes and explain how, if your values and attitudes clash with those of the organisation, you can find yourself not fitting into the organisation's culture. This conflict can cause you stress and lead to you performing less well and even leaving the organisation.

Work–life balance

As countries like the UK and the US create long-hours cultures, the stresses and strains between work and home life mount. Strong evidence reveals that working long hours not only damage your health and family life but also your productivity.

Since the early 1990s, the annual working hours across the globe have declined – by as much as 11 per cent for Japan, and 6 per cent for the UK, although only 2 per cent for the US. This decline is in part because more females are working, and as they often work part-time the average number of hours worked reduces. However, this trend is beginning to reverse with employees now reporting working longer hours than before the recession. According to a 2011 survey, 30 per cent of UK employees are working longer hours, with 42 per cent of this group working three hours extra per day and 26 per cent working more than three hours extra per day. And a survey of 300 organisations in the US and Canada reports that two-thirds of employees are working longer hours than three years ago.

Smoking breaks

Some employees appear to work fewer hours than others. According to a UK survey, smokers take about four 15-minute breaks a day to get their nicotine fix. This means that smokers work on average 240 hours per year less than non-smokers. The Chartered Institute for Personnel Development suggests that one way to overcome resentment between those who do and those who don't smoke is to restrict smoking to statutory breaks. A healthier option, though, is for employers to provide support to encourage employees to live a healthier lifestyle.

A survey in 2007 found that 56 per cent of managers reported that long hours damaged their health; 54 per cent said that these hours adversely affected their relationship with their children; 59 per cent said that it damaged their relationship with their partner/spouse; and 64 per cent said that it had an adverse affect on their social life.

The UK umbrella group Working Families did a study of 625 working people and found that nearly 40 per cent of those consistently working over 45 hours a week spent less than an hour a night with their children. In addition, a major discrepancy existed between their contracted hours and their actual hours. For women, 15 per cent were contracted to work over 40 hours, while only 44 per cent actually did. For men, 27 per cent were contracted to work over 40 hours, while 67 per cent actually did.

Work–life balance is now a major issue in most employee surveys carried out in both the public and private sector as a result of these long hours, and more employees are calling for more flexible working arrangements to deal with them.

In addition to long hours, another reason why work–life balance is seen as increasingly relevant to workplace stress is because of the increasing number of dual-career households, which makes balancing home and work life more difficult, especially if you've child or elder care responsibilities.

Work–life balance conflict can be in both directions:

✔ The demands of work can create problems at home.

✔ The demands at home can create problems at work.

Personality

People are different and react to stressors in different ways. The sources of stress influence the individual, and people's personalities influence what the likely effect of the stressors will be. (You can find out more about personality and individual differences in Chapter 3.)

Personality can affect stress in three main ways. It can have a

- ✔ **Direct effect:** If you're an anxious person, you're generally more likely to experience stress.

- ✔ **Moderating effect:** Some personality characteristics can lead to you being more likely to experience stress in a particular job. For example, if you're an outgoing extroverted person, you may find a job where you work on your own a lot more stressful than an introverted person would. On the other hand, your personality may cushion the affect. For example, being extroverted is linked to positive wellbeing, so a more extrovert employee may find a stressful job situation less stressful.

- ✔ **Direct perceptual effect:** Personality can affect your perceptions of your job. For example, if you've a high need for control, you'll be very conscious of being in a situation where you've low control and be more bothered by it than somebody else who has less need for control.

In Chapter 3, we introduce models of personality. Two are particularly relevant to discussions of stress:

- ✔ **Locus of control:** This trait affects the extent to which you think that you've control over your life. An internal locus of control is good because it can encourage you to do something about a stressful situation. However, if you can't change your situation, an internal locus of control can increase stress.

- ✔ **Type A behaviour:** If you're a high type A personality, you're probably very competitive, high achieving, and impatient. You're also at a higher risk of stress than Type B personalities, who tend to be more relaxed and less competitive.

Seeing How Stress Affects Employees and Employers

The financial costs of stress are high – and we mean really high. For example:

- ✔ The costs of ill-health in the working age population are estimated by us to cost the UK well over £100 billion a year.

- ✔ Mental ill health alone costs the UK around £28 billion.

- ✔ Stress was estimated to cost $3 billion in decreased productivity and $19 billion in lost employment annually in the United States.

- ✔ Effectively managing mental health at work in an organisation with 1000 employees can save as much as £250,000 per year.

- In 2009, workers in the UK took sick days at a cost of an estimated £3.7bn.

- Stress, depression, or anxiety is the largest cause of absence attributable to work-related illness in the UK and accounted for 13.8 million days lost in 2006–07.

You can look at the cost of stress from two angles:

- Individual costs, such as behaviour change and ill health

- Organisational costs, such as poorer performance and absenteeism

Impacting individuals

Table 6-1 outlines commonly reported feelings and behavioural symptoms of stress. If you've ever experienced stress at work, then you may recognise some of these symptoms!

Table 6-1	Common Signs of Stress
Feeling . . .	*Finding It Hard to . . .*
Like a bad person	Take an interest in others
Like a failure as a person, employee, or parent	Make decisions
Frightened of failure, illness, the future, or being alone	Concentrate
Neglected	Express true feelings, including anger
Like the target of other people's animosity	Have a sense of humour
A lack of confidence	Confide in others
Unable to cope	Be patient with people
Uninterested in life	Finish one task before rushing to another

The impact of stress at work on the health and wellbeing of individuals is huge. Stress follows a three-stage process:

- **Behaviour change:** Acting out can occur when you're near the dividing line between pressure, which is stimulating and motivating, and stress, which means that the pressure has exceeded your ability to cope. You may lose your sense of humour, have difficulty concentrating and become more socially withdrawn. Sometimes people can also become more aggressive when experiencing stress.

- **Physical symptoms of stress:** These symptoms can manifest themselves in a number of ways, such as feeling constantly tired, having frequent headaches and having difficulty sleeping at night. Stress-related behaviours, such as increases in smoking, alcohol consumption, and eating too much or too little, can worsen physical symptoms. Also, research indicates that musculoskeletal disorders have been found among call centre employees with high workloads, and premature births among women with low job satisfaction.

- **Serious illness:** If the sources of your stress are very deep-rooted and persistent, it can lead to a range of more serious illnesses, such as heart disease, gastrointestinal disorders, and migraines.

Obstructing the organisation: Absenteeism and presenteeism

Organisations experience a number of problems as a result of employees experiencing high levels of stress at work. Table 6-2 illustrates the problems stress causes and their cost for an organisation.

Table 6-2	How Stress Affects an Organisation
Result of Stress	*Cost to the Organisation*
Compensation claims by stressed individuals	Financial
High turnover of staff	Financial (cost of recruitment), disruption
Low morale	Performance problems and reduced commitment, so less effective and reliable employees who may work slower and produce work of lower quality
Sickness absence	Financial (loss of productivity, cost of sick pay, and replacement workers)

Of the problems described in Table 6-2, the two big factors that affect organisations are

- **Absenteeism:** According to estimates by the Chartered Institute of Personnel Development and the Confederation of British Industry, workplace stress is one of the biggest causes of absence in the UK workforce.

- **Presenteeism:** People are at work, but they aren't performing to the best of their ability or contributing to the bottom line.

Estimates of the costs of absenteeism and presenteeism range from £2 billion to over £20 billion per annum in the UK, depending on whether they're direct costs, such as sickness absence, and/or indirect costs, such as lack of added value to products or services and the costs to the NHS of treating people who have a stress-related illness precipitated by work.

Table 6-3 shows the estimated annual costs of poor mental health to UK employers. These figures are based on common mental health disorders, which include depression, anxiety, and stress (depression and anxiety can be outcomes of stress). Note that presenteeism costs the UK nearly twice what absenteeism costs.

Table 6-3	Estimated Annual Costs to UK Employers of Poor Mental Health		
	Cost Per Average Employee (£)	*Total Cost to UK Employers (£billion)*	*Per cent of Total*
Absenteeism	335	8.4	32.4
Presenteeism	605	15.1	58.4
Turnover	95	2.4	9.2
Total	1035	25.9	100

Source: Sainsbury Centre for Mental Health, 2007.

We can conceptualise presenteeism into a two-by-two matrix to get a picture of the extent of the problem. (See Table 6-4, which is based on a sample of 39,000 UK workers.) Table 6-4 shows that of these workers, 28 per cent of people turn up for work even if they're ill (sickness presenteeism). Thirteen per cent are healthy but not always present (job dissatisfied), whereas only 35 per cent of them are fully functioning.

Table 6-4	Presenteeism	
	Health Good	*Health Not Good*
No absences	Healthy and present – 35 per cent	Unhealthy and present sickness presentees – 28 per cent
Some absences	Healthy and not always present – 13 per cent	Unhealthy and not always present – 24 per cent

Source: Sainsbury Centre for Mental Health, 2007.

Rooting Out Stress in an Organisation

The Do-it-Yourself approach that we recommend organisations follow to identify and deal with stress at work isn't complicated. You follow four simple steps:

1. **Conduct a stress audit.**

2. **Identify stressed groups.**

3. **Involve affected groups in finding solutions to the stress problem.**

4. **Report on problems and recommended solutions.**

The following sections take you through each step in turn.

Conducting a stress audit

Before you start a stress audit, establish in the organisation a stress or well-being *working party,* comprised of management and representatives of workers/unions, to oversee the process and report back to senior management with the results and recommended actions.

To carry out a workplace stress audit, use an established stress psychometric. The most used stress psychometric is ASSET, an organisational stress-screening tool composed of a number of subscales. Each scale has several questions. The scales are aggregated up so that you receive a single score for each scale. Here are the three outcome measures:

✔ Job satisfaction

✔ Mental wellbeing

✔ Physical wellbeing

Seven scales represent workplace sources of stress:

✔ Control

✔ Job security

✔ Overload

✔ Pay and benefits

✔ Resources and communications

✔ Work relationships

✔ Work–life balance

These scales relate to the areas we detail in the 'Understanding the Causes of Stress' section, earlier in this chapter. For example, you may look at

- ✔ The extent to which employees are troubled by
  - • Their pay and benefits
  - • Their relationships at work (with their boss, colleagues, customers, clients, and so on)
  - • Aspects of their workload (whether overloaded or underloaded or unrealistic deadlines for the work)
- ✔ How much control or autonomy they have in their job
- ✔ How secure they feel in their organisation and job
- ✔ Whether they've adequate resources
- ✔ How effective the organisational communications are within the workplace
- ✔ Whether they're getting adequate work–life balance, including the hours they work and their feelings about the flexibility provided by the organisation

The final two ASSET scales look at the perceptions of employees in relation to

- ✔ How committed the organisation is to them
- ✔ How committed they are to the organisation

You can also download stress audit instruments developed by the Health and Safety Executive in the UK from www.hse.gov.uk and by the National Institute for Occupational Safety and Health from www.cdc.gov/NIOSH.

Identifying stressed groups

In order to identify which parts of the organisation, level, or group within the organisation has a stress-related outcome and what that problem is, you need to break down the audit data (see the previous section) by demographics.

Department 1 may have a problem of a long-hours culture that is causing stress. Department 2 may have a bullying boss, and Department 3 may have difficulties juggling work and outside life because employees have no flexible working arrangement options. Or perhaps no problem exists across departments, but a particular demographic within the organisation, such as older workers, experience more stress because they don't feel supported within the organisation. You can compare stress levels across numerous demographics, which can help you to identify any problem areas.

The stress psychometric ASSET (which we introduce in the previous section) has extensive norms from thousands of workers in a variety of sectors, so that each department or demographic can have their scores compared to the norms of the general working population or by the sector concerned (for example, IT, police, hospital, or finance sector). The norms help you diagnose accurately which part of the workplace has problems, as measured by poor mental or physical health, for example, and the source of that problem (for example, poor relationships, lack of control, or poor communications). Check out the ASSET publisher at www.robertsoncooper.com.

Finding solutions

After you know where the stress hot spots are and what they are, you can form focus groups of workers affected by the issue.

If the problem is a glass ceiling for women in Department 1, then form a representative group of women in that department. Ask them to consider how the organisation can deal with that issue to reduce the stress. If new staff have increased stress levels, then form a focus group of these staff and get them to come up with a solution to ease them into the organisation. This way, you've involved those individuals specifically adversely affected, and they've ownership in the solution.

Reporting and recommending

Get the working party on stress/wellbeing to put together a report on where the stress is, the sources of the problem, and their recommendations of how to solve the issue. This group can present their report and recommendations to senior executives, which hopefully includes the HR Director or some other senior role holder.

To ensure that the implementation has been successful, keep the working party on board as the recommendations are rolled out.

Intervening in Stress

So what can organisations do to manage the stress levels? Professor Cary Cooper and Professor Susan Cartwright, both leading work psychologists in the area of work stress, suggest a three-pronged strategy to deal with stress at work in their book *Managing Workplace Stress* (Sage Publications, Inc):

> ✔ **Changing the job (primary prevention),** such as carrying out stress or wellbeing audits and then intervening where a problem occurs.
>
> ✔ **Supporting the employee (secondary prevention),** such as stress management and resilience training.
>
> ✔ **Dealing with the fallout (tertiary prevention),** such as workplace counselling or employee assistance programs

A fully comprehensive strategy incorporates all three of these approaches.

Changing the job

Primary intervention strategies are often a means to change culture and are about taking action to alter or remove sources of stress inbuilt in the work environment, therefore reducing their negative impact on the individual. Possible strategies include

✔ Redesigning the working environment

✔ Setting up flexible working schedules

✔ Involving the employee in career development

✔ Improving managerial behaviour and competencies

✔ Providing social support

The critical focus of primary interventions is in adapting the range of factors, such as those we list here, in individual organisations that can help reduce stress. This type of approach is likely to need to be customised to a specific situation and as such should be guided by a prior diagnosis or stress audit (see the earlier section 'Rooting Out Stress in an Organisation') to find out what specific factors are responsible for employee stress.

Supporting the employee

Secondary prevention requires a quick response to find and manage the experienced stress. You can do so by making individuals more aware of the signs of stress and developing their skills to manage stress through training and educational activities.

Employees respond to exposure to workplace stress in different ways as individual factors can change how you perceive and respond to the working environment. And as everyone has their own personal stress threshold, which means some people suffer and others seem to flourish in the same environment, designing stress-awareness activities and skills training programs (for example, techniques to improve relations at work, and skills to change thought processes and modify work–life balance in order to improve an individual's physical and psychological resources) to improve how individuals cope is important.

Although the aim of secondary prevention is to help employees to adapt to their environment, this type of prevention is really a damage limitation exercise. In a number of instances the working environment is still stressful, so the individual has to develop their own strategies to resist the stress. This has been called a *band-aid* approach.

Dealing with the fallout

Tertiary prevention is all about getting individuals, who have suffered from, or are suffering from, serious ill health as a result of stress well again. This stage involves potential treatments that can assist the individual's recuperation and recovery.

Typical interventions include the provision of counselling services that help employees deal with work or personal problems. These services tend to be provided by in-house counsellors or outside agencies, and offer information, support, and counselling and/or referral to suitable treatment and support services. Research evidence indicates that counselling is an effective way to improve the psychological wellbeing of employees and has substantial cost benefits.

Taking Inspiration from Successful Stress Management Examples

Many organisations have carried out successful stress or wellbeing audits. The following sections give examples of different interventions in very different sectors, based on the work of Robertson Cooper Ltd, one of the leading providers of wellbeing solutions for organisations.

De-stressing the police

In 2007, a UK police force identified that numerous problems, such as relatively high sickness absence, reported work overload, and the like.

The police force decided to carry out a force-wide stress audit using ASSET online. (See the section 'Rooting Out Stress in an Organisation,' earlier in this chapter, for more on ASSET.) They discovered that they had high levels of overload, relatively poor physical and mental health (benchmarked against other police sector norms), worrying levels of bullying (which isn't uncommon in the police service), low levels of productivity, and a gap between commitment by the force to the officers versus their commitment to the force.

Following these results, the groups with the relevant problems designed interventions to tackle the stress problems identified. A range of interventions emerged from a bicycling to work and weight loss campaign to tackle the physical health issues, to controlling the work overload through 'switch off your mobile phone' scheme, to helping officers to prioritise their workloads. In addition, managers attended resilience training sessions to help them cope with many of the issues.

Two years after the interventions were implemented, a follow-up stress survey took place and found

- ✔ An 11.1 per cent decrease in reported work overload
- ✔ An 8.3 per cent improvement in physical and mental wellbeing
- ✔ A 6.9 per cent reduction in workplace bullying
- ✔ A 6 per cent increase in productivity
- ✔ A significant reduction in the commitment gap between the organisation and the individual
- ✔ A reduction in sickness absence figures from 6.3 per cent in 2003 to 3.0 per cent in 2010

Based on these numbers, this program was considered a success.

Improving absenteeism in a healthcare trust

Absenteeism from sickness, issues of engagement, and wellbeing in general tend to be high in the hospital and healthcare sector.

At one healthcare trust, a stress audit, using ASSET, identified hot spots sources of stress, with the goal of determining the nature, location, and severity and to develop follow-up activities for improvement. The stress audit discovered that 50 per cent of all staff reported having a major stressful event, with 66 per cent of these stressful events related to work. Employees had low levels of wellbeing scores and high levels of sickness absence in specific departments, which highlighted the need for targeted wellbeing initiatives.

After engaging their staff, the Trust developed action plans and implemented them, based on the ASSET stress-screening tool and focus-group discussions. A year later, staff turnover was reduced by 3.6 per cent, stress-related sickness absence was down by 7.0 per cent, and the reduction in sickness absence saved the Trust over £70,000 after only six months.

Looking to a stressful future

It is safe to say that we have, at the start of this millennium, all the ingredients of corporate stress:

- ✔ An ever-increasing workload
- ✔ A decreasing workforce
- ✔ A climate of rapid change
- ✔ Control over the means of production increasingly being exercised by bigger bureaucracies
- ✔ A downturn in the economy
- ✔ Emerging threats to stabilising and job security

The end result is that more people are working in job-insecure environments and fewer people are there to do the work.

And the pressures on everyone are likely to get worse. As we move away from our own internal markets and enter larger economic systems, individual organisations will have less control over business life. Rules and regulations are beginning to be imposed in terms of labour laws; health and safety at work; methods of production, distribution, and remuneration; and so on. These concerns are all laudable issues in their own right, but nevertheless, these workplace constraints will inhibit individual control and autonomy.

It appears, therefore, that stress is here to stay and can't be dismissed as simply a bygone remnant of the entrepreneurial 1980s and 1990s. The challenge for human resource management in the future is to understand a basic truth about human behaviour. Developing and maintaining a 'feel-good' factor at work and in our economy generally isn't just about bottom-line factors. This factor is, or should be, in a civilised society, about quality of life issues, such as hours of work, family time, manageable workloads, control over one's career, and some sense of job security.

As the social anthropologist Studs Terkel suggests in his book *Working* (published by The New Press), 'work is about a search for daily meaning as well as daily bread, for recognition as well as cash, for astonishment rather than torpor, in short, for a sort of life rather than a Monday through Friday sort of dying'.

Managing stress in the Council of Europe

The Council of Europe is an intergovernmental body based in Strasbourg, with 47 member countries throughout the whole of Europe. In December 2009, the Council commissioned an organisation-wide wellbeing audit. All employees throughout Europe, in 28 workplaces from Paris to Warsaw to Moscow, took the questionnaire. The Council's purpose was to assess their strengths and weaknesses in an effort to improve wellbeing among their employees.

The Council discovered lots of positives. It showed high engagement and commitment levels, a relatively physically healthy workforce, and relatively high productivity.

The Council identified two areas of concern:

- ✔ Employees were slightly troubled by their work relationships.
- ✔ Employees had high levels of presenteeism.

The Council then effectively and quickly communicated the results and got engagement from areas that needed improvement by localised action plans. The Council is still in the process of rolling out and implementing their action plans with the strong support of senior management and the employees themselves. Maud de Boer-Buquicchio, Deputy Secretary General of the Council of Europe, said of this exercise:

> *The work we have done with this study has enabled us to get to grips with the challenge of managing the wellbeing of a diverse workforce. Our organisation is complex and the work brings unique challenges, but we are now confident that the wellness of our people will contribute to, rather than hinder, its work.*